Charles Archibald Anderson Scott

Ulfilas, Apostle of the Goths

Together with an account of the Gothic churches and their decline

Charles Archibald Anderson Scott

Ulfilas, Apostle of the Goths
Together with an account of the Gothic churches and their decline

ISBN/EAN: 9783337087593

Printed in Europe, USA, Canada, Australia, Japan

Cover: Foto ©Lupo / pixelio.de

More available books at **www.hansebooks.com**

ULFILAS

APOSTLE OF THE GOTHS

TOGETHER WITH AN ACCOUNT OF

The Gothic Churches and their Decline

BY

CHARLES A. ANDERSON SCOTT, B.A.

NADEN DIVINITY STUDENT AT ST. JOHN'S COLLEGE, CAMBRIDGE

"He would not discount life, as fools do here,
Paid by instalment"

Cambridge
MACMILLAN AND BOWES
1885

CAMBRIDGE

PRINTED BY J. PALMER

JESUS LANE

To my Father

PREFACE.

THE flood of barbarian invasion, which for the first
six centuries of our era was beating round the Roman
empire, is broken by a few towering crests; in all the
indistinguishable sea of human beings there appear
two or three men whose genius and majesty have made
an impression on the memory as well as on the history
of Europe. Attila, Alaric, and Theodoric have found a
place among the household names of history, as well
as a niche in popular mythology. These all planted
their renown on the field of battle; by their achievements as chieftains, generals, and conquerors, they
"made themselves for ever known." There is one
name alone which rests its claim to be remembered on
a different foundation. Sole among all these countless
numbers, Ulfilas is known and remembered for works
of peace, for achievement in literature, for the triumph
of the Cross.

The race to which he belonged, and for which he
worked, provides a background not unworthy of this
unique figure. The fortunes of the Goths in the history of Europe command an interest such as few other
episodes in that great epic can surpass. Of no other

Teutonic race were the conceptions so bold, the achievements so great, and the ultimate failure so complete. Geographically their line of influence extends from the Bosphorus to the Pillars of Hercules. Chronologically their history covers the transition from the Roman empire to modern Europe. In the history of religion they are contemporaries and spectators of the passage from paganism to papacy. Their position from these different points of view is strangely similar. Driven like a wedge into the eastern side of Europe by the superincumbent weight of the Huns, they pass along the whole length of it, to be similarly thrust out at the west by the Franks. During this whole course they hold a place intermediate between barbarism and civilisation. They are not nomads, yet they are not able to found a state. Their political fate is matched by their ecclesiastical. They are not heathens, yet they are not acknowledged as Christians. Planted in an indefensible position by their Arian creed, they are crushed between the opposing masses of heathendom and Catholicism.

It is this additional quality, the relation between their fortunes and their faith, which gives to the history of the Goths its crowning interest. Almost alone among the "barbarians," we see in them the working of a conviction. In all physical respects equal to any race in that long series, in material achievement surpassed by none, they present also a quality of mind to which, so far as we know, there was no parallel in any of their competitors. It may indeed be said by some that the thought which they appropriated and presented was a trifle, a crotchet at most, and their adhesion to it only to be reckoned as obstinacy. But even obstinate adhesion to a crotchet would be sufficiently unique among the nations of that period; while, if their faith be regarded from their own view-point under all the dignity of a worthy conviction, bitten in indelibly upon the national consciousness, then such a national apprehension and tenacious grasp of an idea is a phenomenon of the highest interest. Such an idea is the one embodied in the Gothic Church. It is the object of this essay to trace the working of this idea in Gothic history, to observe its first planting through the teaching of Ulfilas, its fostering under the power of his influence and memory, and its great and fatal effect upon the political development of the people.

Its ultimate effects upon the history of the Goths are not far to seek. The map of Europe bears no trace of their wanderings or their settlements. Three Gothic kingdoms, the most short-lived of which endured at least a century, passed away without leaving a sign. For two centuries they professed themselves Christians; yet their Church left fewer marks of its existence even than their State. The annals of the Christian Church record with honour the one name of that Gothic king who broke with the traditions of his people to become a Catholic. In our own century their name has been ingenuously borrowed as a term of reproach wherewith to brand an unpopular style of architecture ! And by popular phraseology they have been planted alongside their Vandal cousins in a pillory of splendid disgrace.

History has done them hardly more justice than tradition. Their enemies are their chroniclers. Their own records have perished. Yet, when all the shreds of information regarding them are pieced together, even in the poor tapestry that results, we see indubitable marks of greatness, the indelible qualities of race. We see in a marked degree the presence of vitality, of tenaciousness, and of the power of initiative.

These three qualities reveal themselves conspicuously, as in the race, so in the representative man. Two great monuments of Gothic history are the memory of Ulfilas, and the fragments of his book. In the following pages an attempt has been made to collect the facts relating to this man, to estimate his position, to note the marks which he left upon his people and his age, and to trace the stream of his influence, as it affected the history of his people, till it was at last exhausted and forgotten.

How imperfectly I have succeeded in this task few can be more conscious than myself. The very extent of the history, the multiplicity of relations secular and ecclesiastical into which the Goths during these three centuries entered, the complications of doctrinal controversy in which every student of the fourth century is involved,—may explain my failure, though they may not excuse my attempt. It is in this consciousness of having left much undone and imperfectly worked out, that I have noted with some fulness the authorities, especially so much of the modern literature bearing on the various sections as has come within my reach. In the usual alternative between a punctilious citation of the authorities and unattested assertion, I have had, as I conceive, no choice. In dealing with a subject where the evidence is so widely spread and so thinly scattered, the paramount desire to bring out the truth makes constant reference to the authorities imperative. It is with this view also that I have collected in the Appendix the most important passages in the Church historians bearing on the ecclesiastical position of Ulfilas, and the vexed question of the conversion of the Wisigoths. A minute comparison of these is very instructive.

In English I do not know of any book which deals directly with either Ulfilas or the Gothic Churches. In German the works of Aschbach, Krafft, Pallmann, and Helfferich are all more or less closely concerned with these subjects. In French there are Maimbourg and Revillout dealing with them from the side of the history of Arianism. I wish, however, to acknowledge especially my indebtedness to Felix Dahn's great work *Die Könige der Germanen* (of which the volumes dealing with the Goths are now complete), to Bessell's very minute study of the authorities for the life of Ulfilas, and to Mr. Gwatkin's *Studies in Arianism.*

I recall also with gratitude the memory of the Rev. John Hulse, through whose benefaction I have been encouraged to study in this by-path of Church history, and enabled to publish these all too unworthy results. Our actual information regarding the life and labours of Ulfilas is still very limited. Of original sources there are probably not more than three. Of his Translation large portions are still lacking. I cannot help cherishing a hope that there is lying buried in some nook of Germany, Italy, or Spain, and yet to come to light, some further record of the great spiritual Father of the Goths.

C. A. S.

Cambridge,
October, 1885.

CONTENTS.

ERRATA.

p. 88, line 9 from below, *for* 'only' *read* 'early.'

p. 127, „ 3 from above, „ '118' „ '188.'

The number of sheets now extant, after being reduced by theft to 177, is restored to 187. See note by Peters, in Bartsch's *Germania*, 1885.

CHAPTER I.

EARLY HISTORY OF THE GOTHS.

AUTHORITIES FOR CHAPTER I.

SOURCES :

Jordanis, *de rebus Geticis*, ed. Closs (Stuttgart, 1861).
Sozomen, *Hist. Eccl.*

LITERATURE :

Pallmann, *Völkerwanderung*, Abth. i.
v. Wietersheim, *Geschichte der Völkerwanderung*, 2nd ed., Dahn (1880).
Dahn, *die Könige der Germanen*, esp. Abth. ii. and v.
Bessell, "Gothen" in *Ersch und Gruber*.
Kaufmann, *die Germanen der Urzeit* (1880).
Platner, *Ueber die Art der Deutschen Völkerzüge in Deutsche Forschungen*, vol. xx.

IF it might be deemed not unworthy of the sobriety of history to give play for a moment to fancy, we might frame for ourselves an allegory of Europe's middle age, a rough generalisation of our period, which might serve to correct the proportions, and illustrate the ultimate value and meaning of the details which follow. We might image to ourselves the prospect of time and its events presented to an observer withdrawn beyond its conditions and the reach of their effects as an avenue of centuries. Down one section of it there moves a man somewhat bowed with years, robed in fine vesture, and bearing treasures of art and thought, the heritage of the past. His step is slow and languid, and his treasures seem ready to fall from his loosening grasp; but ever and anon he collects himself, erects his head, gathers with a firmer hand his "foot-catching robes," and makes a determined effort to throw off the dull languor and the feebleness of age. To join him there

1

comes down a branching alley a child clad in simple white, carrying in his hand a book. He is young, hardly yet conscious of himself; but his frank eyes have a look of confidence and assurance that claims for him the future. Of his book, as yet his sole possession, he has mastered the letters, but hardly yet begun to grasp the meaning. The man beholds the child at first with undisguised scorn, then with suspicion which changes to alarm. He knows not how to treat him; tries indifference, harshness, and cajolery in turn,—then gives him his hand. So they move on together, now joined, now separate, as the old man recognises his own feebleness and need of support, or is dismayed by the growing vigour of his companion. One by one the possessions of the old man are transferred to the boy. Yet there remains a danger, a double one, between the boy and the fulfilment of the destiny which appears written on his face. The old man's strength is still more than a match for his, and in a fit of jealous fury he may fall upon him and kill or cripple him. Again, his treasures are too many and too various for the boy to bear as yet, and should the old man fail now or soon, his gifts must perish with him.

So, behind and between them steps a third, out from another alley,—a true son of the forest, rough handed, gentle hearted, obstinate in opinion, pliable in sentiment. He looks with wonder and amazement on the gems and robes with which the old man is decked; with wonder and awe on the face of the child, with its " tranced yet open gaze." This second figure is received by the old man at first with contempt of the great childish giant who is dazzled by the jewels, and subdued

by the glance of the child; then, recognising the value
of his arm as a stay for himself, he tolerates his presence
with a blustering mien of mingled arrogance and humiliation. Nor does the boy here shew himself much more
generous. He views his new companion at first with distrust, and grudgingly accepts his proffered aid and protection. He has shared already in some of the old man's
possessions, and despises now the plain homeliness of the
new-comer; besides, he is conscious of his own coming
vigour, and will not be hampered by any alliance now,
that might lead to inconvenient claims in the future. The
new-comer resents this treatment. He snatches at the
old man's treasures, lays sometimes a rough hand upon
the child, or again relapses into humble submission and
henchmanship, trying all means to overcome the puny
arrogance of the one and the cold and cautious reserve
of the other. Meanwhile he is doing his appointed
work, supporting the old man's tottering footsteps,
helping and protecting, half unconsciously perhaps, the
growing youth, bearing and transferring gradually the
possessions of the Old World to the New. He is the
" Barbarian," so called in contempt by both those whom
he served; he is the "Scourge of God," but also the
Sheath over God's new graft. It was under cover of
his protection that the New entered upon the heritage
of the Old. When the transfer has been made sure,
the old man drops aside, the son of the forest falls
behind; but the child, now grown to manhood and
consciousness of self, marches forward, bearing the gifts
of the Ancient, reaping the strength of the Barbarian.

Some such picture might the stage of Europe present during the first five centuries of our era, if viewed

through an "inverted glass." Such, or something like it, was the *rôle* played during that period by the Barbarian in relation to the Old World and to the New.

Foremost among these barbarians (whether we take account of numbers, of weight and duration of influence, of intensity of national consciousness, or of the long roll of world-renowned leaders of men) stand those tribes which, though classed under various names, are yet derived from the common Gothic stock. Their history may be roughly divided into two parts. The great epoch in their national life, as in that of the other Teutonic stocks, is the hour of their first contact with the Roman Empire, the rich depositary of Latin traditions of law and government, as of Greek achievements in art, literature, and philosophy; the depositary also since the Christian era of Hebrew Monotheism, and of the cosmopolitan Christian faith, which claimed government and law, philosophy, literature, and art as its subjects, and all the world for its throne. This turning-point in their history came to the Goths about the beginning of the third century, when Rome was losing her right to be considered the centre of the Roman empire, when the State religion of heathenism had long degenerated from a faith to a superstition, which was supported by indifferent rulers and sceptical philosophers only as a safeguard against popular enlightenment and liberty; at a time, too, when the new faith had differentiated itself in the eyes of the Roman world from Judaism, but had raised furious indignation and alarm by proclaiming the pernicious doctrine of equality for all men. It was on the edge of an empire thus pregnant with change that the Goths arrived towards the beginning of the third century.

Their history up to this point is involved in obscurity. Whence they had come; whether they were autocthonous in Europe, or had migrated thither from the East some time in the dim past; what place they held, in the latter case, in the sequence of Aryan stocks, and how long they had been in Europe—these and many similar questions must remain unanswered. There are no records. Only on the question of the quarter whence they started on their great out-wandering do the legends of the people, and a few vague statements of early travellers and topographers, throw a little dubious light. Of their origin and wanderings, of their habits of life and thought, of their constitution and religious ideas and practices we can have no knowledge more secure than the inferences drawn from long-descended and highly-embellished legends, and from a comparison of what we know of other related stocks.

It is true that much information may be gathered from various sources, which seem to refer authoritatively to Gothic history; and modern writers have actually constructed out of the numerous references in old historians and chroniclers to Goths, Scythians, and Getae a long and continuous account of Gothic history, constitution, and religion. Such accounts are all but valueless. As sources of Gothic history, these references are open to a double objection. Many of them are untrustworthy in themselves, and the application of any of them to the Goths rests upon an untenable assumption. This is the ancient and persistent assumption which identifies the Goths of the third and following centuries with the Getae of the earlier empire,[1] and through them with the Scythians of a still more distant period. This ethnological theory, which must have arisen from chance similarities of name, locality, and relation to the empire, is of very early origin, and has given rise to most serious confusion. Critical or even careful enquiry was no part of the early annalist's accepted task, and when a people bearing a name so similar appeared in the same locality as the Getae were known to have occupied, he concluded without question that they belonged to the same stock. A theory countenanced by the very earliest and contemporary writers of Gothic history was naturally accepted by their successors, and the usage of Scythicus and Geticus, Scythia and Getica for Gotthus and Gotthicus is in some writers undeviating.[2] Many later accounts of the Goths illustrate the effects of the natural converse tendency to refer to them all the notices in earlier historians of both Getae and Scythians. Apart from the natural

[1] Thus Shakespeare, referring to Ovid's banishment, " I am here with thee and thy goats, as the most capricious poet, honest Ovid, was among the Goths " (*As You Like It*, III. 3).

[2] The opinion, Gotthi = Getae, has received in recent times the weighty support of Jacob Grimm on philological grounds; cf. *Gesch. der Deutschen Sprache*, cc. 9 and 13. Krafft, *Kirchengesch.*, etc., follows Grimm, and adduces evidence from history, common religious ideas, customs, etc. On the other side stand all later writers of note—Pallmann, Bessell, Wattenbach (*die von J. Grimm vertheidigte Identität kann als antiquirt betrachtet werden*, p. 59, note); but see esp. v. Wietersheim, vol. i., and Dahn's Excursus at end of Wietersheim-Dahn, vol. i. The greater part of Krafft's book stands or falls with this theory.

confusion of the names, and the absence of critical interest or skill among the early chroniclers, a distinct motive for this identification can be traced in the desire to provide the Goths with a famous ancestry, and to shew that they were not the "parvenus" in Europe which they were supposed to be, but were lineally descended from races which had fought the Romans for centuries, and figured even in the pages of Herodotus and Thucydides.[1]

Another fruitful source of confusion lies in the great number of names by which different sections of the Gothic stock were known,[2] and the loose way in which the annalists use them sometimes of particular sections, at other times to denote the whole nation.

But when all historical notices of Getae and Scythians have been excluded, except those where it can be shewn that the writer under one of these names meant to refer actually to the Goths, the materials for their history are very much curtailed, and the date of their contact with the Roman empire brought down to the reign of Caracalla.[3] From this point onwards they appear ever more frequently on the pages of the historian, as the necessity for expansion, want of means of

---

[1] That this was the "tendency" of the work of Cassiodorus, which is the foundation of Jordanis *de Rebus Geticis*, is antecedently probable, Theodoric being anxious to reconcile the Romans to submission to his dynasty; and it is further confirmed by Athalaric's message to the Senate concerning Cassiodorus (Varr. ix. 25), " Iste Amalos cum generis sui claritate restituit," etc.

[2] *e.g.* Greutungi, Thervingi, Rugii, Vandals, Taifali, Victohali, and many others.

[3] See v. Wietersheim-Dahn ; Dahn, ii. 52. Others find the first indications of their presence fifty years earlier.

subsistence, hunger after the good things of the empire, and the pressure of peoples behind them, urged them forward first to skirmishing inroads, then to a close-locked struggle, and finally to conquest. It might be thought that under these circumstances the history of the Goths, at any rate after the date of their arrival on the frontiers of the empire, would have attracted the attention of their contemporaries in the empire, and ensured us a trustworthy account of the people at this important stage. But this is not the case; apart from the fragments of Dexippus, there is no account of the Goths written by a contemporary till the last years before their entrance within the empire, while the authorities most relied upon are actually separated from the earlier period of their history by one, two, or three centuries.

Of the sources available for the pre-Christian era, the most valuable is that contained in the work of Jordanis (or Jornandes, as he is also called). Under the title of a history of the Getae he compiled an account of the Gothic peoples extending from their earliest myths or traditions down to the fall of Vitigis. Jordanis was apparently a bishop, settled in the south of Italy about the middle of the sixth century. That he was himself a Goth lends interest, but does not of itself add to his authority as an historian of the people. Living and writing three centuries after they began to play a part in Roman history, and many centuries after they had left the early home of which he gives an account, he was eye-witness and contemporary only of events which are sufficiently well known from other sources; and for the rest, the value of his statements

must be measured by the value of his authorities and
his skill in using them. His own account of his work
shews that it was a compilation, and that he had not
even his main authority before him when he wrote.
This was the history of Cassiodorus, the minister and
secretary of Theodoric. Jordanis, before he began to
write his own history, got the loan of the manuscript
for three days, and seems to have made copious though
hurried extracts, which he afterwards incorporated in
his text. The rest of the work was made up from
other authorities, from the traditions and folk-lore of
the people, and, for the later period, from the records
of his own memory. The work of Cassiodorus in its
turn was drawn from various older sources, chiefly from
historians whose works are now lost, but also to some
extent from popular songs and traditions.[1]

Through this mingling of Saga that may be partly
history, and history that is more than half Saga, the
beginnings of the Gothic peoples are dimly portrayed
to us. The Saga and the history are so intertwined,
however, that they may be distinguished only herein
perhaps, that while the story tells us too little the Saga
accounts for too much. Through this misty haze we
see the ancient home of the race, that to which they
looked back as their earliest, on the shores of the
Baltic Sea.[2] Some of their accounts stopped short at

---

[1] For Jordanis and his history see especially the following:
Schirren, *de ratione quod inter Cassiodorum intercedat et Jor-
danem;* Köpke, *Deutsche Forsch.* 1859, pp. 50 ff.; v. Sybel, *de
Fontibus Jordanis;* Wattenbach, *Geschichtsquellen,* i. 62 ff.;
Hodgkin, *Italy,* vol. i. pp. 43 ff. "He is careless and uncritical."
—(Freeman.)

[2] Jord. c. 1, § 3.

the southern coast, others looked beyond and across the
sea to Sweden itself (Scanzia). This gives occasion to
refer the three most famous divisions of the stock to
the crews of the three ships which carried the migrat-
ing people,[1] and the laggard progress of the third boat
earned for her crew and their descendants the name of
Gepidi.[2] Whether there be a kernel of fact embedded
in this legend of migration from Sweden or not, the
land to the south of the Baltic was undoubtedly the
point of departure for their migration to the south.
At what time this took place cannot now be ascertained,
and the different dates assigned by different historians
depend on the date they fix for the first appearance of
the Goths on the borders of the empire, and on the
time they allow for their progress across the centre of
Europe.

The first distinct mention[3] of Goths in connexion
with the Roman empire is in the reign of Caracalla
(A.D. 215), against whom the sarcastic jest was made that
he ought to be called Geticus Maximus, "because he
had killed his brother Geta and conquered the Gothi,
who were at that time called Getae." Bessell, however,
has shewn good reason for referring this rather to the
Dacians, who even in the time of Dion Cassius were
confused with the Getae. Passing over this and another

---

[1] Jord. c. 4, § 17. See Bessell, *Pytheas und Seine Zeit.*
Sweden is frequently mentioned as the early home of German
tribes. Their familiarity with the sea and seamanship when they
reached the Black Sea has also been observed as evidence of a
previous home by the sea.

[2] Hodgkin translates "Torpids."

[3] Spartianus, *Vit. Caracallae,* c. 10.

doubtful allusion, we may fix the first appearance of the
Goths on the edge of the Roman empire in or about
A.D. 238.[1] And, as it is scarcely credible that they had
settled down and remained as peaceful neighbours for
any length of time, while there is at least one instance
of a tribe moving from the North Sea to the Roman
boundaries within the space of a year, their migration
from their northern settlement may very well have
taken place in the early years of the third century.
Impelled by what motives we know not, whether by
fear behind or by hope before, they streamed up the
basin of the Vistula, over the watershed, and down the
valley of the Pruth, till they reached the Euxine and
the frontiers of the Roman empire. Here they settled
in the ill-defined district known to the historians as
Scythia, which included the south-east corner of Russia
as far as the Maeotis or Sea of Azov, and the country
north of the lower Danube, answering to what was in
much later times known as Moldavia and Wallachia.

Whether[2] the distinction between Ostrogoths and
Wisigoths arose first in their new settlement, or (as is
more probable) was already existing when they left
their northern home; and whether again these names
were originally based on the relative geographical posi-
tions of two tribes, or were connected with the names
of kings or royal families;—these are questions that do
not concern us here: at any rate, the relative position
of the two peoples in their new settlement was in
accordance with the geographical interpretation of their

---

[1] Dahn, accepting the account of the parentage of the Emperor
Maximin, places the arrival of the Goths as early as A.D. 160.

[2] See especially Dahn, *Könige*, ii. 83 ff.

names. For whether the Ostrogoths, according to the alternative offered by Jordanis,[1] were so called after one of their kings, Ostrogotha, or because they dwelt to the east of their kindred, the latter explanation at least agreed with the fact. The dividing line, though it cannot be supposed to have been very rigidly observed, must have been at or near the river Pruth; eastwards lay the Ostrogoths, and westwards the Wisigoths. The usage of these and other names for different sections of the Gothic race is obscure. Besides the main division into Ostro- and Wisigoths, there are many other names recorded, applying to larger or smaller sections; and among the Wisigoths especially there was a tendency after the break-up of the joint kingdom to split off into separate tribes each under their own chief. The names Ostrogoth and Wisigoth were not applied by either nation to themselves; each side called themselves "Goths" and their neighbours "west" and "east Goths" respectively. The same two peoples were distinguished in their earlier history under the names of Greutungi and Thervingi, which are still used by the historians of the empire simply as alternative names for the Ostrogoths and Wisigoths. Each section had, moreover, its royal house. The Amalungs among the Ostrogoths and the Balthungs among the Wisigoths were held in the highest honour, and had an hereditary claim to the headship of their respective peoples; while, so long as the two sections were ruled by one king, he

---

[1] Jordanis, c. 14 : "pars eorum qui orientalem plagam tenebant, eisque praecerat Ostrogotha, incertum utrum ab ipsius nomine an a loco, id est orientali, dicti sunt Ostrogothae, residui vero Vesogothae in parte occidua."

was chosen from the Amalung stock. The question of the "United Kingship" among the Goths has given rise to much debate. It has been held, on the one hand, that down to the fall of the kingdom of Hermanaric the Ostrogothic kings held double sway over both Ostrogoths and Wisigoths; but this has been called in question by later writers; the passage in Jordanis which it is founded upon can bear another interpretation, and the continuous existence of a united kingdom down to Hermanaric would involve contradictions with other statements of the same writer. The best supported account appears to be that the two peoples came to a political as well as a local separation after the joint rule of Ostrogotha; and though the widely extended authority of Hermanaric cannot fail very early to have reached his own kinsfolk and immediate neighbours the Wisigoths, yet whatever submission they made to him, there was no real surrender of independence, and they continued to make peace and war with the Romans or among themselves, uncontrolled by the Ostrogothic overlordship.[1]

We find this race, therefore, at the date of their first inroad upon the empire (A.D. 238), occupying a territory in central Europe of undetermined depth, but in length extending from the Crimea to the Sereth; divided about the middle of this line by some far-descended distinction into east and west folks, and ruled by princes of two royal houses.

Of their religion as of their manners and mode of

---

[1] For full discussion of the "Gesammt Königthum" see Pallman, p. 10 ff.; Dahn, *Könige*, ii. p. 84 ff.

thought, at and before this epoch, nothing can be ascertained with certainty. Attempts have indeed been made to find the names of deities in those of the traditional fathers of the stock, by connecting, for example, Gapt[1] or Gaut with Geat (one of the names of Wotan), or Balthen with Balder; but the very nature of the attempt is an index of the poverty of our information. Traces of a mythology and of a worship of some sort are perhaps to be found in two passages of Jordanis,[2]— in one of which he states that after a great victory the chiefs of the people, through whose good fortune it had been gained, were hailed not as simple men but as demigods, that is *Anses*, where there can be little doubt that we have an allusion to the "Aesir,"[3] or upholding deities of northern mythology. In a second passage,[4] he relates a similar case where the king and conqueror Tanausis was "worshipped after death among the deities of his people." Of sacred objects or of a national cultus there are very few traces. In the account given by Sozomen[5] of the persecution under Athanaric we read of a wooden image set upon a wagon, which was carried round from one village to another to receive worship. This recals the procession of Freya among the northern peoples, when an image was simi-

---

[1] See Grimm, *Deut. Myth.* 4th ed. i. p. 20.

[2] Jordanis, c. 13.

[3] Goth. "anz," plur. "anzes." Cf. Luke vi. 41, where it = "beam." Grimm, *Deut. Myth.*, ut supra.

[4] Jordanis, c. 6.

[5] Sozomenus, 6, 37. λέγεται γὰρ ὥς τι ξόανον ἐφ᾽ ἁρμαμάξης ἰστὼς καθ᾽ ἑκάστην σκηνὴν περιάγοντες . . . . ἐκέλευον τοῦτο προσκυνεῖν καὶ θύειν.

larly carried through the country,[1] and also the account
given by Tacitus of the rites of the goddess Nerthus
or "Mother Earth" among the Lombards.[2] And if
credence may be given to the details of the description
in Eunapius[3] of the passage of the Danube in 380
(? 376), the heathens who were then crossing brought
with them both sacred objects and heathen priests and
priestesses. Lastly, in a highly interesting passage in
Jordanis,[4] we may find traces of a belief among the
Goths in certain supernatural beings well known in
northern mythology. The popular legend of the origin
of the Huns is there given; namely, that they were the
offspring of a union between certain witches whom the
Gothic king "discovered among his people, and holding
them in suspicion ejected from the country" with certain "unclean spirits wandering through the desert."
It has been conjectured that here, under the phraseology of Cassiodorus coloured by his biblical knowledge,
there lies an allusion to the Teutonic dwarfs or "skohls"
dwelling in this case not in the caves and holes, but on
the outlying uninhabited steppe.

These scanty indications of the stage of religious
consciousness which the Goths had reached at the time
of their first contact with Christendom are yet sufficient
to warrant the assumption that their natural religion
was similar to that of the other Teutonic races, that
their Valhalla was tenanted by gods removed from

[1] See Krafft, p. 370.

[2] Tacitus, *German.* c. 40: "vectamque bubus feminis multa
cum veneratione prosequitur," etc.

[3] Eunapius, frag. 46, ed. Niebuhr, p. 88.

[4] Jordanis, c. 24.

humanity more by the heroism of their deeds than by
their morality, benevolence, or even their all controlling
power; while the earth and the darkness were peopled
by unknown beings, partly benevolent and partly
malicious. It was a brave, simple-hearted people,
panting for the treasure, the comfort, and the secure
sustenance to be found only within the Roman empire.
To them Christianity came with winning grace, with
gifts in her hand of knowledge, of power, and of peace.

CHAPTER II.

THE BEGINNINGS OF CHRISTIANITY AMONG THE GOTHS.

AUTHORITIES FOR CHAPTER II.

Sources :
Philostorgius, *Hist. Eccl. Photii epitome.*
Zosimus, *Hist. Eccl.*, book i.
Theodoret, *Hist. Eccl.*, book i.
Basilius Magnus, *Epistolae.*

Literature :
Kraft, *Kirchengeschichte der Deutschen Völker*, Abth. i. (1854).
Waitz, *Ueber das Leben und die Lehre des Ulfilas* (1840).
Bessell, *Ueber das Leben des Ulfilas, und die Bekehrung der Gothen zum Christenthum* (1860).
H. M. Gwatkin, *Studies of Arianism* (1882).

The necessity, laid upon us by the results of modern inquiry, of withdrawing from the theory of the early writers who connected Gothi with Getae, deprives us at the same time of a great deal of information on the early history, mythology, worship, and civilisation of the Goths; for the history and habits of the Getae are comparatively well known. From their first appearance in the narrative by Herodotus[1] of Darius' march against the Scythians in B.C. 456, allusions to them are frequent in the historians. It cannot escape notice that the very length of continuous existence in one district, which is assumed by those who accept the chain, Scythians—Getae—Goths, the persistency of this one nation, while all the peoples round them were being moved, subdued, annihilated, or absorbed, is in itself so unlikely, that the burden of proof lies fairly upon those who

[1] Herodotus iv. 93.

2

maintain such a continuity of more than 600 years, rather than on those who call it in question. More than one writer,[1] after accepting or demonstrating the reality of this connexion, has been able to give a full and interesting account of the ancestors of the Goths, and especially of their mythology; but as this can no longer be maintained, we are thrown back for information on the very slender sources of Jordanis, and scanty allusions in other historians. From these, as well as from the natural probability arising from their close relationship, it may be gathered, as we have seen, that the Gothic mythology corresponded pretty closely to the well-known system of the German peoples. Polytheists they certainly were; their gods were of the Homeric stamp, raised above mankind solely by their power; while even that was limited by fate, either personified or impersonal.

The introduction of Christianity among this people took place during the space of 130 years, less or more, when they were settled north of the Danube and of the Euxine. Standing thus in contact with the Roman empire along their whole southern boundary, they were also in contact with Christianity. But the time for missionary enterprise, the age of devoted bands of missionaries going out from the empire to work among the barbarians, was not yet. In the third century the new faith was still struggling for recognition, from time to time struggling for very existence. Its prospect of ultimate supremacy was to all appearance very slight. It was held in the balance against the heathenism,

---

[1] *e.g.* Krafft, *Kirchengeschichte d. Deutschen Völker*, Part I.

which rested on the traditions of centuries,—and not rarely within these two centuries, during which the Goths played their great part without and within the Eastern empire, did it seem likely, as far as men could judge, that the old faith, aided by chance, by the policy of the imperial court, and by dissension within the young church, would succeed in crushing its rival. It would scarcely be expected that a church, struggling for patronage, with difficulty holding its own against heathenism, and distracted by controversy, if not yet rent by schism, should shew any great aptitude or enthusiasm for missionary work; the seeds of Christianity were carried beyond the Danube by no organised effort, by no church-supported labourers detached for the work, but, to all appearance, accidentally, and certainly at the cost of much misery and suffering.

It has been observed that the first indisputable appearance of the Goths in European history must be dated in A.D. 238,[1] when they laid waste the South-Danubian province of Moesia as far as the Black Sea. In the thirty years (238—269) that followed, there took place no fewer than ten such inroads. Emperor after emperor marched against the same devastating barbarians, and whether he achieved victory, or encountered defeat, his successors had alike to reckon with the same foe,—a people, who descended like locusts upon the fertile plains of Moesia, urged not by desire of conquest, nor as yet by hope of settlement, but by the imperious necessity of obtaining food, and by the reports of a land of plenty and riches, lying across the dividing

[1] See Capitolinus, *Vita Maximi*, c. 16; cf. id. *V. Gordiani*, c. 22.

stream. The attempt to satisfy these craving hordes. with an annual subsidy failed no less than the attempt to hold them in check by force of arms. A victory cost the Emperor Decius 30,000 men. A defeat cost the lives of the whole Roman army and of the emperor himself.[1] Nor had the enemy themselves tilled fields, valuable cities, or rich treasures to lose, through which retaliation might be inflicted and a warning brought home to them. It became at length the despairing hope of the Roman subjects south of the Danube,[2] that the winter might pass without the ice on the river becoming strong enough to afford the barbarians a safe and easy passage, wherever they chose to cross. Nor were they content with the plunder of Moesia alone; but, extending their range, took shipping on the Euxine, and scoured the coasts of Asia Minor from Trebizond to Ephesus.[3] Achaia was attacked both by land and by sea. Even large and fortified towns did not escape their furious onset or patient blockade, however long they might have defied their arts of siege;—Philippopolis and Athens, in Europe,[4] Chalcedon, Nicomedia, and Ephesus, in Asia, fell into their hands.

From these expeditions they returned with immense booty,—corn and cattle, silks and fine linen, silver and gold, and captives of all ranks and of all ages. It is to these captives, many of whom were Christians, and not a few clergy, that the introduction of Christianity among

[1] See Gibbon, c. 10.

[2] cf. Libanius, *Orat. in Constantium et Constantem*, ed. Reiske, iii. 303; Pallmann, p. 49.

[3] A.D. 257, Zosimus, i. 32.

[4] A.D. 267, Zosimus, i. 39.

the Goths is primarily due. Of this we have direct
testimony. Sozomen,[1] relating how, at the time of
Constantine, "the church multiplied throughout the
whole Roman world," adds as follows : "To almost all the
barbarians the opportunity of having Christian teaching
proclaimed to them was offered by the wars which took
place at that time between the Romans and the other
races, under the reign of Gallienus and his successors.
For when, in those reigns, an untold multitude of mixed
folk passed over from Thrace, and overran Asia, while
from different quarters different barbarian peoples did
in like manner by the Romans alongside them, many
priests of Christ were taken prisoners and abode with
them. And when they were found healing the sick
there, cleansing those who had evil spirits, by simply
naming the name of Christ, and calling on the Son
of God, and, further, holding a noble and blameless
conversation, and overcoming their reproach by their
manly walk, the barbarians marvelled at the men, their
life and wonderful works, and acknowledged that they
themselves would be wise and win the favour of God,
if they were to act after the manner of those, who
thus shewed themselves to be better men, and, like
them, were to serve the Right. So, getting them to
instruct them in their duty, they were taught and
baptised, and subsequently met as a congregation."

It is of course not to be mistaken that this account,
written nearly a century later, is coloured, especially in
its details, by the ecclesiastical experience of the writer,
and is, in these particulars, little more than a statement

[1] Sozomen. *Hist. Eccl.* ii. 6 ; cf. *de Vocatione gentium*, ii. 33 ;
Krafft, p. 213.

of probabilities; but there can be no doubt about the main fact, that the Christian captives spread the knowledge of their faith among their "masters." This is further attested by Philostorgius,[1] who both lived nearer to the events he described, and was himself a native of one of the districts of Asia Minor which the Goths had laid waste. His account is similar to that of Sozomen: in the reign of Gallienus and Valerian a great body of Goths had overrun Europe and even crossed into Asia, Galatia, and Cappadocia, and had carried off from thence many captives, including members of the clergy; this "captive and pious crowd" had turned "not a few of the barbarians" to a life of piety and a Christian way of thinking.

The influence of such captives on their captors, and their means of obtaining the respect and affection of their masters, may be illustrated by the case of the Iberians, which is given with much detail by Sozomen.[2] A captive Christian woman (perhaps a virgin or nun), named Nouné, first by her blameless and self-denying life, then by her skill or simple prudence exerted in healing the sick wife of the king, and finally through certain strange deliverances and successes, which were ascribed to her prayers, brought to the faith both the king and the people, and it is recorded that they built a church, and sent to Constantine to ask him to provide them with priests and teachers. Whatever may have been the foundation for this story, which appears in a highly-elaborated form, it is easy to see how knowledge

---

[1] Philostorg. *Hist. Eccl.* ii. 5.

[2] Sozomenus, ii. 7; cf. Theodoret, *Hist. Eccl.* i. 27; Moses Chorenensis, ii. 86; Revillout, p. 17.

and skill would come to the aid of devotion and purity
of life, in winning for the Christians from the south
a powerful influence over the simple, unlearned barbarians of the north.

These accounts are confirmed, and the sympathy
excited by the fate of the captives throughout the whole
Church is shewn, by an allusion to the circumstances of
this period, which is preserved in one of the letters of
Basil. In a letter,[1] which he addressed to Damasus,
bishop of Rome, beseeching the sympathy and support
of the churches in the west for the churches of his own
diocese, which were suffering from various causes, he
reminds him that there is a precedent for such help in
the assistance rendered by a former bishop of Rome,
Dionysius; for, at that time of the Gothic inroads, he
had condoled with the church in Cappadocia on their
losses and sufferings, and had sent envoys to "redeem
the brethren who were captives."

The period of the inroads, which so strangely formed
a sowing-time for Christianity, was followed by a long
period of tranquillity, during which the new faith took
root and spread. The great victory won by Claudius,[2]
after he had almost despaired of the state, was followed
up with the greatest persistency and military skill; and
Aurelian, his successor, had given proof in the same way
of his strength and courage, before he signalised his
wisdom also by withdrawing his garrisons from Dacia,
and deciding henceforth to defend the Danube as the
frontier of the Roman empire. The province thus
abandoned was occupied chiefly by the Thervingi or

---

[1] Basil. Mag. *Ep.* 70, ed. Migne.

[2] At Naissus, A.D. 270 (Gibbon, c. xi.).

Wisigoths;[1] though some part of it came into the possession of the Taiphali or Victohali, who were probably smaller branches of the same stem. On the Goths, thus at peace with the empire, and established on its borders, the influence of the Roman world now began to be more freely exercised. It was one of the conditions of peace that they should provide a large body of troops, chiefly cavalry, to serve under the emperor; and though Aurelian's early death would shorten the period of their service under himself, yet the arrangement was continued, and it became more and more the practice for bodies of Goths[2] to take service alongside the Roman legion, and even in the emperor's body guard. While these emigrants thus came into contact with Roman manners and Roman opinions, a lively commercial intercourse, which sprang up between the north and south banks of the Danube, would bring the same within the reach of their countrymen at home. The cession of Dacia had been followed by the withdrawal of most of the Roman settlers; but not a few, on the other hand, had preferred to trust their new masters rather than leave their old home. These would now become agents and distributors of the products of the southern province, and of the luxuries which a generous treaty of peace, as well as the security of numerous hostages, hindered the Goths from carrying off by force.[3] So important indeed did this commercial intercourse be-

---

[1] Eutropius viii. 2.

[2] cf. Jordanis, c. 21: "nam sine ipsis dudum contra quasvis gentes Romanus exercitus difficile decertatus est." .

[3] J. Capitolin. *in Maximin.* 139: "cum Gothis commercia exercuit."

come, that its enforced cessation during the war of A.D.
369 was one of the most effective inducements to the
Goths to sue for peace.[1]   But if I am right in my conjecture as to the reason which had induced some at
least of these "Romans" to remain in the country of
their adoption, they must have had more than an indirect
influence on the propagation of Christianity.   The persecutions of the Christians, which occurred at intervals
throughout the third century (notably in 235 and 250),
together with the general insecurity of life and property
which they experienced at all times, led many of them
to seek from the barbarians the welcome and protection
which they failed to find in the empire.   There has been
preserved a remark of Constantine,[2] which shews that
these migrations had attracted the attention of the emperor, and had withdrawn from the empire worthy and
valuable citizens.   "The barbarians," he said, "are now
boasting over these very men, even they who received
the men who at that time fled from among us."   It may
easily be supposed that settlers who had left the southern
province for such a cause would be not improbably
found among those who refused to follow the garrisons
when they were withdrawn from the Roman outposts.

It is to the faithful work and pure lives of men such
as these, who had fled from Roman civilisation for conscience sake, to the example of patience in misfortune
and high Christian character displayed by the captives,

---

[1] Amm. Marcell. 27, 5, 7: "quod commerciis vetitis ultima
necessariorum inopia barbari stringebantur."

[2] ap. Euseb. *Vit. Const.* ii. 53: "Αὐχοῦσι νῦν ἐπ' ἐκείνοις οἱ
βάρβαροι οἱ τοὺς κατ' ἐκεῖνον καῖρον ἐξ ἡμῶν φύγοντας ὑποδε-
δεγμένοι, καὶ φιλανθρωποτάτῃ αἰχμαλωσίᾳ τηρήσαντες."

and to the instruction of the presbyters sprinkled among them, that we must look, as the source of Christianity among the Goths.[1]

The peaceful relation between the Goths and the empire remained undisturbed, except by occasional raids made by small parties of Goths on the southern bank, until the reign of Constantine. Nor is it very easy to trace the causes or the progress of the hostilities which then broke out. The transference of the capital from Rome to Constantinople, and the necessity of securing the frontier, which lay comparatively near to the new capital, no doubt made Constantine more ready to take the offensive; but the conditions of peace,[2] which were offered and accepted, as well as the statement[3] that he agreed to pay a subsidy to the barbarians, give weight to the supposition that his object was not so much to subdue or terrify them as to enforce a favourable alliance and obtain guarantees for their conduct. Campaigns were carried on against the Goths probably in the years 323 and 332 (in the latter case under the younger Constantine), and at the conclusion of the latter the Goths submitted, gave hostages for future good behaviour (amongst whom was found the son of the king Aorich), and further agreed to provide a contingent of 40,000 troops for the imperial army.[4]

---

[1] cf. Bessell, *Goths*, p. 132 (in *Ersch und Gruber*).

[2] Sozomenus i. 8; Eusebius iv. 5; Socrates i. 18.

[3] Julian. *Caesares*, c. 24.

[4] Jordanis, c. 21, who adds, "quorum et numerus et militia usque ad praesens in republica nominantur; id est Foederati." These "Foederati" were still extant in the reign of Zeno (A.D. 477); cf. Malchus, *Hist. Byz.* ed. Niebuhr, i. 237.

Up to this point we have found no direct allusion in the writers of the time either to Christianity or to a church among the Goths; and the coincidence is certainly remarkable that the earliest distinct reference to them as Christians comes from the champion of the orthodox faith against the heresy which they afterwards adopted. Athanasius, writing before the Council of Nicaea,[1] mentions among the list of barbarian peoples who had received the gospel of Christ both Scythians and Goths. They, together with Aethiopians and Armenians, had shewn the power of Christianity by changed lives, by abandoning cruelty and massacre. Even wars they no longer loved, but had betaken themselves to peaceful pursuits; and the hands that had grasped the sword they now stretched out in prayer. Nay, so strong was their faith, they even despised death, and some of them had already become martyrs of Christ.

The allusion in Cyril[2] is less direct; for though among the races whom he claims as Christian the Goths certainly find a place, yet the challenge is expressed in such general language, and is so obviously rhetorical, that we should hardly be justified in concluding (as some have done) that he meant to assert that among them also was found a fully-organised church, possessing " bishops, presbyters, deacons, monks, virgins,

---

[1] *De Incarnatione Verbi* (§ 51, 52), A.D. 320. Cf. Neander, trans. iii. 177, Bessell, *Ulfilas*, p. 116, and Krafft, p. 214, all of whom connect this passage with the Goths. Cf. also Libanius, ed. Reiske, iii. 303, where he states the problem, and gives his own solution, viz. what induced the Scythians "τοὺς ὄρει τετελεσμένους καὶ ἐνστύχημα τὴν ἡσυχίαν κρίνοντας εἰρήνην μὲν ἀγαπῆσαι καταθέσθαι δὲ τὰ ὅπλα."

[2] Cyril, *Cat.* xvi. 22; cf. xi. 19 and xiii. 40.

and laity besides." Nor can we refer even the statement of Athanasius to the Goths of the Danube; far more probably had he in mind a community and a church in the Crimean peninsula. The fact (to which we shall have to refer later), that, of all the sea raids undertaken by the Goths between the years 238 and 269, the Wisigoths took part in only two, while the Ostrogoths, who were settled in Southern Russia along the coast of the Euxine from the Crimea to the Dneister, were engaged probably in all of them, makes it very unlikely that the captives mentioned by Philostorgius were carried anywhere else than to the eastern settlements. To the influence of these Asian Christians, exerted mainly, if not entirely, upon the Ostrogoths, must be added the ever-increasing intercourse carried on by sea between the Crimea and both the southern shore of the Euxine and Constantinople. To these probabilities has now to be added the fact that the only traces of an *organised* Gothic Church existing before the year 341 are clearly to be referred to a community in this neighbourhood. Among the bishops who were present at the Council of Nicaea (A.D. 325), and who signed the symbol which was then approved, we find a certain Theophilus,[1] before whose name stand the words " de Gothis," and after it the word " Bosphoritanus." There can be little doubt that this was a bishop representing a Gothic Church on the Cimmerian Bosphorus; and if, following the Paris MSS., we read further

---

[1] *Concilior. coll. ampl.* ed. Mansi, ii. 696; Socrates ii. 41; vide Tillemont, *Mem. p. Serv. Hist. Eccl.* x. 2; Waitz, p. 35. Krafft (p. 216) alone, so far as I know, tries to connect Theophilus with the Byzantine Bosphorus.

down the list the name Domnus Bosphorensis or Bos-
phoranus,[1] we may find here another bishop from this
diocese, and regard Theophilus as chief or arch-bishop
of the Crimean churches. The undoubted presence
at this council of at least one bishop of the Goths, and
the conclusion drawn therefrom in favour of the ortho-
doxy of the Gothic Church in general, led afterwards
to the greatest confusion. Failing to distinguish between the Crimean and Danubian communities, the
historians often found their information contradictory,
and altered it in the readiest way to suit the condition
of the Church which they had specially in view.

One other figure, which is little but a shadow, must
be placed between the Nicene Council and the general
conversion of the Goths. In the touching and affec-
tionate letter of Basil to Ascholius,[2] thanking him for
the gift to the Church of Cappadocia of certain relics of
Gothic martyrs, we hear for the first and only time of
Eutyches, a Cappadocian, a friend and probably contemporary of Basil, who had gone to Europe, and in some
way become a missionary among the Goths. These
martyrs had been fruits of his ministry. The letter of
Ascholius had reminded Basil of his friend, for he says,
" You gladdened me by the remembrance of the old
days, while you saddened me by the testimony of what
I saw; for no one of *us* stands near to Eutyches for worth
—we, who are so far from bringing to gentleness the
barbarian by the power of the spirit and the exercise of
the gift received from Him, that even those who are

---

[1] Bessell, *Ulfilas*, p. 116.
[2] S. Basilii Magni, *Epp.* pp. 254, 255; *Ep.* 164. ed. Migne.

gently disposed are made fierce by the exceeding number of our sins."

Eutyches, being dead, had yet spoken to his old friend through the relics and in the story of the sufferings of his disciples; and perhaps Basil half regretted that his lot had kept him in an organised Christian community, whence "love was fled," and where, though there were "heavy tribulations," there was found none of the martyr spirit. He wrote this letter during his bishopric, that is to say, between 370 and 379, and as he was himself born in 329, we may place the activity among the Goths of Eutyches his friend between the years 355 and 365.

We are now met, almost simultaneously, by the fact, of which the consequences were most serious, and by the man, whose influence for good and evil was most momentous, for the Gothic Church,—by the personality of Ulfilas and by the Arianism of the Goths. For it was soon known in the Christian world that the Gothic Church was Arian in its creed, fatally and stubbornly attached to some form of that teaching which had been condemned at Nicaea, and thus hopelessly alienated from the party which had triumphed there, and eventually made good its claims to represent the only orthodox faith. It was also widely known that the conversion of that section of the nation, which became the Gothic Church, was due to the apostolic labours of one of their own race,—the great missionary bishop Ulfilas. But to him too was to be traced the heresy in which they stopped short on the way from heathenism to a complete Christian faith. To the ecclesiastical mind of the fourth century this was a condition more desperate, and an attitude more hostile to the true Church, than open heathenism or blatant infidelity. It was a battle for life and death between the two parties, and certain even of those courtesies which obtain between ordinary foes were suspended in this internecine struggle. The victory fell ultimately to the Athanasians; and the Arians suffered by the fortune of war, what there is no reason to doubt they would have inflicted had victory been theirs, the fate of having their history written by contemptuous and unscrupulous enemies. Thus, in the period which we now approach—the first age of the Gothic Church—there is added to the insecurity which inevitably belongs to the statements of historians writing from fifty to eighty years after the events they record, the distrust which is raised by the obvious and even avowed partisanship of the writers. In the matter of the Arian Gothic Church of Ulfilas, the relation of these three terms, the Church, the Man, and the Creed, is presented in every possible variation. Each one of them appears in turn as the parent of the others, and it is only too clear that, when the events in their historical sequence did not coincide with the ecclesiastical (or anti-ecclesiastical) views of the writer, they were not seldom re-arranged, or even distorted to that end. It is fortunate, however, that historical works dealing with this period, and founded to some extent at least on contemporary authorities, are preserved in sufficient numbers to make a comparison possible. Such a comparison ought to yield a precipitate of truth; and while we must decline to follow the most thoroughgoing foreign critic the full length of his destructive criticism in this field, it may prove possible to construct a harmony of the authorities, and to ascertain with some nearness to certainty what were the events, and what their sequence, which lie behind these apparently contradictory accounts. We must be prepared to find that round Ulfilas, as the central figure in the Gothic Church, or rather as the only name of a spiritual leader of the Goths known to most of the historians, much has gathered that does not of right belong to him. His was the name that suggested itself to be attached to any nameless ecclesiastic who crossed the stage of Gothic history; his influence the *deus ex machinâ* to be summoned to solve all historical puzzles. In like manner, when attempts came to be made in much later times to collect the scattered scraps of information regarding the Gothic Church, his is the figure round which they have all been grouped; so that, to take one example, we are gratified by a list of four or five Gothic bishops, "successors of Ulfilas," though he in all probability had no successor, or at most but one, who can be identified.

The materials for a life of Ulfilas and an estimate of his character and position, inadequate as they are even now, were still more unsatisfactory till within the last fifty years. Up till 1840 we were dependent entirely upon the Church historians of the fifth century, whose unfriendly attitude towards a heretic of the preceding century, and uncritical handling of the traditions on which they founded, furnished but a meagre and untrustworthy account of the great bishop. It was the good fortune of Waitz to discover, in a MS. in the library of the Louvre, a new and authentic account, written by an Arian, a contemporary, and indeed a scholar, of Ulfilas. The importance of the discovery is obvious. We can now behold the man, and the ecclesiastic, from two sides, as he had left his mark on the memories of his opponents, and as he was known by his intimate friend, adherent, and pupil, Auxentius.

The foundation of an enquiry into the history, of which Ulfilas was the centre and the pivot, will perhaps best be laid by an account of this document. For, though it is true that of the points in dispute in regard to his life but few are touched on by Auxentius, yet in his evidence we shall find firm ground from which to approach the debated questions. This memoir is contained in a MS.,[1] the proper contents of which are certain writings of Hilary, two books of Ambrose *de fide*, and a copy of the proceedings of the Council of Aquileia, held in 381. The object of this council, where the Catholics were led by Ambrose, was to bring to reason or submission the western Arians, who were represented by Palladius and Secundianus. There was little courtesy shewn to opponents in such councils, and small respect for the rights of minorities. Ambrose, no doubt, conducted himself overbearingly towards the heretics, but what they resented most bitterly was that their pleadings and replies were misrepresented or omitted in the official account of the proceedings. To correct these misrepresentations and supply the omissions, another Arian has made use of the broad margin of his copy of the *Acta* to make a fresh copy of his own,

---

[1] In the Paris Library, Supplement Latin No. 594, partially deciphered and edited by Georg Waitz in *Ueber das Leben und die Lehre des Ulfilas* (Hanover, 1840); described and critically examined by Bessell, *Ueber das Leben des Ulfilas*, etc. (1860)

inserting remarks and corrections, as well as some longer documents bearing on the proceedings of the council.[1] This marginal script extends over fifty-two pages, with a wide interval of twenty-five pages in the middle, whose margin is left blank. It is unfortunately much injured. For not only has one whole line at the top and at the bottom of almost every sheet been cut away in the binding, as well as many letters from the fore-edge, but the text itself also has been defaced in several places, and that so systematically, that it can hardly have been caused by accident. The writing is an autograph of the compiler himself, and from his regular expression in introducing his own remarks,[2] we learn that his name was Maximin, and that he was a bishop. That he was also an Arian is clear from the whole scope of the document, and from the tendency of these remarks, which is uniformly to correct the *Acta* in favour of the Arian representatives.

The fragmentary character and partial illegibility of the MS. is very unfortunate, and a hiatus frequently occurs just where it was most important to have a continuous text; for Maximin took occasion to add to, or introduce into, his version of the *Acta* sundry documents, whose character and relation to the council could only be ascertained with certainty if the context were complete. But one consequence of the mutilation of the MS. is that it is no longer possible to discover exactly at what point, and by what connecting link, the

---

[1] Cf. *Actt. conc. Aquil.* p. 399, and Waitz's MS.: "et his apparet quomodo pro sua voluntate scripserunt, quod eos libuit"; see Bessell, p. 3.

[2] e.g. " Maximinus episcopus interpretans (*vel* disserens) dicit."

writer passes from his revised or annotated copy of
the transactions' to the document, which is of such
value and importance for the life of Ulfilas. Nevertheless, from references which are made to it in other
parts of the MS., both its author and its subject may be
ascertained beyond doubt.[1]

The writer was Auxentius, an Arian bishop of
Dorostorus (Silistria), and it is Ulfilas whom he describes
thus: "A man whom I am not competent to praise
according to his merit, yet altogether keep silent I dare
not. One to whom I, most of all men, am a debtor,
even as he bestowed more labour upon me. For from
my earliest years he received me from my parents to be
his disciple, taught me the sacred writings and manifested to me the truth, and, through the tender mercy
of God and the grace of Christ, brought me up both
physically and spiritually as his son in the faith."[2] In
the first line, which is legible, of this account, drawn up
by Auxentius, he is found distinctly referring to one,
who can be no other than this his master, as "of most
upright conversation, truly a confessor of Christ, a
teacher of piety, and a preacher of truth." To this there
follows immediately an exposition of the doctrinal
position of Ulfilas, and of his teaching regarding the
qualities and relations of the Father and the Son.
This is very full, and includes a description of his
attitude towards each of the parties which were prominent in the Church at that time, with reasons for his
dissent from each. Leaving the doctrinal position of

[1] Waitz, ut sup. p. 33; Bessell, p. 1, seq.
[2] MS. fol. 284.

Ulfilas for future examination, we find the epochs of his life given by Auxentius thus. He died at Constantinople at the age of seventy, when he had been bishop and preached "in the one and only church of Christ" for forty years, having been consecrated at the age of thirty, the earliest canonical age. Previous to his consecration he had been a "lector" or reader; as bishop he worked for seven years among the Goths on the far side of the Danube, till, a cruel persecution having risen against them, he sought and obtained leave from "the emperor Constantius" to move his flock across the Danube, and settle with them in Moesia; here he spent (so far as we learn from Auxentius) the remaining three and thirty years of his bishopric and his life, till he undertook his last journey to Constantinople "upon imperial request," and died almost as soon as he reached the city.

The facts of his life are given very briefly and tersely, especially when compared with the account of his teaching; and it is worthy of note that no direct mention is made of his great work of translation; hence we feel that the object of the writing was not primarily historical or biographical or even commemorative, but doctrinal if not polemic. It is quite in accordance with this view that the climax and the close of the work is the creed of Ulfilas, solemnly introduced by the words:[1] "And he, moreover, at his departure, even in the moment of death, through his testament, left for the people committed to him a statement of his faith." Then follows the creed, and though the conclusion is unfortunately lost through the defective state

[1] MS. ed. Waitz, fol. 286.

of the MS., yet enough remains to shew that it was distinctly Arian in its tendency; while, on the other hand, it corresponded exactly with none of the many creeds which were at the time the watchwords of as many parties. Of the utmost importance, however, for the history of the Gothic Church is the first clause, which runs,[1]—"I, Ulfilas, bishop and confessor, have always thus believed." Ulfilas was at no time in his life an adherent of the Athanasian party.

It will at once be seen that the most important date for fixing the chronology of his life is that of the year when he journeyed to Constantinople, and died. The object of his visit has been lost through the fragmentary state of the MS. at this point; but at the very end of the MS., the second part of which consists of a polemical work by Palladius addressed to Ambrose, we find an independent allusion to Ulfilas,[2] and to a journey which he made to Constantinople, attended "by the other bishops."[3] It is also stated that their object was to induce the emperor to summon a general council. They obtained his promise; whereupon the leaders of the opposite (Athanasian) party were alarmed, and brought so much pressure to bear upon the emperor that he not only withdrew his promise, but also issued a decree[4] forbidding the holding of any discussion con-

---

[1] "Ego Ulfila episcopus et confessor semper sic credidi, et in hac fide sola et vera testamentum facio ad Dominum meum."

[2] Bessell, *Ulfilas*, p. 17.

[3] "ceteris consortibus."

[4] "Ut lex daretur quae concilium prohiberet, sed nec privatim in domo, nec in publico vel in quolibet loco disputatio de fide haberetur."—(MS. ed. Waitz, fol. 327, p. 23.)

cerning the faith "either in private at home, or in public, or in any place whatsoever."

The date of the composition of the principal work which Maximin has inserted in this marginal script— that of Palladius, which forms the second part of the MS. (ff. 314—327)—could be fixed with some certainty, (1) between the death of Auxentius, bishop of Milan,[1] and the appointment of an Arian successor, Mercurin (Auxentius II.), that is between 374—386; (2) between the Council of Aquileia and the death of Damasus, bishop of Rome, that is between 381—384. Taking note of the fact that the writing contains no reference to the Acta Concil. Aquil., which could scarcely have happened, if it had been compiled *after* the publication of the *Acta*, and further that the interest in the whole controversy subsided very rapidly after the same council, we should date the work nearer to 381 than to 384. If it could be assumed, therefore, that this clause, which brings the MS. to a conclusion, is in vital connexion with the rest of the work, and part of the same composition, the date of Ulfilas' death would be ascertained to within one or two years; for it would be mentioned in a document which cannot be placed earlier than 381 or later than 384. But, however probable this date may on other grounds be shewn to be, it cannot be supported from the general date of the composition of this polemic of Palladius. The last clause is not homogeneous with the whole work. It is preceded in the MS. by a passage of impassioned appeal, which might most fitly form a peroration by itself. After a rhetorical allusion to Italy

---

[1] MS. Waitz, "an de mediolanensi (*scil.* Auxentio) qui sine successore decessit." cf. Tillemont, *Hist. Eccl.* x. 165, 746.

and Rome, "which have been held worthy to behold
the martyrdoms of apostles, and to hold their sacred
relics in possession," Palladius challenges the Athanasians, "if they have any assurance of faith," to meet
their adversaries in public disputation before the senate
at Rome, and promises on behalf of the Arians that
their defences, drawn up at all points according to the
authority of all the Scriptures, should then be forthcoming. Amongst the audience he hoped they would
permit the presence of "followers of heathenism" as
well as Christians, citing the mission of Paul to the
Gentiles, and of Peter to the Jews, as a proof that the
"Apostolic summons excluded none from hearing of
religion." "For, so it shall come to pass, that when
truth, which is in the meanwhile crushed by your
hostile attack, begins to breathe again, those who now
appear to be without will become servants of God."
Finally, he declares that, wheresoever it may please
them to hold a council, by the help of God through
His only begotten Son, Palladius of Ratiara, and
Auxentius, out of the rest of the bishops, will not be
found wanting. It is at the close of this impassioned
address to Ambrose that there follows immediately the
notice of the last journey of Ulfilas to Constantinople,
which is related in the matter-of-fact style of an
annalist, and supported by a reference to the narrative
of "Saint Auxentius," which had been inserted in the
first section of Maximin's MS.

The conclusion cannot be avoided that the notice of
Ulfilas forms no integral part of the writing of Palladius,
but is, in truth, a pendant to it added by Maximin.
Hence the date of the composition of Palladius' polemic

cannot be taken to define the date of the death of
Ulfilas, which must be ascertained upon independent
evidence. Now, the tenour of this concluding paragraph is as follows: " When they (presumably Palladius
and Auxentius), together with Ulfilas and the rest of
their fellow-bishops, had reached Constantinople, and
the emperors, moreover, were present there, after that a
council had been promised to them, as Auxentius has
set forth, the heads of the heretic party did use all their
influence to have a decree issued to forbid a council,
and to provide that neither privately at home, nor
publicly, nor in any place whatsoever, should any disputation concerning the faith be held—as is shewn
by the text of the decree." Regarding this statement
by itself, we would gather that Palladius pursued his
plan of a council, but wished it now to be held not at
Rome, but at Constantinople. The Arian bishops, with
Ulfilas amongst them, met in the capital. If this is
called a council or synod by Maximin, it is, nevertheless,
nothing more than a conference of Arian bishops.
They had come not to meet or form a general council,
but to demand one; and, furthermore, the presence
of the emperors in Constantinople seems to be regarded by the chronicler as an accident, and one
favourable to their design.[1] Their mission appeared at
first likely to be crowned with success. The much-
desired council was promised to them. Upon this the
Athanasians (here called " heretics," according to the
common practice of the Arians, who regarded themselves
as alone the true Church), took alarm, and brought such
pressure to bear on the emperors that not only was the

[1] " ibique etiam et imperatores adissent."

promise rescinded, but a decree was issued, which finally crushed the hopes of the Arian party by prohibiting religious discussions of any and every kind. This important statement is now attested by a reference to two decrees of Theodosius, which profess to embody the legislation referred ·to in the text, the origin of which has been thus described. Now these laws are dated in 388 and 386 respectively. The former of the two, however, is seen to refer more directly to such circum-stances; and, on the evidence of this law, and its date in the Codex of Theodosius, the year of the journey of the bishops, the year of the death of Ulfilas, has been fixed at 388.

It cannot be denied that there appears to be cir-cumstantial evidence here of the strongest kind; so much so that, in spite of the convergence of many other lines of proof on 381 as the date of Ulfilas' death, Waitz[1] was compelled, with not a little reluctance, to accept the year 388, and to assign dates to the different events of his life by reckoning backwards from that year as the year of his death. Thus his birth falls in 318, his consecration as bishop in 348, and his flight with his people in 355.

The reluctance to accept the date thus forced upon him by the connexion set up between Ulfilas' last journey to Constantinople and the laws of 388 and 386, is well founded; the difficulties and contradictions that follow are many and insuperable. In the first place, there is no trace of an assembly of bishops at Constantinople in 388. The church historians, well-informed as they are on the events of the time in question, have no mention

[1] Waitz, p. 47 f.

of it, and, moreover, a council in that year can be shewn to have been out of the question, since the emperor, who, according to Auxentius, must have been at Constantinople, was absent from the capital during the greater part of the year.[1] In the next place, the legislation of the year 383 had been already such as to destroy all possibility of a council for the settlement or even for the discussion of the Arian question. In fact, the policy of suppression, which had been persistently and systematically followed out by Theodosius since his accession, had long before 388 'so reduced the numbers and influence of the Arian party in the Church that proposals for a council at that time would have been absurd, even if they had been legally possible. Thirdly, the laws quoted at the end of the MS. prove, on examination, to be quite inappropriate, and even futile in regard to their ostensible purpose,—namely, to rescind a promise just given, and absolutely to forbid the proposed council.[2]

But these very laws thus quoted, which give rise to the difficulty, contain also the clue to its solution. It is admitted that, in the MS. of Waitz, we have the actual autograph of the compiler, Maximin, who made use of the wide margin of his copy of the *Acts of the Council of Aquileia* to engross thereon some portion of the same *Acta*, with a few

----

[1] This had not escaped Waitz. "Freilich wissen wir nichts von einer Versammlung von Bischöfen zu Constantinopel im Jahre, 388." p. 47.

[2] It is true that Waitz reads, "Nulli . . . . concilii aliquid deferendi patescat occasio," but, apart from the difficulty of construction and sense involved, the text of the codex gives *consilii* without any v.l.

remarks of his own interjected, a quotation from
Cyprian, the writing of Auxentius, and the letter which
Palladius had publicly addressed to Ambrosius. Who
Maximin himself was, there is nothing beyond his own
writing to shew; but from this it appears that he was
a bishop, an Arian, and had been in all probability a
personal friend of Palladius, Secundian, and Auxentius,
with whose ephemeral works he is so well acquainted,
and whose opinions he defends so earnestly. At what
time he collected for himself these documents, bearing on
the Arian controversy, cannot be distinctly ascertained.
On the other hand, there can be no doubt that the
appended laws, together with the statement derived
from Auxentius, of which they are offered in confirmation, and which has been shewn above to be independent of the foregoing Palladian document, were
not written here before 438. The evidence for this
statement is very curious. The second of these two
laws (the year of whose issue has unfortunately been
defaced in the MS.) is identical in its wording with
the law of 386, Codex Theodosianus XVI. 4, 1.
The most cursory examination of this law, however,
shews that it is incomplete; for neither has it any
grammatical construction, nor does it convey any
effective sense. In fact, a comparison with Cod. Theod.
XVI. 1, 4, shews that it is nothing more than an
incomplete sentence taken from that law, which here
appears as independent and complete. Thus, not only
is the ostensible application of the second law discredited, by which it is referred to the prohibition of
Arian conferences at Constantinople, but it proves to be
a fragment of a law issued by Valentinian at Milan,

under special circumstances, and actually in favour of the Arian party, while this particular clause was directed against the Catholics, "who think that to themselves alone the liberty of assembly has been granted." Now, since it cannot be supposed that this detachment of a sentence of the law Cod. Theod. XVI. 1, 4, and the erection of the fragment into an independent law, took place twice—once in the hands of the collator of the Codex, and again in those of Maximin—it follows that the latter drew his quotation from the published Codex. But the Codex was not collected and published till the year 438. With this second law we must connect also the first one, which immediately precedes it in the Codex, and assume that Maximin, having the statement of Auxentius before him, searched the Codex for an edict or edicts to confirm it, found these two in immediate proximity to one another, under the very appropriate title, "De his qui de fide contendunt," and hastily added them to his text.

If, therefore, the connexion of the year 388 with the last journey of Ulfilas to Constantinople depends only on the evidence of Maximin, writing later than 438, and conjecturally assigning the laws he quotes to the circumstances in the text, we are at liberty to neglect this evidence in favour of the otherwise converging testimony in favour of a date between 381 and 383. One of the objections to the date of 388 for the futile application for a council was, that there was no trace of such negotiations in the historians, nor would such an attempt have been possible under the historical circumstances as we know them. This objection does not apply to 381. We are aware of a situation and 'a

course of events which, though differing in detail,
are yet in striking agreement with the situation and
events described by Auxentius. Sozomen,[1] in introducing a story of readiness and address displayed by an
aged bishop in the presence of Theodosius, explains
that "the Arians, being still a considerable body, on
account of the support given them by Constantius and
Valens, were assembling with more boldness, and holding
public discussion concerning God and the divine substance; and they were for persuading the officers
of the palace, who were like-minded with themselves,
to make trial of the emperor. For they thought to
succeed in their attempt, having regard to what happened in the time of Constantine. But this also raised
anxiety and alarm in the party of the Catholics."
From this point the account goes on to speak of
Eunomius as the object of special fear among the
Catholics, in relation to the emperor; and describes
how, by the influence of his wife, and the parabolic
instruction of a courageous bishop, "he became more
cautious, and did not admit those who held the contrary opinion;"[2] and a decree was issued, forbidding
discussion and assemblies in the public market, and
"making it very unsafe to discuss the nature and substance of the Godhead in the same way as before." The
correspondence of this account with Auxentius is sufficiently remarkable. In both, the emperor is the

---

[1] Soz. vii. 6; cf. Theodoret, v. 16; cf. Tillemont, *Mem. Hist.
Eccl.* vi. 627, and note 104. The reasons put forth for disregarding
the chronological arrangement of Sozomen are insufficient.

[2] ἀσφαλέστερος γενόμενος οὐ προσίετο τοὺς παρὰ τοῦτο
ἐπξάζοντας.

central figure; inclining at first to admit the heretics to negotiations, raising thereby the alarm of the Catholics; being diverted, through their influence, from his tolerant purpose, and destroying all hope in the heretic party by the issue of an edict forbidding all public discussion. This account is placed by Sozomen between the arrival of Theodosius in Constantinople and the consequent banishment of Demophilus, and the meeting of the Great Council of Constantinople, that is to say, between[1] November, 380, and June, 381. Turning now to the Codex Theodosianus, XVI. 5, 6, we find an edict of January 10th, 381, which answers exactly to the circumstances and the foregoing negotiations as described by both Auxentius and Sozomen, while we cannot but find a distinct reference to the promise hastily given by the emperor in one of the opening sentences: "Let all men know, that even if anything have been obtained by men of this kind by any special authority whatever, craftily obtained, it is of no value."

Finally, the transfer of the date of Ulfilas' death, from 388 to 381, provides an immediate solution of a very perplexing statement in another historian.[2] In an account of Ulfilas, given by Philostorgius (368—430), who, after Auxentius, stands nearest to him in point of time, and is further connected with him by the ties of a common creed, his consecration to the bishopric is described thus:[3] "Having been sent by the rulers of

---

[1] Bessell, *Ulfilas*, p. 30. [2] See Waitz, p. 36.

[3] Philostorg. *Hist. Eccl.* ii. 5, ὁ τοίνυν Οὐρφίλας οὗτος καθηγήσατο τῆς ἐξόδου τῶν εὐσεβῶν, ἐπίσκοπος αὐτῶν πρῶτος καταστὰς· κατέστη δὲ ὧδε, παρὰ τοῦ τὴν ἀρχὴν ἄγοντος τοῦ Ὀθροὺς ἐπὶ τῶν Κωνσταντίνου χρόνων εἰς πρεσβείαν σὺν ἄλλοις

the nation on an embassy, with certain others, in the
time of Constantine, . . . he was appointed by Eusebius,
and the bishops with him, to be bishop over the
Christians in Gothia." As the history of Philostorgius
is preserved only in the epitome which is given of it by
Photius, who is, moreover, of opinion that Philostorgius
thinks too highly of Ulfilas, and may therefore not have
taken much pains to mould the extracts he made into a
harmonious account, it is not difficult to understand
how the embassy, and the selection for the office of
bishop, are carelessly put together in one sentence, and
made to appear as if both took place in the reign
of Constantine (who died in 337). But no similar
account can be given of the express assertion that
Ulfilas was made bishop by "Eusebius, and the bishops
with him." That is a fact on which Philostorgius is as
likely to be accurate as Photius is unlikely to have
invented it. And as Eusebius, of Nicomedia, who
alone can be referred to,[1] died in 342, to place the
consecration of Ulfilas in 348 involves a hopeless contradiction to the authoritative statement of Philostorgius. On the other hand, if 381 be accepted as the
year of Ulfilas' death, reckoning back the forty years of
his bishopric, we arrive at 341 as the year of his
consecration, and that is within the lifetime of Eusebius.
Nor was a fitting opportunity lacking in that year. At
the Council of the Dedication, held at Antioch in 341,[2]

ἀποσταλεὶς—καὶ γὰρ καὶ τὰ τῇδε βάρβαρα ἔθνη ἐπεκέκλιτο τῷ
βασιλεῖ—ὑπὸ Εὐσεβίου καὶ τῶν σὺν αὐτῷ ἐπισκόπων χειροτονεῖται τῶν ἐν τῇ Γετικῇ χριστιαναζόντων.

[1] Eusebius of Caesarea died circa 338.

[2] See especially Gwatkin, p. 114 f.

there were present some ninety bishops of the Eusebian party, and Eusebius was the leading spirit there. ' It can, of course, be only a conjecture, but if the consecration of Ulfilas took place at this time, and during this council, then the expression of Philostorgius, ὑπὸ Εὐσεβίου καὶ τῶν σὺν αὐτῷ ἐπισκόπων, becomes fully intelligible.

These are the grounds upon which the conclusion of Waitz may be set aside, and the year 381 accepted in place of 388 as the year of Ulfilas' death. The other dates follow accordingly. He was born in 311, consecrated bishop of the "Christians in Gothia" in 341, and migrated with his persecuted flock into Moesia in 348. In 380 he journeyed to Constantinople in obedience to a summons from the emperor, and there he died, either. at the end of the same year, or in the very first days of 381. ' So much may be established upon the testimony of Auxentius, the simplicity of whose account, together with the entire absence of "tendency," which is implied in the fact that the biographical notice is quite apart from, and subordinate to, the main purpose of the document, entitle him to the fullest credit. Unfortunately, he went no farther; and from the man, whose familiarity with the people, the scene, the circumstances, and the chief actor, would have enabled him to give most valuable information, we have, so far as regards the outward history of Christianity among the Goths, little more than the bare facts collected above.

Seeking now to fill in these outlines, we have to depend on less satisfactory authorities, who wrote, for the most part, fifty or sixty years after the death of Ulfilas,

and had views of church history, and of church and state
policy, to support, which were an almost irresistible temptation to accept or reject statements according to their
bearing on these points, if not in some cases to modify
them in the direction of their own sympathies. The
passage in Philostorgius, to which reference has already
been made,[1] supplies important information concerning
Ulfilas, which goes far to fill up the outline given
by Auxentius. Beginning with the remark that " about
this time Ulfilas (Ourphilas) is said to have brought
across into Roman soil a large body of people from
among the Scythians beyond the Danube (whom the
ancients called Getae, but the moderns, Goths),"—he
proceeds to describe the origin of Christianity among
this people, as has been shewn above, and refers especially
to Asia, Galatia, and Cappadocia, as districts from
which Christian captives were carried off. " To this
body of captives belonged also the forefathers of Ulfilas,
being Cappadocians by race, from a township near to
Parnassus, and a village called Sadagolthina." This
very exact statement, which has been accepted without
cavil by most of the historians,[2] gains an apparent support, sufficient almost to induce conviction, from the fact
that Philostorgius, as a Cappadocian and an Arian himself, may be presumed to be well-informed on the point
in question. But this support is only apparent, and the
statement itself, in the absence of attestation from any
collateral evidence, can at best be regarded as a tradition
preserved by a writer to whom it was a matter of personal interest. The following points are to be noted:

[1] Philostorg. *Hist. Eccl.* ii. 5.
[2] Waitz, p. 36.

4

First, the connexion of Philostorgius with Cappadocia does not really add weight to his testimony regarding the descent of Ulfilas from a Cappadocian captive, carried off thence to some place beyond the Danube. He stands even less near to original information on this point than a Byzantine writer would do. Indeed, such a fact could hardly be known to any one, writing forty or fifty years after the death of Ulfilas, except by a tradition derived from Ulfilas himself.[1]

Secondly, it is to say the least, highly improbable that any captives carried away from Cappadocia were so carried away by the Goths of the Danube; still less probable that such could be the case in the expedition to which Philostorgius refers the captivity of an ancestor of Ulfilas. This expedition, in the reign of Valerian and Gallienus, took place in 267, and in so far as it was the only one which penetrated to Cappadocia, the account of Philostorgius is confirmed. But in all the sea-expeditions, except that of 258, in which the Wisigoths also took part, but which reached no further than Nico-media, the marauders were Ostrogoths from the Crimea and the coast of the Euxine, who had quickly learnt to make use of the highway of the sea,—perhaps had only to recall their experience acquired on the Baltic. Hence we should naturally look for Cappadocian captives, and traces of their influence, in the Crimea, but not among the Goths of the Danube.

Thirdly, it is not easy to understand how the descendants of a captive family could, in the third generation, have risen to such importance among the Goths that one of them, at the age of 17 or 23, should

[1] See Pallmann, i. 64.

represent the people at the court of Constantinople, either as a hostage or as an ambassador. Yet this is what Philostorgius has related of Ulfilas just before. His object in connecting Ulfilas with Cappadocia was, no doubt, to enforce the idea that Arianism was a much earlier factor than had been supposed (compare the immediately following account of Theophilus, also ordained by Eusebius as deacon to go to the Indians); and the groundwork of the account may probably have been the work among the Goths of the undoubted Cappadocian, Eutyches, and the testimony borne thereto in the letters to and from Basil, and in the martyr relics presented to the Church in Cappadocia.

Leaving undetermined the question of the credibility of Philostorgius on this subject of the nationality of Ulfilas, we thank him, nevertheless, for the following. Sometime in the reign of Constantine, Ulfilas was "sent by the ruler of the nation on an embassy, with others." This event in his life is the earliest of those mentioned by Philostorgius, and was no doubt taken by Photius as the point round which to collect his excerpts from that writer on the subject. If this be so, the phrase with which the whole passage is introduced, κατὰ τούτους τοὺς χρόνους, may be pressed so as to give a clue to the date of the event which was earliest, but is thus by Photius confusedly combined with the event which was most important,—his consecration by Eusebius. The "times" referred to are seen, from the chronological position of the narrative, to be those immediately succeeding the Vicennalia, hence the year 327 or 328. And if, as seems probable, the anxiety of Constantine to secure the frontier, to which his newly-

founded capital was in perilous proximity, determined
him first to over-awe, and then to make peace with, the
Goths on the Danube, the presence at his court of representatives of that nation, either as hostages or as envoys,
would readily be explained.[1] If this were not the occasion,
however, the conclusion of the important treaty in 332
would provide another opportunity. From this time we
must suppose that Ulfilas resided, possibly as a hostage,
at Constantinople or, at any rate, within the empire;
for to this period, and the opportunities which such a
residence would offer, we ascribe his knowledge and
command of both Greek and Latin, and the commencement of his great task of the *Translation*, his work as
"lector," and his acquaintance with Eusebius, which led
to his appointment as bishop. His command over three
languages is doubly attested by Auxentius, who describes
him as preaching constantly in the Greek, the Latin,
and the Gothic tongue, and also as having left behind
"several treatises and many expositions in those very
three languages"; and if in explanation of this, and
other indications of opportunity for study and familiarity
with the Roman world, we assume for Ulfilas a sojourn
of some years within the empire, we can find room for
his activity as a "lector" either among the large body
of Goths, who were, after the peace of 332, attached to
the Roman army, or among those of his countrymen
who were drawn in ever-increasing numbers to settle in
the empire, where, since the peace, they were admitted
to many high offices. Whether his conversion to

---

[1] See Bessell, *Goths*; the building of the bridge across the river
took place in 328. *Chron. Alex.* Law of July 13th in this year
shews that Constantine was at Discos, on the Lower Danube.

Christianity is to be ascribed to the same period or not, there can be little doubt that it was then that he first learnt and embraced the Arian doctrines, which in one form or other would be found wherever he might be stationed in the empire.

The question of the form of Arianism, adopted and represented by Ulfilas, must be reserved for later discussion; sufficient for our present purpose that he had become an Arian, and had worked as a "lector" among his countrymen before his ordination by the semi-Arian Eusebius. In the latter circumstance we may find the simplest and readiest motive for the undertaking of the great work, which marks Ulfilas as a leader among men, the Luther as well as the Moses of his people, the father of all Teutonic literature, the first translator of the Scriptures into the mother tongue of the barbarians, in whose hands was the future of the world. The need of such a work would be obvious from the first moment of his undertaking to be a "reader" of Christian truth among his own countrymen. Nowhere else, and at no other time of his life, would the opportunity be so favourable for both conceiving and carrying out such a design. Living, as I imagine him to have done, in some part of the province of Asia,[1] possibly moving

---

[1] That Ulfilas worked at this period of his life elsewhere than in the land of his birth, is supported, I think, by general probability, and also by Auxentius (Waitz, p. 50): "ita et iste sanctus, ipsius Cristi dispositione et ordinatione et in fame et *penuria predicationis indifferenter agentem* ipsam gentem Gothorum secundum evangelicam et apostolicam et profeticam regulam emendavit," etc. A passage which could hardly have appeared in this form had he been active there before. Cf. also Philostorgius: χειροτονεῖται τῶν ἐν τῇ Γετικῇ χριστιαναζόντων.

from one garrison to another with the Goths who served under the Roman standard, he would come in contact with many men, especially of 'the Eusebian party, from whom he would obtain both encouragement and assistance; and his ordination by bishops of that party, at the earliest canonical age, is indirect proof both of their intimate acquaintance with him, and of zeal and ability displayed by him in his previous work.

The death of Constantine, the persistent and powerful champion of union in the Church, was the signal for renewed activity among the Eusebian party ;[1] they held a council at Antioch in 338 for the purpose of deposing Athanasius, and met there again in 341 to consecrate the Golden Church of Constantine, and also to reply to the letter of Julius. At the same time we find Philostorgius relating, in immediate connexion with these councils, the appointment by Eusebius of two men to work among the heathen, of Ulfilas as bishop and of Theophilus[2] as diakonus, wherein we cannot fail to see striking evidence of a determination among that party to widen their influence by missionary enterprise.

Under such auspices was Ulfilas sent forth to preach the Gospel to the large body of his countrymen on the far side of the Danube, possibly with some part at least of his translation completed and in his hand. The Wisigoths, or Thervingi, were at that time ruled by a prince or chief,[3] whose great figure, looming through the haze, makes us wish that some of the historians had been at pains to tell us more, and more accurately, about

---

[1] See esp. Gwatkin, p. 111.

[2] Philostorgius, *Hist. Eccl.* ii. 6; cf. iii. 3 and 12.

[3] See note at the end of this chapter.

him and his deeds, and sufferings. The political connexion of these Wisigoths and their prince with the
Ostrogoths, and the wide-ruling Ermanaric, is very
obscure, but[1] it seems probable that if any dependence
at all were admitted by the former, it was little more
than nominal.[2] When the gentile, or topographical,
distinction between Ostrogoths and Wisigoths deepened
into a political separation, which took place either during
or before the reign of Ermanaric, and certainly before
the onset of the Huns, the Wisigoths did not apparently
come under the rule of one king, chosen from among
themselves, but fell into separate tribes, whose chiefs or
princes were independent of one another, and shortly,
if not immediately, became independent of the Ostrogothic king. The ruler of the people, among whom
Ulfilas went to work, bore the title not of king, but of
"judge,"[3] which may, according to Grimm's suggestion, be
a Latin attempt to render the Gothic " faths," *i.e.* herr, or
" over-lord." Among a Gothic people, thus ruled by an
" irreligious and impious over-lord," Ulfilas worked
until the success of his efforts roused the alarm or suspicion of the ruler, and gave rise to a cruel persecution,
" so that Satan," as Auxentius quaintly phrases it,
" who was eager to work mischief, against his will
worked weal; for those whom he hoped to make

---

[1] See Dahn, *Könige*, ii. 84, 92 ; v. 1 seq.

[2] Jordanis, c. 24, " rex Hunnorum in Ostrogothorum partem
movit procinctum, a quorum societate jam Vesegothae quadam inter
se contentione sejuncti habebentur."

[3] Gibbon, c. xxv.; Themistius, *Orat.* 10; Ammian. Marcell.
27, 5, 6, " Athanaricum judicem potentissimum"; 31, 3, 4,
" Athanaricus Thervingorum judex." But see Dahn, in *Forsch. z.
D. Gesch.* xxi.

deniers of the faith and renegades, Christ aiding and
defending them, became martyrs and confessors. Whereupon, after the glorious martyrdom of many servants
and handmaids of Christ, because the persecution was
still in terrible fashion over-hanging them, after ful-
filling only seven years in his bishopric, this most
saintly man, Ulfilas, of blessed memory, was driven
forth by the barbarians, together with a great body of
the faithful, and received with honour on Roman soil by
the then reigning emperor, Constantius; so that just as
God, by the hand of Moses, did set free his people from
the power and violence of Pharaoh and the Egyptians,
and caused them to pass through the Red Sea, and
procured them to be his servants, so did God, by
the hand of Ulfilas, set free from the barbarian the
confessors of his own only begotten Son, and caused
them to pass over the Danube, and to serve him
according to the manner of his holy ones." What
follows in the narrative of Auxentius is rather fragmentary, but it is clear that he carries out the parallel
between the two leaders, pointing out that Ulfilas also
judged the people forty years in all. This account
is confirmed by Philostorgius in the passage already
referred to, though, in consequence of the confusion
introduced by Photius' epitome, the migration is made
to take place under Constantine. Ulfilas settled with
his Christian Goths in Moesia at the foot of the range
of Haemus, round about Nicopolis, and near the site of
the modern Tirnova. Here Jordanis, or his authority,
knew them,[1]—"a very numerous people, but poor and

---

[1] Jordanis, c. 51, "populus immensus, . . . gens multa sed
paupera et imbellis nihil abundans, nisi armento diversi generis,

unwarlike, rich in nothing except cattle of different kinds, pastures, and forest trees; not having much wheat, though the soil is fertile in all other kinds of produce." This is evidently the picture of a peaceful pastoral people, drawn probably by the hand of one (not Jordanis himself) who could not appreciate the gentler manners of the once terrible barbarians, or the hidden source of their new civilization. It is not a little remarkable that this is the only place where Jordanis mentions Ulfilas. "There were," he says, "other Goths indeed, who are called 'Gothi Minores,' a numerous people, with their chief priest, or primate, Ulfilas, who is also said to have taught them letters." The meagreness of this account, his only reference to the famous bishop, is an indication in itself of the narrowness of the sources from which the historian of the Goths drew his information.

We must now leave Ulfilas working among his people, safely and peaceably established at the foot of the Balkan mountains, preaching, writing, and carrying on the work of his translation; his people were Arians, because he himself held Arian doctrines in some form or other, and on his death-bed he could say, "I, Ulfilas, have always thus believed."

The Gothi Minores do not again appear in history; no doubt their settlement became a rallying point for Arians of other nationalities, and when the severe legislation of Theodosius forced the adherents of the

pecorum et pascua silvaque lignorum; parum habens tritici, ceterarum specierum est terra foecunda. Vineas vero nec si sunt alibi certe cognoscunt, ex vicinis locis vinum negotiantes; nam lacte aluntur plerique."

defeated party to leave the capital, it was in Moesia that many of them took refuge, among whom Demophilus, the late bishop of Constantinople, was the most noteworthy. Possibly some of the Gothi Minores were swept along with Alaric's host, and found their way to Greece and Italy. Otherwise the people became absorbed in the ordinary population of Moesia. Of Ulfilas himself, from the time of the migration, we hear nothing for twenty years, except that in 360 he was present at the synod of Constantinople, at which the creed of Ariminum was accepted and confirmed.[1] But we may see traces of his influence on his fellow-countrymen across the Danube in their subsequent history; and whether or not we claim for him all the active participation which is ascribed by the historians, we can well believe that during these twenty years he built up that great influence, described by Socrates, which, from that historian's point of view, he used for evil. " For the Goths having been instructed by him in the things belonging to the faith, and having been by him made sharers in a more civilized way of life, readily obeyed him in all things, being fully persuaded that nothing of what was said or done by him was bad, but that all tended to the advantage of the zealous believer."[2] The part taken by Ulfilas in the events following 367, and the questions arising in that connexion, are so intimately connected with the general conversion of the Wisigoths, that they can be best discussed in a subsequent chapter.

---

[1] Socrates ii. 41; Sozomen. iv. 24; vi. 37.

[2] Sozomenus vi. 37, p. 273, *ad fin.*

NOTE.—Although it has been generally, and almost tacitly, assumed, since the publication of Waitz's MS., that the " irreligiosus et sacrilegus judex," by whom Ulfilas was persecuted and forced to quit the country of the Wisigoths in 348 (355 according to Waitz's own chronology), was no other than Athanaric, yet it must be pointed out that there is no direct evidence for the identification; in fact, the evidence in this case is no more complete than that which connects Ulfilas with the "presbyter Christiani ritus" of the negotiations before the battle of Adrianople. The passages from Ammian and Themistius prove that Athanaric was known as "Judex," or δικαστής, or the Gothic equivalent to these titles, and he was also "barbaricus," a heathen, and a persecutor; but this was in 370, and the earliest mention of him by name is at the commencement of his war with Valens in 366 or 367, that is to say, twelve years after the date of the persecution of Ulfilas, even according to Waitz's date. It is quite possible that "Judex" was the title of several Wisigothic chiefs, and of some predecessor of Athanaric, unknown to us by name; and in view of the great length which his connexion with the persecution of Ulfilas would demand for his reign (348—381), it is at any rate better to leave it an open question.

CHAPTER III.

THE GOTHS AND THE EMPIRE.

AUTHORITIES FOR CHAPTER III.

SOURCES:

Ammianus Marcellinus.
Eunapius.
Socrates and Sozomen (as before).

LITERATURE:

Kaufmann, *Kritische Untersuchungen zu dem Kriege Theodosius des Grossen mit den Gothen* in *Deutsche Forschungen*, xii.
Gueldenpenning, *Theodosius der Grosse*.
Richter, *das Weströmische Reich unter Gratian, Valentinian und Valens*.
Dahn, *Könige der Germanen*, Abth. ii. and v.
Gwatkin, *Studies in Arianism*.
Pallmann and v. Wietersteim (as before).

THE history of Christianity among the Goths in the succeeding period is so closely bound up with their civil and political history, that it will be necessary, even for the proper understanding of the questions which have to be treated, to give here a short sketch of the relations of this people to the empire, reserving for the present any point that is held in dispute.

The peace of 332, "the last of Constantine's great services to the empire,"[1] governed the relations between the Goths and the Romans for many years. It was certainly to the advantage of both parties to preserve it unbroken. Apart from the security they had given in their hostages, the Goths had motives of self-interest, binding them to good behaviour, in the advantages of a peaceful intercourse with the empire, and the career which was opened up to many a barbarian in the army

---

[1] See Gwatkin, p. 83.

or in the palace. On the other hand, the emperor,
besides the services of the auxiliaries, whom the Goths
were bound to provide, enjoyed, through their tranquillity, a security along the northern frontier, which
was of the utmost importance at a time when the
empire was engaged in frequent struggles with Persia.
These peaceful relations continued throughout the
reign of Constantius (337—361).[1] In the reign of Julian
the sounds of discontent and coming danger first made
themselves heard. But it was not till the reign of
Valens that hostilities actually broke out.[2] The causes
and the details of the war of 367—369 are very
obscure, and do not concern us here; it ended in a
peace concluded between Valens and Athanaric, which
was arranged and ratified on board a ship moored
in the river.[3] From this time forward there appears on
the scene a new and famous figure,—another chief of
some section, tribal or otherwise, of the Wisigoths,—
namely Frithigern, whose relations to Athanaric on the
one hand, and to Christianity on the other, form one of
the kernels of the whole question. But whatever was
the position of the parties, now three in number, in the
years immediately after the peace of 369, all these
relations were thrown into the greatest confusion by the
sudden appearance on the stage of European history of
the Huns.[4]

[1] See esp. Libanius iii. p. 303, ed. Reiske.

[2] See Bessell, *Goths*, p. 137; Gwatkin, p. 237; Dahn, *Könige*.

[3] Ammianus Marcell. 27, 5, 7—10.

[4] For the Huns, see Jordanis, c. 24; Ammian. Marcell. 31, 2;
31, 3, 1, etc.; Eunapius, ed. Niebuhr, p. 48; Dahn, *Könige*, i.
214; and v. Wietersh. ii. 25.

At what time the terrible "riding folk" first passed the Gate of the Nations, and entered Europe, cannot be ascertained with certainty, but in or before the year 375 the shock of their onset upon the Goths of the Volga made itself felt upon the banks of the Danube. The empire, or great federation, governed by Ermanaric went to pieces. One part of the Ostrogoths submitted to the dominion of the new comers, and was absorbed in the great wave that rolled forward toward Europe. Another part fled before the wave, and, falling back upon their brethren, the Wisigoths, crushed Athanaric and his subjects back into the Carpathians, while they thrust Frithigern and his people forward to the very waters of the Danube. From the far side of the dividing stream, while the whole people, men, women, and children, were massed up to the banks, looking back with terror for the approach of the dreaded foe behind, a homeless, starving multitude, stretching out their hands to the land of plenty and of safety which lay in front, Frithigern[1] sent envoys to Valens, asking him to receive his flying people, and give them leave to settle on Roman soil. Valens, after long debate with his advisers, gave his consent, and, almost before the negotiations were completed, the impatient people began to cross. Some plunging into the river were drowned in an attempt to swim over; others crossed on rafts; while the main body were transported by boats, the passage lasting "through days and nights,"—200,000 fighting

[1] Alavivus in Ammian; probably both. For the whole, see esp. Ammian. Marcell. 31, 3 and 4; also cf. Eunapius, *ut supra*, and see Pallmann, p. 111. The whole account in Eunapius is full in detail, and very graphic.

men, according to Eunapius, with their weapons and their families.

Whatever were the conditions on which the barbarians were allowed to enter the empire, it is certain that they were not observed on either side. Valens was in distant Antioch; and the carrying out of the whole operation was necessarily entrusted to officials. They scandalously abused their position. On the one hand, the Goths were not compelled to lay down their arms; and on the other, the provisions which had been promised, and which were absolutely necessary for the starving multitude, were cruelly withheld till the people were fain to part with their gold and their jewels—nay, even with their children—to buy a piece of meat.[1] The madness of such conduct is inexplicable. Lupicinus and Maximus were blinded by their greed, and they saw their own folly too late, when the people who had gradually been stripped of their goods, their treasure, their children, and their honour, of all but their arms, rose against their oppressors, destroyed the small force which Lupicinus had at his command, and poured forth over the whole peninsula, carrying back as they returned not only much booty, but their own treasure and their own children from every town.[2] The Emperor Valens, engaged on the opposite frontier of the empire in negotiations and hostilities with the Persians, and most unwilling to leave that quarter till he had brought affairs to an issue, trusted to the lieu-

---

[1] Jordanis, c. 26.

[2] Eunapius, ed. Niebuhr, p. 51; Chrysostom, *ad Vid.* i. 421: χορεύοντες μᾶλλον ἢ πολεμοῦντες; Themistius, *Orat.* 14 and 16: "an Iliad of Misfortune."

tenants whom he sent, and to the assistance of Gratian, emperor in the west, to subdue the revolt of his new subjects.   But his generals Profuturus and Trajanus were defeated in the Dobrudscha, and Gratian, after reaching the frontier, was compelled to divert his forces to meet a sudden inroad of the Alemanni on the Rhine; and not till Valens himself returned to the seat of war were the Goths compelled to desist from plundering far and wide, and to fight not only for land and liberty, but for their very existence as a nation.

The opposing armies drew together in the neighbourhood of Adrianople. Whether from fear at the greatness of the stake, which depended for him and his people on the issue of the conflict, or from an honourable desire to obtain by negotiation and without bloodshed all they demanded—namely, the fulfilment of the late compact, securing to the Goths a free settlement in Mœsia, and proper sustenance till they could support themselves—Frithigern, under whose leadership the other tribes seem to have united themselves with the Wisigoths, made several attempts to come to terms.[1] The envoy, who passed between the camps, is described by Ammian as "a presbyter, as they themselves call him, of the Christian religion," who was sent by Frithigern "as an envoy with other humble men."   This presbyter[2]

---

[1] Ammianus Marcell. 31, 12, 8: "Christiani ritus presbyter ut ipsi appellant, missus a Fritigerno legatus cum aliis humilibus venit ad principis castra."   What persons precisely are referred to as "humiles" it is difficult to say; probably it means only "suppliants," but perhaps "monks."

[2] Bünau, *Teutsche K. u. R. H.* i. p. 826 (who thinks the bishop's name is also mentioned by Ammian under the corrupted form of Alavivus); Waitz, p. 40; Bessell, *Ulfilas*, 58.

has been commonly identified with Ulfilas, but only on the ground that he would be a *persona grata* to Valens, and the most likely and competent man to undertake the mission. Pleasing as it would be to find Ulfilas on so rich an opportunity using his great influence for the highest good of both nations, we must point out that the idea is quite unsupported by any ancient authority. Even Socrates and Sozomen, who are elsewhere very ready to introduce Ulfilas into their account of other transactions, know nothing about him on this occasion. On the other hand,[1] Isidore, deriving his information, no doubt, from the source common to himself and Jordanis, represents the relation between the immigrant Wisigoths and their former countrymen, the Moeso-Goths, as decidedly hostile. The latter absolutely declined to form an alliance with the new comers (and had even to defend their independence with the sword); and though, for reasons which appear later, we must reject (perhaps as a private comment of the compiler) the concluding sentence, which tacitly contrasts these Moeso-Goths as Christians and Catholics with the later immigrants as heathens or Arians, yet the passage, as a whole, points to a relation between the two peoples, such as would make it very improbable that Ulfilas would be found in the camp of Frithigern. Ammian states distinctly that the envoy, besides the public demands of the Goths, was entrusted with a private message from Frithigern. It has been conjectured that this referred to the question of religion, and perhaps included an offer to conform to Valens' wishes in the matter, but in the absence of any

---

[1] Isidore, era 416.

information on this point, and, above all, of any results
that followed, the speculation is unnecessary, if it be not
precluded by the previous fulfilment of all such conditions as Frithigern might have offered.

The envoy was dismissed with an ambiguous reply
(this again was scarcely likely if Ulfilas had been the
man); and a smilar attempt, twice renewed, only met
with similar success. A fierce, and for a long time
a doubtful, battle ensued. But a furious charge of barbarian cavalry, under Alatheus and Saphrax, decided
the day. The defeat of the Romans was so complete
that Adrianople was called the second Cannae. Two-
thirds of the army perished by the sword or in the
morass; and the emperor himself was carried wounded
to a small hut, to which the barbarians, ignorant of
their opportunity, set fire, and so destroyed the enemy
of their nation and the champion of their faith.

Valens was succeeded by Theodosius, who displayed
both high military skill and great political shrewdness in
his treatment of the Goths. The victory of Adrianople
had put south-eastern Europe at the mercy of the barbarians; but with the danger that had threatened them,
there disappeared the only bond that held them together.
Having failed in one attempt to take Adrianople by
assault, and in another to seize Constantinople by surprise, they broke up into roving bands who scoured the
whole peninsula, succeeded in doing much damage, but
often fell victims to the cautious and watchful generals
of Theodosius. It is probable also that about this time
the uniting influence of Frithigern was withdrawn by
his death,—at any rate, he is not mentioned later than
the year of the great battle. The serious and prolonged

illness which attacked the emperor at Thessalonica, and
detained him there from February to December, 380,
obliged him to leave the work of clearing the province
of Thrace of the barbarians to his generals. Moreover,
several of the other tribes, who were always moving up to
the Danube to take the place of those who had crossed
the river, emboldened by the perilous condition of
Theodosius, forced their way across, and strengthened
the barbarian resistance in Moesia. But the emperor did
not confine himself to the attempt to drive the Goths
out of Thrace by force, but opened negotiations with
them, which led even sooner to a complete pacification,
the barbarians receiving permission to settle in different
places along the line of the Danube, from Pannonia to
Moesia. The Goths were now fairly established within
the empire, and the crowning proof and symbol of the
new relations established between the two was the
appearance at Constantinople of the fierce old heathen
Athanaric,[1] who, coming in his old age to make submission to the power which his nation had conquered,
was received by Theodosius with most distinguished
honour. He entered the city on January 11th, 381;
but fifteen days afterwards the old chief died, and was
buried with the greatest pomp. It were strange indeed
if, as we have reason to believe, he died in the same
month, in the same city of strangers, and under similar
circumstances with Ulfilas, the Christian whom he had
persecuted and driven from his fatherland.

NOTE.—Bessell's account of the movements of the Goths after
the battle of Adrianople is far from satisfactory: his ultimate

---

[1] Jordanis, c. 28.

object being to shew that the general conversion of the Wisigoths under Frithigern took place in 380, and *that*, on the occasion of their crossing the Danube, he has to shew how Frithigern and his subjects were on the far side of the river at all at that time. But there is really no authority for supposing that Frithigern re-crossed the river; if it be Zosimus on which Bessell relies (he gives no references, vid. article *Gothen* in *Ersch und Gruber*, 181 *a*), the passage (iv. 24, 34) is full of the greatest contradictions and improbabilities (see esp. Pallmann, 141), and even for a fact, not in itself improbable, would supply very little confirmation. On the other hand, the fact is in itself very improbable, for what course was more unlikely than that, after a victory like that of Adrianople, which laid open to the Goths possibilities far greater than they can ever have conceived, the victorious general should withdraw with his people from the very ground they had fought to obtain? It could be neither to seek for provisions that they went from a land of plenty to one of scarcity, nor to obtain reinforcements that he crossed the river, on the other side of which whole tribes were waiting for a signal; strangest of all would be the reason alleged, that he crossed to give battle to Athanaric.

Again, how could so striking a success as the expulsion of the dreaded enemy beyond the frontier they had crossed three whole years before fail to have been celebrated by the historians, chroniclers, and panegyrists of Theodosius' reign? And we have to go no further than Jordanis himself to see the unlikelihood, if not the implicit denial of such a theory; for on the one hand, after the death of Valens, he tells how the Wisigoths at that time began to settle in the provinces of Thrace and Dacia by the river, "as if they were holding the land of their birth."[1] And on the other hand, the success which he attributes to the troops of Theodosius,[2] encouraged as they were by the advent of an emperor of better stamp than Valens, is explicitly limited by him to "driving them from the

[1] Jordanis, c. 26, *ad fin.* "Quo tempore Vesegothae Thracias Daciamque ripensem post tanti gloriam tropaei tanquam solo genitali potiti coeperunt incolere."

[2] Jordanis, c. 27. "At vero ubi milites principi meliore mutato fiduciam acceperunt, Gothos impetere tentant eosque Thraciae finibus pellunt." We lose the guidance of Ammian after the repulse of the Goths from Constantinople.

frontiers of Thrace," that is to say, back over the Balkans into Moesia. This is immediately followed by the renewed advance into the southern provinces of the Goths in two divisions, Frithigern leading his section towards Epirus and Greece.

It is, therefore, on a review of these facts, impossible to accept the theory that Frithigern and his Wisigoths crossed the Danube twice, once in 376, and a second time in 380. Those who crossed in the latter year were new tribes, attracted by the success and perhaps by the invitation of Frithigern, and may have belonged partly to the Wisigothic and partly to the Ostrogothic stock.

CHAPTER IV.

THE PERSECUTIONS OF A.D. 370—375. AUDIANISM.

AUTHORITIES FOR CHAPTER IV.

Sources :

Basilius Mag. *Epp.* 164 and 165.
Hieronymus, *Chronicon.*
Orosius, Jordanis, and Isidore.
Epiphanius, *Adv. Haereses*, ed. Oehler.
Acta S. Sabae ; Acta Sanctorum, April 12th.
Acta S. Nicetae.
   The references are collected in Tillemont, *Mem. Hist. Eccl.* x. 2.
Ammianus Marcellinus, } for crossing of Danube.
Eunapius, }

Literature :

Waitz, *Ulfilas*, p. 39.
Wietersheim-Dahn, ii. 9, 10.
Krafft, *Kirchengeschichte der deutschen Völker*, esp. p. 309.
Köpke, *Deutsche Forschungen.*

On the persecutions, the best handling of the sources is by Pallmann, though he rejects the evidence of the Acta SS. too completely. Bessell, on the other hand, claims too much certainty for the results of his analysis (*Ulfilas*, p. 80).
   For the crossing of the Danube, the sources are critically examined and the subject ably discussed by Bessell; but his conclusion is altogether untenable, and the importance which he attaches to Eunapius, on whom he mainly relies, is unfortunate, considering the open and malicious hostility of this writer to Christianity. See also Pallmann, pp. 76, 110; Dahn, *Könige*, v. 1; Krafft, 223; Aschbach, 46; Richter, *das Weströmische Reich*, p. 444; v. Wietersheim, 1st edit. iv. 98.

HAVING thus sketched the external history of the Wisigoths from the peace of Constantine to their pacification and settlement within the eastern empire under Theodosius, we return to trace the progress of Christianity and the fortunes of the Church among the Goths during the latter part of the same period. The earlier part of this period is marked by the work of Ulfilas on the far side of the Danube, and perhaps by that of Eutyches. The middle part, from the flight of Ulfilas to the second persecution, is unfortunately a perfect blank in the records preserved to us, and it is not until the year 370 that we can take up the thread at a point twenty years after Ulfilas dropped it. In the year 370, or possibly in the year immediately preceding, the opposition of the heathen governor of the Wisigoths to the ever-growing body of Christians broke out in fierce persecution. The date is fixed by evidence converging from several independent sources.[1] Jerome, in his chronicle under the year 370, relates that Athanaric, king of the Goths, raised a persecution against the Christians, slew a great number, and drove out the Christians from their fatherland on to Roman soil. An opportunity for such persecution would be found after the conclusion of peace with Valens; and in the ill-success that had attended Athanaric we may perhaps see the motive for his taking vengeance on the unbelievers, to whose presence among the people the anger of the heathen gods was frequently ascribed.

This persecution of Christians among the Goths is not to be confounded with the previous one which had issued in the migration of Ulfilas with his flock. Both are sufficiently attested as independent persecutions, taking place at an interval of over twenty years. Ulfilas, with his Arian Goths, had been settled all that time in Moesia. Who, then, were these Christians who fell under the displeasure of Athanaric in 370 ? Who had planted the seed that was bearing such fruit, and was their steadfastness to the credit of an Arian or of an Athanasian creed ?

It is clear that these same questions were raised by those who were all but contemporaries of the persecuted

---

[1] Cf. letter of Basil, 164, written in 373; Orosius vii. 32; Isidore, era 407, though the latter may depend on Jerome.

Christians, and were not satisfactorily answered even then. But there can be no doubt that the orthodox opinion was that the Gothic Christians who suffered at this time were not Arians but Catholics. Thus Augustine, referring to this persecution, distinctly claims its victims as Catholic martyrs; and so strongly emphasizes the fact that none but Catholics were exposed to it, giving as his authority "certain brethren who had been present there as boys," and were eye-witnesses of their sufferings, that he even appears to be controverting a different opinion.[1] Thus Theodoret also speaks of the Goths as having been brought up in "the teaching of the Apostles."[2] Jerome would never have alluded to them in such an unqualified way if he had had any inkling of unorthodoxy in their Church. Nor would Basil have received so gratefully the relics of an Arian martyr. And, not to multiply the indication of this opinion,[3] Ambrose, in the commentary on Luke, mentions the Gothic martyrs in direct distinction to those who tolerated even the discussion of the Arian doctrines.

---

[1] *De Civitate Dei,* xviii. 52. Nisi forte non est persecutio computanda quando rex Gothorum in ipsa Gothia persecutus est Christianos crudelitate mirabili, cum ibi non essent nisi Catholici, quorum plurimi martyrio coronati sunt. Sicut a quibusdam fratribus, qui tunc illic fuerant . . . . audivimus.

[2] Theod. iv. 37. τοῖς ἀποστολικοῖς ἐνετρέφοντο δόγμασι.

[3] Ambrosius, *Expos. evang. Sec. Luc.* i. c. 37. "Gothis non imperabat Augustus, non imperabat Armenis, imperabat Christus. Acceperunt utique Christi censores qui Christi martyres ediderunt. Et ideo fortasse nos vincunt, ut praesentia docent, quoniam quem illi oblivione sanguinis fatebantur, huic Ariani quaestionem generis inferebant."

On the other hand Socrates, describing the general conversion of the Wisigoths, which he places at any rate before 375, mentions a persecution cruelly carried on against the Christians by Athanaric, and especially adds,[1] "So that there suffered martyrdom at that time barbarians who were of the Arian party." And yet another sect claims a share in the persecution, if we add the statement of · Epiphanius that the Audians, whom he knew on the banks of the Euphrates in 375, had been driven out of "Scythia, that is the land of the Goths," four years before.

Taking a general view of these and similar passages that might be added, we cannot escape the conclusion that the persecution which lasted, with alternations of greater or less severity, from the end·of 369 till 373 or 374, fell upon both Catholics and Arians, and found victims among Athanasians, Arians, and Audians alike. And the supposition is not in itself an unlikely one. The withdrawal of Ulfilas with his Arian flock need by no means necessarily have left Christianity unrepresented among the Wisigoths. Not a few of his own followers even might prefer to take their chance of the persecution dying away when the great body of confessors and their energetic leader were departed; and even if we have not any direct evidence on the point, we can scarcely believe that Ulfilas left either his converts who remained behind or his heathen countrymen uncared for. No doubt those twenty years after the

---

[1] Socrates, iv. 33. ὁ Ἀθανάριχος ὡς παραχαραττομένης τῆς πατρῴου θρησκείας πολλοὺς τῶν Χριστιανιζόντων τιμωρίας ὑπέβαλλεν ὥστε γενέσθαι μάρτυρας τηνικαῦτα βαρβάρους Ἀρειανίζοντας.

first migration, though a blank to us as regards Ulfilas, were filled with active missionary work, carried on by his converts and scholars who were sent out from the Arian community in Moesia. Again, the Catholic Christians, of whom we must always assume the presence among the Goths of the fourth century, whether as individuals or as small communities, would be unaffected by the departure of Ulfilas except in so far as they shared in the general cessation of persecution that followed. And with the ever-increasing communication in both directions between the barbarians and the Romans, these Catholic Christians must have received both encouragement and support from their co-religionists within the empire. Of this we shall find indirect proof in the bonds of familiarity and sympathy which undoubtedly existed at this time between the " Church in Gothia " and the Church in Cappadocia.

Lastly, there were the Audians,[1] who were probably a more important factor in Gothic Christendom than the meagreness of our information would lead us to suppose. Our chief source of information concerning the sect and their founder is Epiphanius,[2] who found them pretty numerous in the neighbourhood of the Euphrates, and devoted to them one of his treatises " against heretics." Audius, we learn, was of Mesopotamian descent, but dwelling in Syria, when, " at the time of Arius," he founded his sect. A man of great purity of life himself, and ardently zealous for the

---

[1] For Audians and their founder Audius, or Audaeus, see Tillemont, *Hist. Eccl.* vi. 691; Richter, p. 446. The principal sources besides Epiphanius are Hieronym. anno 341, and Theodoret, 4, 10.

[2] Epiphanius, ed. Oehler, vol. iii. pp. 11—39.

purity of the Church, he did not hesitate to expose the
irregularities and lash the vices of the clergy by whom
he was surrounded. Encountering, as was natural,
great dislike and misrepresentation, he nevertheless
persisted in his work as censor, "studying in the meanwhile to be separated as little as possible from the
fellowship and society of the Church," until actual
violence, to which he and his disciples had been exposed, forced him to leave the communion where his
strict morality and shrewd tongue were so unpopular.
The influence of his life and his earnestness was, however, strong enough to attract to his side many of the
laity; and the bishops of Syria,[1] alarmed lest a serious
schism should arise, laid a complaint before the emperor,
who sustained it, and banished Audius to Scythia. Up
to this time it would appear that he had not at any
rate published the opinions which afterwards marked
him out as a heretic; but they were probably known
to a few of his supporters, and must have been rapidly
developed after his banishment. From the land of his
exile he exercised an influence which must have been
great indeed to produce such results as are described
by Epiphanius. He speaks of monasteries, convents,
and congregations spreading as far as the Taurus
mountains, Palestine, and Arabia, though at his own
day the Audians were reduced to an insignificant sect,
having then only two settlements.[2] But what chiefly

---

[1] Epiph. c. 14.

[2] *Ibid.* ἐκεῖ δὲ μάλιστα διατρίβων καὶ εἰς τὰ πρόσω βαίνων
καὶ εἰς τὰ ἐσώτατα τῆς Γοτθίας πολλοὺς τῶν Γότθων κατήχησεν,
ἀφ' οὗπερ καὶ μοναστήρια ἐν Γοτθίᾳ ἐγένετο καὶ πολιτεία καὶ
παρθενία τε καὶ ἄσκησις ἡ οὐ τυχοῦσα.

concerns us is that Audius made his way into the very
interior of Gothia, "and instructed many of the Goths
in Christian doctrine." In fact, it is on the side of
Audianism alone that we have a picture of a real
ecclesiastical organisation among the Goths, for Epiphanius goes on to describe how, through Audius, there
arose monasteries and an organised religious life, recognised vows of virginity, and a general discipline of no
common kind. But Audius was an old man already
when he was sent into exile, and most of this work
must have been done by his successors. Several bishops
joined his communion, and carried on his work after his
death, among whom one Uranius is specially noted.
But the Goths also were not backward in this respect,
and it appears that Audius himself, who had been
ordained by a bishop in Palestine (one who had left
the Syrian Church for similar reasons), ordained Goths
to the same office;[1] and the succession must have been
maintained, for we hear of a certain Silvanus, "bishop
in Gothia," after whose death the churches dwindled.
But the principal cause of the decline of the Audians
in Gothia was a severe persecution which they under-
went together with other "Christians of our own communion." And the way in which Epiphanius describes
the persecution leaves no doubt that it was the same as
that which fell on all Christians alike in 370. "Moreover, the most part of them were chased out of Gothia,
and not they alone, but also our own Christians in the
same place, through a great persecution which arose

---

[1] Epiph. c. 2. ὕστερον δὲ μετὰ τὸ ἐξεωσθῆναι τῆς ἐκκλησίας
ἀπὸ ἄλλου ἐπισκόπου τὰ αὐτὰ συζητοῦντος καὶ ἀναχωρήσαντος
τῆς ἐκκλησίας χειροτονεῖται οὗτος ἐπίσκοπος.

under a barbarian king." The cause of the persecution, he adds, was the anger of the king against the Romans on account of their emperors being Christians. In this remark we may find remarkable confirmation of the reason suggested for Athanaric's persecution,[1] namely, chagrin at the conditions of peace imposed on him by the Christian king, Valens. In consequence of the persecution, many Audians among the Goths fled from their country and betook themselves to Mesopotamia, where they had been living already three or four years when Epiphanius wrote.

In judging Audius and the Audians,[2] Epiphanius finds more. to blame in their schism than in their false doctrines. After describing the latter, he adds, "What is worse than all the rest, and more terrible, is that they do not pray with any one, even if he be known to be a virtuous man, if only he be connected with the church," that is, with the Catholic Church. Nevertheless, the doctrinal position and the ritual of Audius, in two points at least, divided him very sharply from the Orthodox Church. He and his followers refused to follow the direction of the Nicene Council regarding Easter, and persisted in celebrating it according to the Jewish calendar, believing themselves herein also to be keeping the purity of early practice in opposition to an innovation dictated by subservience to Constantine. A more

---

[1] cf. Köpke, *Deutsche Forschungen.* "Ein Rückschlag des Volkslebens gegen die Niederlage die es soeben erlitten hatte."

[2] τὸ δὲ δεινότερον πάντων καὶ φοβερώτερον ὅτι οὐκ εὔχονται μετά τινος, κἄν τε τῶν δοκίμων φανείη, καὶ μηδὲν εἰς κατηγόρησιν ἐχόντων μηδὲ μέμψιν πορνείας ἢ μοιχείας ἢ πλεονεξίας, ἀλλ' ὅτι ὁ τοιοῦτος ἐν τῇ ἐκκλησίᾳ συγάγεται.

serious point of difference lay in the opinion held by
Audius concerning the corporeal nature of God. Taking
the account given in Genesis of the creation of man,
and especially the texts Genesis i. 27, and ii. 7, as the
basis of his teaching, he sought to shew that, man being
made in the image of God and at the same time formed
out of the dust of the ground, therefore God Himself
must be conceived as possessing a corporeal existence.
For this theory he sought further support in such
anthropomorphic expressions as Ps. xxxiv. 15: "The
eyes of . the Lord are upon the righteous, and His ears
are open to their cry."[1] This teaching was not a new
thing in the Church, as Krafft points out, for one
Melito,[2] bishop of Sardes, had written a work entitled
περὶ ἐνσωμάτου Θεοῦ, in which the same doctrine was
propounded. A reference to it may perhaps be found
also in Augustine,[3] who classes with the Anthropo-
morphites a certain sect called Vadiani, which may be
a corruption of Audiani. Modern writers point out
that an anthropomorphic conception of the Deity would
recommend itself to the heathen Goths, both as easier
to comprehend, and as more nearly related to their own
conception, wherein the full deity was only a step
beyond the demigod, and removed from the hero more
by antiquity than by omnipotence, infinity, or incom-
prehensibility. But there is no ground for supposing
that Audius deliberately adopted this view in order to
effect more quickly the conversion of the Goths. On
the other hand, there can be no doubt that the austere

---

[1] He laid stress also upon Isai. lxvi. 1; Dan. vii. 9.

[2] In the second century. See Krafft, p. 365, and reff.

[3] August. *de Haeres.* c. 50.

life led by the monks of Audius would deeply impress
the barbarians, and appeal, moreover, to sympathies
buried deep in the heart of the Teutonic race. Epiphanius has nothing but praise for the Audians in this
respect. "For indeed," he says, "this method is altogether admirable in its fashion, and everything within
these monasteries is ordered well, apart from these
controversies."

We believe, therefore, that all these forms of belief
had representatives among the Christian Churches and
communities on whom Athanaric's anger broke forth,—
Nicenes, Arians, and Audians; and all alike, no doubt,
furnished victims to the roll of martyrs. Tradition has
preserved to us the names of some of these; while of
many others we know only the perseverance and the
cruel fate. Nor is it necessary to attempt, as some have
done, to claim the heroes of the persecution for any
particular church. Those within hearing of the conflict, but outside the ring of the flames of persecution,
might grasp eagerly at proofs of the steadfastness shewn
by adherents of their own creed. But upon the very
field of battle, and within reach of the fire that tried
all parties alike, such distinctions would surely melt
away. When the scorned and hated idol was drawn
through the village, and they were called to do homage
to it, Arian, Nicene, and Audian, who were there
to glorify one Master, and looked with steadfast eyes to
receiving the same eternal crown, would hardly stay to
think of the trivial points that distinguished them from
their neighbours, such as whether the Creator made
man in the image of a divine body, and whether the
Lord God the Son were begotten or made, equal or

second to His Father in the Godhead. Those who died, died not in defence of the creed of a council, nor of the teaching of a bishop, however noble, but as subjects of one King, confessors of one Redeemer, children of one God.

After the great work of Ulfilas, the most interesting monument of the Gothic Church is the document which forms the basis if not the entire contents of the Acts of St. Saba,[1] one of the Gothic Christians who fell in this persecution by Athanaric. This is the letter which was sent by the suffering Church in Gothia to the Church in Cappadocia, accompanying or following the remains of the martyr, which they had sent to their sympathetic fellow-Christians in testimony of their steadfastness and gratitude. The salutation runs thus: "The Church of God which is in Gothia to the Church of God which is in Cappadocia, and to all Christians of the Catholic Church wheresoever in the world they dwell—mercy, peace, and love of God the Father and Jesus Christ our Lord be fulfilled." Then follows a quotation from Acts x. 35, which leads at once to the mention of Saba as one who feared God and worked righteousness, and had indeed been accepted by Him. He was a Goth by birth, who had been a Christian from boyhood, and had led so holy and noble a life, and witnessed so glorious a confession, that the Church was moved to describe his works and sufferings for the instruction and edification of the faithful. After a eulogy on his character, in which his justice, devotion, and peaceableness are celebrated in turn, the third paragraph takes up his

[1] Acta Sanctorum, April 12; edit. Paris, 1866. April. Vol. iii. and Appendix.

history at the beginning of the persecution "by the
princes and magistrates of Gothia," who insisted on the
Christians renouncing their faith publicly by eating
meat that had been sacrificed to idols. Some of the
heathens, touched with compassion for their Christian
neighbours, combined to give them means of escape by
substituting secretly for the forbidden meat portions of
meat that had not been thus polluted; but Saba, when
he understood the subterfuge, refused to profit by it,
and openly warned the Christians that no true Christian
could accept escape on such a condition, "and thus he
warned them to avoid the snare of the devil." The
heat of the persecution seems then to have cooled for a
season, but broke out again with a general inquisition
for Christians, from which Saba's would-be friends again
sought to shield him by swearing that there were no
Christians in the village. But Saba broke into the
assembly and loudly exclaimed, " Let no one swear for
me, for I am a Christian." Summoned before the chief
persecutor, he was contemptuously dismissed, on the discovery of his great poverty, as one who could do neither
good nor harm. Afterwards there arose a third and
more determined persecution, during which the holy
man set out to keep the feast of Easter with a presbyter
named Gutthica; but, commanded by a vision which
met him on the journey, turned back to find another
presbyter named Sansala, unexpectedly returned to his
native country, and with him he kept the festival. On
the third night after the celebration, " Atharidus, the
son of the King Rhotesteus," broke into the village
with a body of impious bandits, and carried off both
the presbyter and Saba bound and naked. Treated by

6

his persecutors with the harshest cruelty, the saint bore with them with steadfast patience. Left for the night bound to a log, he was released by a woman who had pity on him, but he refused to make his escape. In spite of both torture and cajolery, he refused to eat the meat offered to idols. At length, after he had several times escaped death as it seemed by a miracle, Atharidus ordered him away for execution. Led away to be thrown into the river Musaeus, he inquired of his executioners what his companion had done "that *he* should not deserve to die," and his last words testified to his faith in God and praised the name of His Son. He died by "wood and water," for a beam was fastened to his neck that he should sink. He was only thirty-eight years old when he thus confessed his Master by his death, and "received the martyr's crown on the fifth day of the week after Easter week," that is to say, on the 12th of April. His body was sought out and obtained by Julius Soranus, "dux Scythiae," who was himself a Christian, "who hath sent it to Cappadocia to your Church by permission of the presbytery, a precious gift and glorious fruit of the faith. Wherefore do ye, holding a celebration on the day of his martyrdom, make this known to the rest of the brethren, that rejoicing with all the Catholic and Apostolic Church they may praise God, who chooseth His own servants for Himself. They salute you who with us do suffer persecution." And this letter from the persecuted Church in Gothia to the sympathising Church in Cappadocia is then concluded with the Doxology.

Most interesting confirmation of this account has been curiously preserved in certain letters of Basil, who .

was Bishop of Caesarea in Cappadocia, from the year
364. The first[1] is addressed to "Julius Soranus," who
was at the time (373) "Governor in Scythia," and appears from the letter to have been a sincere Christian,
and held in high honour by the bishop. It is at the
conclusion, after discussing matters of purely personal
interest, that he writes: "But in all the good thou
doest, thou layest up treasure for thyself; and if thou
providest relief for them that are persecuted for the
name of the Lord, that thou preparest for thyself
against the day of reward.[2] But thou wilt do well if
thou do also send to thy fatherland relics of the
martyrs, since, as thou hast reported, the persecution
is even now causing martyrs for the Lord." This is
clearly in answer to a letter from Soranus offering
to procure some of the precious relics for his native
Church. That he did so, and that they were those of
the martyr Saba is clear from two other letters of Basil,[3]
one addressed to Ascholius, and the other to Soranus
himself. The first is in answer to a letter from Ascholius,
which must have had reference to the Church in Gothia
and the martyrdom of Saba. Basil, in his despair at the
state of his own Church, the coldness of the love, the
strife of parties, the zeal which caused bitterness, but

---

[1] Basil Magni, *Ep.* II. 145 (Migne).

[2] καλῶς δὲ ποιήσεις, ἐὰν καὶ λείψανα μαρτύρων τῇ πατρίδι
ἐκπέμψῃς.

[3] Basil, as above, 164 and 165. The title of the latter is, " To
Ascholius, Bishop of Thessalonica"; but that this is a mistake is
clear from the contents; esp. μάρτυρι . . . . τὴν ἐνεγκοῦσαν
ἐτίμησας. Ascholius was a native of Thrace, but Soranus of
Cappadocia. See Krafft, p. 380.

neither roused nor could support persecution, had been
encouraged by the testimony to the faith of the Church
in Europe, conveyed by the relics of a martyr from
among the barbarians beyond the Danube.[1] And when
he recurs further on in his letter to the letter of
Ascholius, he takes up some of his language: "Thine
own relation also, the agonies, the bodies that were
torn for the 'sake of the Faith, the anger of the barbarian when he was despised by the men of unquailing
heart, all the various tortures of the persecutors, the
steadfastness through all of the sufferers, the wood,
the water, which were the final trials of the martyrs."
The reference here to the sufferings of Saba, if not to
the actual narration of them, in the letter to the Church
in Cappadocia, is too distinct to be called in question,
and it has been supposed that the letter of Ascholius,
to which Basil was replying, was the identical narrative.
The second letter, addressed to Soranus, conveys to him
directly the thanks of Basil for the precious gift that he
had made to his fatherland, "like a grateful husband-
man sending of his first-fruits to those who had provided
the seed."

Another record of the same persecution is contained
in the Greek Calendar, which celebrates, on March 26th,
the martyrdom of six-and-twenty Goths, of whom two,
Bathusis and Verékas, were presbyters, and the rest
were of the laity, both men and women. These
suffered, according to this record, in the reign of
Valentinian and Valens, through the cruelty of the

---

[1] μάρτυς δὲ ἡμῖν ἐπεδήμησεν ἐκ τῶν ἐπέκεινα Ἴστρου βαρβάρων, δι' ἑαυτοῦ κηρύσσων τῆς ἐκεῖ πολιτευομένης πίστεως τὴν
ἀκρίβειαν.

Gothic king, Jungerich (Athanaric), by whom they were burnt together in a church. Then follows a long account of the removal of the relics by a pious queen, who, with her daughter, brought them to Cyzicum. The memory of the same event is also preserved in the fragments of a Gothic calendar,[1] which were discovered in the library at Milan early in this century. One of the seven festivals therein noted is on the 29th of the month preceding November,[2] which is marked as "Remembrance of the martyrs among the Goth-folk who were burnt with Veréka, a presbyter ('papa'), and with Batvin, the servant of the Catholic Church."[3]

In the same month the calendar also commemorates the many martyrs among the Goth-folk, and "Fripareikeis,"[4] where it has been proposed, either with or without a change of reading, to find an allusion to Frithigern, not indeed as a martyr, but as a champion of the faith. This would be illustrated by the dedication of a day in November to "Constantine, King," but the reading seems established, and, apart from the first syllable, it is hard to find the name of the Gothic chief underlying the word in the MS. The other persons commemorated are "Dorotheus, Episcopus," "Philip, Apostle in Hierapolis," "the forty venerable virgins in

---

[1] Mai, *Ulphilae partium specimen*, Massmann, *Ulfilas*, p. 590; Bernhardt (ed. 1884), p. 200.

[2] Not October, since it has only 30 days. See Massmann.

[3] "Gaminpi martyre pize be Verekan papan jah Batvin bilaif aikklesjons fullaizos ana Gutpidai gabrannidai." The meaning of "fullaizos" is doubtful, but even if it = "catholic" it would apply equally to Arians in an Arian document. See below.

[4] "pize ana Gutpidai managaize martyre jah Fritpareikeis."

Beroea," and "Andrew, Apostle."[1] This curious relic of the early Gothic Church appears to belong to its Thracian period, and hence to the close of the fourth century.

This persecution of Athanaric would seem to have been prolonged with varying intensity over several years; and while the death of Saba and the persecution of the Audians, described by Epiphanius, must be placed in or before 372, the death of Nicetas, which is also commemorated in the Acta Sanctorum, belongs apparently to the year 374, or the beginning of 375. The accounts given of Nicetas in the Acta, and of the persecution in general by Sozomen, are obviously connected,[2] and refer to the same period. But it is clear on the face of it that the account of Nicetas in the Acta has been "edited" by a later redactor, and has received copious additions, suggested by the editor's knowledge or ignorance of the history of the time.

Passing over for the present the perplexing questions that arise in this connexion, we learn here something about the later stage of the persecution. Nicetas, like Saba, was by birth a Goth, and brought up in the midst of barbarian surroundings. "All men know the Ister, renowned among rivers for its size, called in the language of that neighbourhood the Danube. It had, moreover, for dwellers on its banks, Goths, who at that time had moved out of their own country." Here lived Nicetas, by birth and nurture, but neither by life, character, nor faith, a Goth. In his youth he had

---

[1] Concerning these, see Krafft, p. 385.

[2] The relation between the Acta and Sozomenus is important, but very obscure. See further below.

drawn from the streams of the teaching of Theophilus. Now in the reign of Gratian, the impious and blood-thirsty Athanaric began to shed the blood of the faithful, and taught his subjects to do the like. Nicetas, in spite of his threats and cruelties, "nothing heeding, persevered in preaching the faith.". At length he was seized and put to torture, but nothing could induce him to abandon his confession, and, after one or two miraculous deliverances from death, he received the crown of martyrdom along with many others. A certain Marianus of Cilicia, who was a believer, having by means of a miracle obtained possession of the body of the saint, transported it to Mopsuestia, where cer-tain miracles followed, of which an account is given. This portion of the Acta (which is included in the §§ 1, 4, 5) is probably, as we shall see later,[1] independent of both of the intervening paragraphs, and perhaps repre-sents the original account, which would be drawn up presumably by Marianus himself. From Sozomen[2] we learn that, of the Christians, some were brought to trial and boldly confessed their faith; others were destroyed without an opportunity being allowed them of speaking. A wooden idol placed upon a waggon was drawn through the villages,[3] and the Christians were summoned to come forth from their houses to worship and offer sacrifice; upon their refusing, the heathens

---

[1] Except the reference to Theophilus. For the whole account, cf. Bessell, *Ulfilas*, p. 80.

[2] Sozomen vi. 37.

[3] Krafft, p. 370, compares the procession of the goddess Nerthus among the Lombards, etc., described by Tacitus (*Germania*, c. 40), and similar processions in the north with an idol representing Freyr.

burnt their dwellings to the ground with the occupants. One act of barbarous cruelty is recorded. Several Christians, who had been driven by fear or force to offer sacrifice, fled with their wives and children " to the tent of the church at that place,"[1] but only to be pursued by their enemies and there burnt alive together. These are probably the victims whose memory is preserved in the calendar.

The statement in the Acta Nicetae that the persecution in which he fell took place under Gratian, if it be a genuine record, would fix the date later than the exaltation of that prince in 374. On the other hand, it may have taken a place at any time between that and the death of Athanaric in 381.[2] The statement that the Goths had then migrated " from their own country " must be regarded as an insertion of the editor to make all his statements tally, and could at no time be true of subjects of Athanaric. On the whole, it seems most probable that this persecution was a continuation of the former one, and took place only in 375. Whatever we may have afterwards to say concerning the concurrent political events, the general results of these persecutions were disastrous to Athanaric, whose power dwindled as that of his rival Frithigern increased.

We have thus observed the appearance of a Christian Church among the Goths under two successive phases: first, as the organised result of the labours of Ulfilas, professing in the main an Arian creed, fleeing

---

[1] ἐπὶ σκήνης τῆς ἐνθάδε ἐκκλησίας.

[2] Bessell contends for 380 (p. 88); but this is part of his generally untenable position that the conversion of the Wisigoths took place in that year.

before the first cruel persecution to settle with their beloved teacher in Mœsia, whence they continued to work for the conversion of their brethren. Secondly, there appears among the Goths, who remained across the Danube, a more sporadic Christianity, scattered confessors, presbyters, and communities owning allegiance to one or other of the various parties, according as they received the seeds of the Gospel from Arians, Audians, or Nicenes. They, too, felt the blast of persecution, and many of them no doubt took refuge with their countrymen beyond the river. Others, however, found a refuge and a rallying-point with Athanaric's rival, Frithigern, who, about this time, proclaimed himself a Christian, or at least a protector of the persecuted. Thus was formed the kernel of the future Christian Gothic state. From this rivalry proceeded the general conversion of the Wisigoths.[1]

This raises one of the most perplexing and debated questions in connexion with the Gothic Church. It is a double one. When and under what circumstances did the Wisigoths as a nation, or the great bulk of them, accept Christianity ?—and why was the Christian scheme of doctrine which they adopted an Arian one ? In answering these questions, if an answer can be found for them, we shall also meet the subordinate yet im-

---

[1] The phrase, "conversion of the Wisigoths," is adopted in default of a more accurate, but not too cumbrous an expression, though it is doubly defective. The "Goths who crossed the Danube under Frithigern" would be more exact ; for they included certain Ostrogothic tribes, but excluded the Wisigoths under Athanaric, and perhaps some other sections. These were the Goths whose conversion and whose creed were so momentous for themselves and the empire.

portant question—What part was played by Ulfilas in
this act of his nation's history?

This conversion of the Wisigoths to Arian Christianity is closely connected with their migrations across
the Danube in 376 and the following years, and also
with the relations between Athanaric and Frithigern.
The rivalry of these two chiefs represents the struggle
between the old faith and the new, between proud
barbarian independence and a subject-alliance with the
empire, between the old national spirit that stiffened
its back against misfortune and distress, and a more
supple statesmanship, with wider views, which per-
ceived how by a small surrender it was possible to
secure an immense advantage. The third political
element in the matter is the Emperor Valens, a prince
of Arian leanings in the hands of a strongly Arian
court. In these circumstances it is hopeless to look for
an impartial record of the events that led to the conversion. None of the authorities except Eunapius and
Ammian can claim to be heard as contemporaries.
Most of them wrote sixty or more years later. Their
partisanship, unchecked by any true historic sense, took
its own way with the facts. Even before comparing
one authority with his fellows, we feel that the accounts
are coloured by the influence of all that has gone
between, affected by the rise of new parties as well as
by the extinction of old ones. Caution has, moreover,
to be observed in handling these authorities, lest too
much weight be given to a manifoldness of concurrent
testimony, which may after all have but one original
source underlying it. This, while it involves much
careful comparison, at the same time opens the door to

much destructive criticism. But between the rocks of partial and ill-supported assertion and the whirlpool of scepticism a course may yet be shaped.

The one undisputed fact is that the Wisigoths professed Christianity and held it under an Arian creed in 381. That it was more to them than a mere outward profession, and that the form was not less important in their eyes than the essence itself, is clear from the facts that they transmitted the faith and the form together to their brethren the Ostrogoths, to the Vandals, and other Teutonic tribes, as well as to their own posterity; and moreover that, rather than abandon the form, they sacrificed opportunities such as were offered to no other barbarian race, foredoomed themselves to failure in the noblest and most patient struggles to invigorate the effete Roman race and decaying empire, and accepted the ruin of one kingdom after another, though it had been erected with an infinitude of patience.

More open to question, but yet extremely probable, is the opinion that the definite transference of their national allegiance from heathenism to Christianity took place on an occasion of their crossing the Danube, and being received within the empire. We are defending a position when we say that it could only have taken place under an Arian emperor, and that he could have been no other than the Emperor Valens; and we are on much disputed ground when we maintain that the occasion was the general immigration in the year 376, that the act was a national act by the chiefs acting as representatives of the nation, and took place by agreement between Frithigern with his fellow chiefs and

Valens, either upon the offer of the one party or on the demand of the other; while it is quite possible that previous communications between Frithigern and the emperor had laid the foundation of Gothic Arianism.

If we turn now to the authorities, we find one group which must be dealt with together.[1] The accounts of the conversion of the Wisigoths given by Orosius, Jordanis, and Isidore are thrown into one group by a curious remark which, with individual variations, is common to all of them, but which could scarcely have occurred to each of them independently.[2] At the close of the account, after the death of Valens, they each remark on the "judgment of God," which inflicted upon Valens in this life the same torture of burning which, by perverting their faith, he had secured for the Goths in the life to come. From this we conclude either that one of these writers was the source from which the others drew, or what is most probable, that all three depended on a fourth authority. In either case we cannot cite two of the three in support of the third. But there is good ground for believing that Jordanis depended either directly or indirectly on a document which carried the history down to 417;[3] and it is important that we can shew that this source was accessible to and in part at least used by Sozomen who might otherwise be looked upon as an independent authority. This is proved by

---

[1] The passages referred to in Orosius, Jordanis, and Isidore are given in Appendix.

[2] A comparison of the passages will shew in the verbal concurrence and divergences the undeniable relation between the three.

[3] Bessell, p. 56.

a comparison of the accounts given in both writers of the first contact of the Huns with the Ostrogoths;[1] the legend of the popular notion that the peoples were divided by an impassable sea, which was only removed when some hunters saw an "infuriated cow" or "a stag" crossing the shallow water, is common to both Sozomen and Jordanis, and undoubtedly betrays a common source; and since Sozomen wrote in 440, this may very well have been the document of 417.

Jordanis' account of the conversion is as follows. The Wisigoths, after being long in perplexity as to what they should do to escape the Huns, "by general consent" despatched envoys to the Emperor Valens, saying that if he would give them a portion of Thrace or Moesia to settle in they would live according to his laws and submit to his authority. "And that he might have more abundant confidence in them they promised, if he would give them teachers in their own tongue, to become Christians. When Valens had heard this, he soon afterwards granted with much satisfaction what he would fain have been the first to ask, and received the Goths in certain parts of Moesia, where he planted them as a wall against other races; moreover, because the Emperor Valens, smitten by the perverted faith of the Arians, had at that time suppressed all the churches belonging to our party, he sent them for preachers supporters of his own creed. And they imbued the Goths, who came thither ignorant and unlearned, with the poison of their own perverted faith; so in this way the Wisigoths, through the Emperor Valens, were

---

[1] Compare Sozom. vi. 37, ἐλάνθανον δὲ προσοικοῦντες ἀλλή-λοις, κ.τ.λ., with Jordanis, c. 24, Hujus ergo gentis, etc.

made Arians rather than Christians. Moreover, they themselves sent preachers to carry the Gospel in the same form to the Ostrogoths and Gepidi, nations of the same stock as themselves; and in this way all the nations of the same speech were drawn into the same sect."

In Orosius the account is much shorter, all details as well as motives being omitted, but the course of events is the same. The Arianism of the Goths is traced to an application made to Valens and acceded to,—that "bishops might be sent to them from whom they might learn the rule of Christian faith." Turning to Sozomen,[1] we find indications that the same original document was at his disposal, and probably formed the basis of his narrative; but he has tried to combine it with, and perhaps to assimilate it to, a supplementary account either written or oral, which added two new factors, a quarrel between the heathen Athanaric and the Christian Frithigern, and the influence of Ulfilas. He diverges from the account of Jordanis at the point where the embassy was despatched to Valens. "The head of this embassy is said to have been Ulfilas, the bishop of the nation." Then, *after* the migration, a quarrel broke out among the Goths, the different sides being led by Athanaric and Frithigern. Frithigern having been beaten in battle, applied to Valens for help. The imperial troops in Thrace having been sent to his aid, he won a great victory, and put Athanaric and his party to flight. Then, out of gratitude to the emperor, he adopted his religion, and induced his followers to do the like. But Sozomen is not satisfied

[1] Sozomenus vi. 37.

that this was the only reason for the Arianism of the
Goths, and accordingly he introduces Ulfilas as another
agent in their conversion. Ulfilas, who was then their
bishop,[1] had originally held the faith in full accordance
with the Catholic Church; and though, in the reign of
Constantius, he had "without due consideration" taken
part with Eudoxius and Acacius at the Synod of Constantinople (360), he had continued nevertheless in
communion with those who held the Nicene faith.
But when he came to Constantinople on this embassy
he met there the chiefs of the Arian persuasion, who
plied him both with arguments, and with promises of
their support in his appeal to the emperor, if he only
would join them, until either from pressure of the
necessity of his mission, or from honest conviction, he
joined the Arian communion, and severed his whole
people from the Catholic Church. For he had boundless
influence over them, through his long devotion to their
cause, and the sufferings and perils he had gone through
for their sake and the Church. This narrative of Sozomen, so far as it is distinct from Jordanis, is related
in a degree too striking to be overlooked to the Acta
of Nicetas, and especially to sections 2 and 3 of that
document, which it is further to be noticed are not
unreasonably suspected of being themselves an insertion made by a later editor into the original account
of Nicetas.

Fortunately, it is not necessary for our inquiry
to decide precisely what is the nature of the relation
between these two accounts, whether one is the parent
of the other, or both are founded upon a third and

[1] τὰ μὲν πρῶτα οὐἐὲν ἐιεφέρετο πρὸς τὴν καθόλου Εκκλησίαν.

earlier document. Nevertheless, I incline to the opinion
that these paragraphs in the Acta Nicetae were probably drawn up *later* than the account of Sozomen,
and were not the foundation of that account. Bessell,[1]
for whose theory of the conversion it is of importance to
shew that the Acta Nicetae were the foundation of the
accounts of the Church historians, lays stress on the
many[2] special traits " in the Acta which he would
regard as indications of greater closeness to the time of
action "; but the traits to which he refers are little
more than stock epithets, and are consistent with the
generally artificial character of the style, which gives an
impression much more of a revision in the spirit of a
triumphant and much later ecclesiasticism, than of the
original work of one who was immediately or closely
connected with the events.[3]

This account, which is common to Sozomen and
the Acta Nicetae, and which we may for convenience
refer to as the second document of Sozomen, was also used
by Socrates,[4] and one obvious blunder of the former

---

[1] Bessell, *Ulfilas*, p. 80; esp. 83.

[2] e.g. Ἀθαναρίχῳ τῷ πάντα δεινῷ : ἀποστάσους τοῦ Φριτιγέρ-
νου : Ὀυάλεντι τῷ μισοχρίστῳ.

[3] Compare : Sozom. οὐ πολλῷ δὲ ὕστερον πρὸς σφᾶς αὐτοὺς
στασιάσαντας, διχῇ διαιρεθῆναι with Actt. Nicet. ἐπεὶ δὲ οὐ πολὺς
ἐν μέσῳ διέβη χρόνος, καὶ τὸ Γότθων ἔθνος εἰς ἀντιπάλους
διερράγη; or Sozom. κακῶς πράξας ἐν τῇ μάχῃ Φριτιγέρνης
δέδιτο Ῥωμαίων βοηθεῖν αὐτῷ with Actt. Nicet. ὅθεν Φριτιγέρνης
ἀπορρηθεὶς πρὸς τὴν ῥωμαϊκὴν ἀπέβλεψε δεξίαν.

[4] Socrates iv. 33, and 34. Bessell (*Goths, E. and G.* p. 140 *b*
and 152; *Ulfilas*, p. 80) rejects this quarrel and civil war, concluded by Roman aid, as altogether unhistorical,—a piece of destructive criticism not justified, and unjustifiable, in the face of the
evidence.

writer, which arose either from an attempt to reconcile his document with some previous notions of his own, or from careless handling of it, is corrected by a reference to the latter. This blunder is contained in the description of strife between Athanaric and Frithigern as breaking out *after* the Hunnish invasion, and after the general migration across the Danube; an arrangement of events which is quite unhistorical, and is contradicted not only by the account in Socrates, but also by the thoroughly trustworthy and fully detailed narrative of Ammian. But having made this obvious correction, there is no reason why we should not accept the civil war between Athanaric and Frithigern as historical, and as leading to important consequences for the Goths. Whether the cause of this discord was originally political or religious it is not easy to decide; but whichever element appeared first, it is certain that the other quickly followed. Whether Frithigern was a rival chief, who strengthened his hands by giving protection to Christians who fled from Athanaric's persecution, or whether he was a Christian of noble family who was driven to appear as a political rival to the heathen Athanaric, the issue was the same. His party were defeated. He crossed the river to ask help from Valens; returned with Roman troops, and retrieved his defeat by a victory which drove Athanaric northward and eastward, and excluded him and his followers from finding asylum with their countrymen in the Roman empire when the Hunnish thundercloud burst upon them.

Passing on to the second part of Sozomen's account, that which introduces Ulfilas as an actor in

the drama, we find it to be open to much suspicion.
A comparison with Socrates shews that this introduction of Ulfilas as an important figure in the
negotiations was either absent from the document with
which he, Socrates, and the editor of Acta Nicetae
were all directly or indirectly acquainted, or was
ignored by the better informed Socrates. Again,
the very clumsy way in which Sozomen introduces
Ulfilas and his influence,[1] as a further explanation of
what has been sufficiently explained already in the
conversion of Frithigern and his influence on his subjects, followed by that most strange account of his
" thoughtlessly " joining Eudoxius and Acacius in 360,
but, nevertheless, remaining in communion with the
Nicaeans, betrays traces not so much of the smooth
course of an original and authentic document as of an
attempt to foist into such a record some previous
opinion or tradition which the writer himself held. It
will suffice to indicate one more point which raises
suspicion against the genuineness of this record. The discussions between Ulfilas and the heads of the Arian party,
and the meetings during which pressure was brought to
bear, and promises were held out of influence to be
exercised with the emperor, are represented as taking
place at Constantinople. Now Valens, to whom the
embassy was directed, was at Antioch;[2] is it then to be

---

[1] οὐ τοῦτο δὲ μόνον οἶμαι αἴτιον γέγονεν εἰσέτι νῦν πᾶν τὸ
φῦλον προστεθῆναι τοῖς τὰ Ἀρείου δοξάζουσιν.

[2] Valens was absent from Constantinople, and in the East .
(principally in the neighbourhood of Antioch) from 371 to 378, when
he returned to Constantinople on May 30th. See Gwatkin, *App.*
2, p. 295.

supposed that Ulfilas, if he had been one of the envoys, knowing the stress and terror of his people on the far bank of the Danube, would pause in his journey to Antioch to discuss points of doctrine with the Arian leaders at Constantinople? But Sozomen is evidently under the impression that the emperor was actually at Constantinople, a place to which he did not return for fifteen months after the Goths had crossed the Danube. By Socrates, Ulfilas is also introduced, but only parenthetically; and all that he has to tell is incorporated by Sozomen in his perverted account. Thus we conclude that of these church-historians, Socrates stands nearest to the original source; that Sozomen, coming next, had access to Socrates' account, and also directly or indirectly to the document on which Jordanis founded his; but that he introduced matter of his own apart from either of these authorities, which is of very doubtful value. Lastly, that the Acta Nicetae, §§ 2 and 3, are not the source of Socrates, but represent either an independent contamination of the same authorities, or, as seems much more probable, a version of Socrates worked up and embellished for insertion in the original Acta.

A fourth writer who discusses the same subject is Theodoret;[1] but as his account shews no indications of resting on different or better authority than the foregoing, and contains only one variation of moment for our enquiry, it need not detain us long. It shews the bitterness, if not also the unfairness, of the *odium theologicum* more clearly than the other historians do.

---

[1] Theodoret, *Hist. Eccl.* iv. 37. For Theodoret, see Bessell, *Ulfilas*, p. 91.

The condition that the Goths should become Arians is
made to proceed from the side of the emperor on
the instigation of "Eudoxius the badly named."[1] For
he said they had long ago received the rays of divine
instruction, and were being brought up in the teachings
of the Apostles; and a common faith would prove a
stronger pledge of peace.   To Eudoxius also (or
Euzoius?) he ascribes the conversion of Ulfilas, whom
he charges with having been brought over by means
not of argument alone, but of bribes.[2] Ulfilas, moreover,
whose influence over his people is here again described
as supreme, lightly persuaded them to adopt the new
form of faith by saying that there was no doctrine
of importance involved in the dispute, which was merely
a matter of party jealousy, and a battle about words.
The greater part of this version falls to the ground at
once when tested with the touchstone of the Auxentian
document; but the suggestion that the proposal that
the Goths should become Arians proceeded from Valens
is quite a reasonable one, though hardly to be preferred
to the statement of the converse.

Finally, we have an interesting and graphic account
given by Eunapius,[3] who was actually a contemporary

---

[1] Εὐδόξιος ὁ δυσώνυμος; but this should almost certainly
be Euzoius, for Eudoxius died at Constantinople in 370 (vide
Socrates iv. 14); whereas Euzoius was bishop of Antioch when
Valens was there. See Annot Valesii, *ad Soc.* loc. cit., and the
introduction to Acta Nicetae, ed. Paris, 1866.

[2] τοῦτον καὶ λόγοις καὶ χρήμασι δελεάσας.

[3] Eunapius, *Frag.* 46, ed. Niebuhr, p. 82.   This account is the
one chiefly relied upon by Bessell in his attempt to shew that the
Goths as a nation were heathen till 380, and first passed over to
Christianity in that year.

writer, of the passage of the Danube, from which Bessell has tried to draw conclusions concerning the date and probable motives of the conversion of the Wisigoths. No doubt he is right in maintaining that the reference here is to a different and later passage of the river than that in 376, namely to one in 380.[1] But if this be the case, according to our conception of the history, the body of Goths who crossed in 380 were not Frithigern's Goths of 376, returned to their country after their great victory, and now hurling themselves anew upon the empire. That is an altogether untenable theory. They were bands of Ostrogoths, and perhaps of remaining Wisigoths, who, either at the summons of Frithigern or upon the news of the disabling illness of Theodosius, flocked to share in the victories and the booty of their comrades who had crossed before.

Statements concerning Christians, or professing Christians, coming from a heathen, and avowedly hostile, writer like Eunapius,[2] are obviously to be received with caution. But some of the details which he gives are too curious to be passed over. After describing the tribes crossing in great numbers, he adds that each tribe brought along with it its national sacred things or idols, together with the priests and priestesses belonging to them. But about these the most deep and "adamantine" silence was preserved, and all the open and ostensible signs of religion were prepared to "deceive the

[1] Though Niebuhr has dated both narratives in 376: but compare the circumstances; the remorseless cutting down of those who swam over on the first occasion with ἐπεδιέβαινον οὐδενὸς κωλύοντος on the second.

[2] See Hodgkin, *Italy and her Invaders*, i. 129.

enemy." They had dressed up some of their number in robes to represent bishops, and made them advance in front and in the middle of the line. Monks also they had provided themselves with, and that without much difficulty, for it "sufficed if they swept along in dark robes and tunics, and both were, and were thought to be, scoundrels." All this was done to deceive some people who met them on the opposite bank, not further specified, who were "so sunk in foolishness that they were clearly and immoveably convinced that they were Christians and followed all the rites."

We are now in a position to collect the evidence thus sifted, and briefly to describe the course of events which we believe to have led to the conversion of the Wisigoths. After the peace of 369 concluded between Valens and Athanaric, the latter was left with his heart full of wrath, and his hands free to avenge upon the Christians the insults which their unbelief offered to his native gods. Ulfilas, through his disciples, had probably carried on the work of evangelisation among his old countrymen, particularly among the dependents of a smaller chieftain, Frithigern; but the faith had also found adherents among the subjects of Athanaric. The cruel persecution of the Christians by Athanaric raised the rivalry of the two chiefs to an open quarrel. Frithigern, whether out of conviction or of policy, took the part of the Christians, who soon learnt to know their champion, and flocked to him. In the war which followed, Frithigern was defeated, and hastened across the Danube to seek help from the Roman emperor. The only pretext for such a request, or for the assistance accorded to him, would be the claims of persecuted

Christians on a Christian emperor. And whether the church-historians are right or not in ascribing the chief's own conversion wholly to his gratitude on this occasion, his convictions would certainly be strengthened and his faith encouraged. The Roman troops led the Goths, who owed allegiance to Frithigern, to a victory which secured the position of the latter as an independent chieftain, and internal peace for the period that intervened before the inbreaking of the Huns. To this period, and to the communications between Valens and Frithigern, I ascribe the application for, and sending of, "preachers from whom they might learn the rule of Christian faith," though the historians, with the foreshortening inseparable from their method, have connected this with the embassy of 376. Before the latter year arrived, these labourers, assisted perhaps by missionaries of Ulfilas, may have converted no small section of the Goths to the simple form which the faith took, outside the reach of theological controversies, and so the famous embassy of 376 may very well have carried sincere proposals for the acceptance by the whole nation of the faith of the emperor, which was already known and accepted by a considerable section. While on the other hand, if the true view lies with Theodoret, it may have been Valens who dictated a condition which could be of service to the peace of the empire only if a large part at least of the incoming people could accept it with sincerity. This seems to me to be the only account of the conversion of the Wisigoths reconcileable with a fair and comprehensive survey of the authorities.

CHAPTER V.

THE ARIANISM OF ULFILAS AND THE GOTHS: THE GOTHIC BIBLE.

AUTHORITIES FOR CHAPTER V.

Sources:

Ulfilas' Version of the Bible, edition of Gabelentz and Loebe.
Arian documents discovered by Cardinal Mai, and edited by him in *Corpus Veterum Scriptorum*, vol. iii.
Arian MS., edited by Waitz.
Skeireins, edited by Massmann.

Literature:

Castillione, *de Ulfilae et Gothorum Arianismo*—Excursus at the end of the Epistle to Philippians.
Krafft, *de fontibus Ulfilae Arianismo*. Review of the same by Bessell in *Göttingen Gel. Anz.* 1861.
Gwatkin, *Studies in Arianism*.
Kölling, *Geschichte der Arianischen Haeresie*.
Lange, *der Arianismus in seiner weitern Entwickelung* in Illgen's *Zeitschrift*, vol. v. 1.

The literature and editions of the Gothic Version are collected in Goedeke's *Grundriss zur Geschichte der Deutschen Quellen*.

THE acceptance of Christianity by the Goths in the modified form of Arianism, as described in the last chapter, was an event of most serious importance for their future development, and, as it proved, of hardly less importance for the future of the Roman empire. Provided thus with a platform that lay between the darkness of heathenism and the light of a full-orbed Christianity, they came to a fatal halt. In this dim twilight of Arianism the figure of the Christ appeared familiar to them, and comprehensible by its resemblance to their own old deities who stood between man and the absolute divine,—the All-Father. It did not cost them much to exchange these demigods, who were just one step removed from heroes, for one heroic figure in whom all the powers and qualities of the rest should combine. But the All-Father remained as far removed as ever from reach and contact of human needs. Christ was not God come down from heaven to reveal the Godhead in the flesh, to deliver man from sin, having made atonement for it, and so to exalt him to an original state of glory and holiness. He was a creature like man—the first and highest of creatures, it is true—and as such worthy to be honoured and adored next to God, but exalted above man by the design and will of the Father, not by virtue of his own divine essence. Least of all was his essence to be regarded as identical with that of the Father, for " the transition from one who walked on earth to equality with the All-Father is so great as to be almost inconceivable."[1] It was thus that the Arian Christ found responsive acceptance in the Teutonic mind. They pictured him as a true king upon earth, moving about the highways of Palestine, attended by troops of loyal followers, from among whom he had chosen the Twelve as captains. When he " went up into a mountain," and took his seat, his captains stood in obedient readiness before him, and all below and around the faithful host was waiting to hear his commands and ready to execute them.[2] Or if at any time the Teutonic mind took a deeper and more spiritual view of the Saviour's work, it was as the Healer that they loved to behold him, moving about among

---

[1] Dorner, *Doctrine of the Person of Christ*, ii. 265.

[2] This is the picture in the Saxon *Heliand* of the ninth century.

suffering humanity, touching for the evil, restoring sight, and power, and hearing.[1]

Teutonic Arianism is nevertheless to be carefully distinguished from Hellenic Arianism. Even if the two could be shewn to occupy the same platform of belief, the moral value of the same faith was very different in and for the two parties who had approached it from different directions. For the Goth, in spite of the assistance he may have found in the likeness between his demigods and the Arian Christ, it was nevertheless a distinctly upward step in faith when he confessed a belief in a historic revelation, and submitted himself to the teaching of the Gospel, through which Jesus was manifested as the Son of God. For the Hellenic Christian, on the other hand, the acceptance of an Arian creed, or any of the post-Nicene compromises, was a step backwards and downwards. He left the high level of conception of the nature of God to which, after a great struggle and, as it were, by a supreme effort the Nicene Council had sprung; and he fell back upon a philosophical heathenism, which began by denying the Godhead of Christ, and afterwards sought to bring about a compromise of faith with reason at the cost of logic by proclaiming Christ to be God, but God " in the second degree."

Nor is the Arian Teuton morally superior to the Arian Hellene in theory only, but still more remarkably in practice. Here the moral tendency of the race came to the aid of a defective faith.[2] In the Arian Church

[1] The " Neriende Krist " of the *Heliand.*

[2] Well described by F. D. Maurice: " The result I arrived at was,—that the feeling of religious awe and mystery was that which

of the empire the surrender to heathen philosophy seemed to be followed by a surrender of Christian morality. At a time when neither party can claim to have illustrated the ethics of the Gospel by their conduct, the Arians distinguished themselves above their rivals in their display of worldliness, and their unscrupulous recourse to treachery and intrigue. In the matter of "works," if we may trust the report of writers like Salvian, the Goths, on the other hand, approached nearer to the full ideal of Christian life than their stunted faith would warrant us to expect. They had learnt to curb their passions, to respect women, and to honour truth. Nevertheless it was a stunted faith, nor was there much hope that it would develop to a fuller, richer form. For the bitterness of schism proved a more impervious barrier to the fostering of a more perfect faith than the ignorance of heathenism had been to the introduction of true light.

The effect of this conversion on the political history of the Goths will appear in subsequent chapters. For the Roman empire also, whose subject-allies they now became, the form of their creed, and the tenacity with which they clung to it, involved important consequences. The conversion of the Goths arrested the decay of the Arian cause, which would otherwise have collapsed, under the pressure of persecution upon its hollow and divided frame, before the fourth century had come to a close. But the same day that planted this new buttress of the party within the empire saw it shattered at its foundation by the death of its champion,

belonged to the Celts, as the moral feeling, reverence for relationships, marriage, etc., especially characterised the Gothic race."

Valens, by the consequent loss of court support, and its ultimate transfer to the opposite party. The gain of a nation could not atone to the Arian party for the loss of an emperor. Three years later the Arian bishop and clergy of Constantinople had to surrender the churches, and submit to laws suppressing all the gatherings of their flocks, or leave the capital. Most of them chose the latter alternative, and the Arian Church became little more comprehensive than the Gothic Church, had few fixed habitations, but wandered over southern Europe with these its latest converts, and only staunch supporters.

But it must not be supposed that the Arianism of the Gothic Church presented that many-fashioned creed in its coldest and most brutal form. The distinctions had been fined down till, on the main point at issue, they might seem to any but a trained theologian practically to disappear, and it is hard to say that the language of homage and adoration for the Son of God, God and Creator of all other created things, which comes from the pen of Auxentius, and came to him from the lips of Ulfilas,—it is hard to say that this is the language of any but a Christian in the full sense of the term. The form of faith which was held by Ulfilas, and taught by him to the Goths, may be studied in the manuscript of Auxentius, to which he appended his beloved master's creed. The latter is unfortunately only a fragment as it has come down to us in the transcription of Maximin,[1] but it may nevertheless honour these pages,—the first Teutonic Confession of Faith. Auxentius introduces it thus: " And he, even at his

[1] Waitz, p. 21.

departure, at the very hour of death, left for the people
committed to his charge a written confession of his
faith, saying thus:

"I, Ulfilas, bishop and confessor, have always thus
believed, and in this one and true faith I make my
testament before my Lord.

"I believe there is one God the Father, alone unbegotten and invisible, and I believe in His
only-begotten Son, our Lord and God, Creator
and Maker of the whole creation, not having
any like unto Him—therefore there is one
God of all, who is also God of our God[1]—and
in one Holy Spirit, an enlightening and sancti-
fying power—(as Christ says for warning to
His Apostles: 'Behold, I send the promise of
my Father upon you; but do ye dwell in the
City of Jerusalem until ye be clothed with
power from on high.' And again: 'And ye
shall receive power coming upon you by the
Holy Spirit')—neither God nor Lord, but the
minister of Christ . . . ."

At this point the MS. becomes fragmentary, and the
sentence is incomplete; only we can ascertain that he
believed the Spirit to be "subjected and in all things
obedient to the Son," and the Son to be "subjected and
obedient in all things to God the Father." Thereafter
the creed seems to have closed with a doxology addressed to the Father "through Christ . . . ." and " by
the Holy Spirit." The creed thus presented is expanded
by Auxentius in the account of his master's teaching,

---

[1] Waitz had read "ideo unus est omnium Deus, qui et de
nostris (?) est Deus," where Bessell (p. 42) would read "qui et dei
nostri."

which fills the greater part of the document.   He had
"never hesitated to proclaim openly and freely to
willing and unwilling hearers alike, one only true God,
the Father of Christ, and the second rank of Christ
Himself; well knowing that this, the alone true God, is
alone unbegotten, without beginning, without end,
eternal, ... incorruptible, incommunicable, of incorporeal essence, not combined of parts, single, unchange-
able, ... incomparably greater and better than all;
who being alone, not unto the division or diminution of
His Godhead, but unto the display of His goodness and
property, by His alone will and power,—passionless did
passionlessly, incorruptible did incorruptibly, immoveable did without motion create and beget, make and
establish an only-begotten God.   According to the
tradition and authority of the divine Scriptures, that
this second God and Author of all things existed of the
Father, and after the Father, and for the Father, and
for the glory of the Father, this was never concealed by
him; but that He was both great God and great Lord,
and great King, and great Mystery, ... Redeemer,
Saviour, ... just Judge of quick and dead, yet
having a greater God, even His Father; this he did
always set forth according to the blessed Gospel." [1]

After this exposition of the positive views of his
master, Auxentius proceeds to define his position nega-
tively, setting forth his condemnation of one party after
another, with the reasons which he added for the sake
of his pupils.   We recognise here at once the man who
joined the synod at Constantinople in 360, and there
signed (not ἀπερισκέπτως, as Sozomen[1] would have it)

---

[1] Sozomenus iv. 24.

the creed of Ariminum with the addendum that the words ὑπόστασις and οὐσία should cease to be used in reference to the Godhead. One after the other the parties, whose watchwords are compounded with οὐσία, are unsparingly condemned.

The kernel of the creed of Nicaea lay in the word ὁμοούσιον, which was inserted after much debate and with widespread reluctance. The objections to it on the conservative side were many. Its value in the eyes of the Athanasian party was that it held the Arians in a vice. There was no eluding its searching analysis of the various compromises proposed; and the efforts of the Arians who had accepted it to disguise its force to their followers, and to explain their own conduct in signing a creed which made use of it to define the relation of the Father to the Son, only served to attest its value as a discerner of the false from the true. Two bishops alone had the courage to refuse their signatures, and to share with Arius the consequences,—removal and banishment. Two others, Eusebius of Nicomedia and Theognius of Nicaea, chose the less heroic alternative, and signed with reservations. But either the reservations became too widely known, or their sympathy with Arius was afterwards too openly displayed, for three months later they had to accept the same sentence as their bolder comrades.

This is the Eusebius who afterwards selected Ulfilas to be bishop among the Goths, and with whose views the young "lector" must have been very familiar, to whose party indeed he most likely belonged. For Eusebius did not long remain in exile, and on his return to his see became one of the leaders of that reaction against

the Homoousion, which set in immediately after the
council had separated.   For the next fifty years the
authority of their creed trembled in the balance.   One
coalition after another attacked and condemned the
Nicene decision, and attempted to set up a watchword
of their own.   "Homoiousion" was the first.   Eusebius,
of Caesarea, had had his own creed returned to him
spoiled by the insertion of one word.   It did not express
his faith, but he signed it, issuing to his flock an explanation of his reasons for doing so.   He took the word to
designate "likeness in respect of essence," not "sameness
of essence"; and the many who felt with Eusebius did
the like, and formed the party who were known as
Homoiousians.[1]   In so far as they represented a protest
against the obnoxious word ὁμοούσιον, they had a large
and increasing body of supporters.   The centre party at
the council had hardly confirmed the new creed before
they began to take alarm at what they had done.   The
new word was not in the Scriptures.   That they had
insisted on before, but had been overruled by the
Athanasians, "who maintained that, if Scripture was to
be limited to any particular meaning, they must go
outside Scripture for technical terms to define that
meaning."[2]   But now the full effect of this innovation
was felt outside the council; and, what was worse, in
the anxiety to repel Arianism, they had sanctioned
a word which was distinctly open to question on the
ground of Sabellianism.   The controversy slumbered,
but the reaction gathered force and volume in the time
that intervened before the death of Constantine.   The

---

[1] Neander, vol. iv. p. 26.   [2] Gwatkin, p. 45.

death of this emperor removed the court and state support, which had done so much to enforce the creed of Nicaea. The Eusebian party were ready and quick to seize the opportunity. The council at Antioch in 339, and the council of the Dedication in 341, follow one another in quick succession. The consecration of Theophilus to work among the Indians, and of Ulfilas as bishop among the Goths, marks a determined missionary activity in the party, and the general adhesion of the men whom they chose to the doctrines they represented. But if Ulfilas was a follower of Eusebius in 341, at a later period of his life he heartily opposed his teaching, and appears to have joined a new party, which took shape and acquired influence before the council of Constantinople in 360.

In Auxentius' exposition of the teaching of his master we learn that he condemned Homousians and Homoiusians alike. Nevertheless, it is interesting to trace in his language a difference in the manner, though not in the measure, of the condemnation. "The detestable and abominable confession of the Homousians he *spurned* and *trampled* on as an invention of the devil and the teaching of demons." But "of the Homoiousians also he *deplored* and *shunned* the error and impiety, being himself most carefully instructed out of the Holy Scriptures, and having also been earnestly confirmed therein in many consultations of saintly bishops." And again, his attitude to the two sects is described, and the same distinction may be traced.[1]

---

[1] Quapropter homousionorum sectam destruebat, quia non confusas et concretas personas, sed discretas et distinctas credebat; omoeusion autem dissipabat quia non comparatas res sed differentes

The sect of the Homousians he would *destroy*, because he believed " non confusas et concretas personas, sed discretas et distinctas." The Homoiusians, moreover, he would *scatter* because " non res comparatas sed differentes adfectus defendebat." There is an obvious softening in the phrasing, even a little touch of tenderness in reference to the errors of the Homoiousians or Eusebian party, which would be very natural in one who in earlier life had been connected with them.

Fortunately, we are not called upon here to trace the history of the parties in the Church in the fourth century, a history of strife and intrigue, of base dependence on court favour, of unsparing and unscrupulous use of any short lease of power. The softer sort of Arianism, which Eusebius represented, held the party together till a slight change of front, in which ὅμοιον κατὰ παντά and ὁμοιούσιον became " more and more the watchwords of conservatism," alienated the fiercer spirits, who formed together a party which, returning to the doctrines of Arius in their most simple form, took or received the name of Anomoeans. The direct contradiction of their doctrine was offered by a party who were naturally known as the Homoeans,[1] and to this party Ulfilas, at least after 360, belonged. Auxentius gives his positive teaching on this point briefly thus: " That the Son is like to His Father, ... according to Holy Scripture and tradition." This party appears, by its leaders, at the parallel councils of

---

adfectus defendebat, et filium similem esse patri suo non secundum Macedonianam fraudulentam pravitatem et perversitatem contra scribturas dicebat, sed secundum divinas scribturas et traditiones.

[1] For the rise of the Homoean party, see Gwatkin, p. 163.

Ariminum and Seleucia. The course of time and the rise of new parties had tended to draw more closely together the Nicenes and the semi-Arians, who were now representing the old Eusebian party, and defended the ὁμοιούσιον against the ὁμοούσιον. But in the face of a new and common foe an alliance was brought about, partially through the judicious mediation of Hilary of Poictiers. The representatives of the new Homoean party met this combination, Ursacius and Valens at Ariminum, and Acacius at Seleucia. Outwardly worsted at both places, they nevertheless contrived to get a creed of their own approval accepted by a joint conference at Constantinople, and confirmed their victory by a council which they held at the same place a few days later (January, 360). At this latter council Ulfilas was present, and took part with Acacius, as we learn from Sozomen.[1]

Thanks to the disunion and weakness of the other parties in the east, and to the court influence and commanding position enjoyed by Acacius and his successor, the Homoeans maintained their superiority until the fall of Arianism with the death of Valens, and the new attitude of the court under Theodosius. That period coincides with the last twenty years of the life of Ulfilas, and during it we must regard him as a steadfast adherent of that party.

Whatever were the views he held, he maintained them with determination and very little tolerance for those who dissented from him. "In preaching and expounding he declared all heretics to be not Christians, but Anti-Christs; . . . . . not in hope, but without

---

[1] Sozomenus vi. 37.

hope; not worshippers of God, but without God; not leaders, but misleaders."[1]　Auxentius adds a list of the heretics whom he denounced, which contains the names of thirteen sects, including both the Homousians and the Homoiusians.　One name on the list, that of Antropiani, may possibly refer to the Anthropomorphite sect of the Audians, against whom the phrase "incorporeal in His substance," which occurs in the account of his teaching, may be specially directed.

On the doctrine of the Holy Spirit, the specific discussion of which, though it was involved in the Arian controversy, was bequeathed to a later age, Ulfilas differed widely from what was subsequently the orthodox belief.　His teaching on that point was,[2]— that the Holy Spirit is neither the Father nor the Son, but made before all things by the Father through the Son ; that He is not first nor second, but placed by the First through the Second in the third rank; that He is not unbegotten nor begotten, but created by the Unbegotten through the Only-begotten in the third rank.　In support of this doctrine he was wont to quote John i. 3, and 1 Cor. viii. 6.　It followed from the foregoing that the Holy Spirit could not be said to be either Advocate, or God, or Lord; but from God through the Lord received power to be not Author nor Creator, but Illuminator, Sanctifier, Teacher, . . . Minister of Christ, and the Distributor of Grace.　Ulfilas further maintained the unity of the Church of the living God, "the pillar and foundation of truth," the unity of the flock of Christ "our Lord and God, one Virgin, one Spouse, one

---

[1] Auxentius, ap. Waitz, p. 19.　　　　[2] Auxentius, ut supra.

Queen"; and, as the converse of this, he firmly declared that, as there was but one community of Christians, " all other conventicles were not churches of God, but synagogues of Satan." For all points of his teaching he relied almost exclusively on the Scriptures (" tradition " is once mentioned by Auxentius). This was characteristic of the Homoeans,[1] who were distinguished for it even in an age which had been put upon its guard against non-Scriptural expressions by the troubles that had arisen from the Homousion. In this short account of Ulfilas by Auxentius, the general appeal to " Holy Scripture " is made four times; four texts are quoted, and at the close he adds: " Let the reader understand that all these things were taught by him, and have been described by us according to the Holy Scriptures."

Such was the teaching of Ulfilas, especially on those questions which were threatening in his day to rend the Church. Our only authority hitherto has been Auxentius. Attempts have been made to deduce confirmation, and perhaps amplification, of his report from Ulfilas' rendering of crucial passages in the New Testament. But the results of this enquiry are slight and dubious at best. There remain one or two Arian documents discovered this century, written in Latin or in Gothic, in which traces of the hand or teaching of Ulfilas have been found. The Ambrosian codices, which were brought to light by the researches of Cardinal Mai at Milan, are two MSS. of great interest and value in

---

[1] And so the Arians in general, whose doctrine has been said to be " supported by alternate scraps of obsolete traditionalism and uncritical text-mongering."

connexion with the Gothic Church.[1] The first is a palimpsest containing, in the upper script, a "thesaurus" of the works of Augustine written about the seventh century. The lower script, the writing of which is " far better and fairer," dates from the fourth or fifth century, and contains large fragments of a commentary on the Gospel of St. Luke, which bears clear traces of an Arian origin. The second MS. is also a palimpsest. The original codex having been broken up, the parchments came to form part of two volumes, one of which lies in Milan and the other at the Vatican. When collected together the original manuscript yielded fragments of a commentary on St. John, written in the language of Ulfilas, and several fragments of dogmatic treatises written in Latin, and even more pronounced than the first document in the Arian character of their doctrine. Reserving for the present the description of the Mœso-Gothic manuscript, we may find in the dogmatic fragments valuable illustrations of the Arianism of the Goths.

The ancient home of both these MSS. had been the famous monastery of Bobio. The monastery of Bobio was founded in 612 by Columbanus,[2] the Irish monk, who left his early home in the monastery of Bangor, and after some years of missionary work with his companion Gallus in Burgundy and Neustria, left the latter to carry on his work on the shores of the Bodensee, and himself pushed on to Italy. Here, in a secluded nook of the Apennines, he planted his new monastery, an outpost of

---

[1] Mai, *Scriptorum Veterum Nova Collectio,* iii. 186.

[2] See Hertel, in *Zeitschrift für historische Theologie,* 1875; Wattenbach, *Geschichtsquellen,* i. 99; Revillout, p. 367.

the Catholic faith, in the midst of the Arian Lombards. Eager and vehement in all he undertook, Columbanus set about to gather round him a magazine of Arian literature,[1] out of which to forge new weapons for the destruction of the stubborn heresy. One of these palimpsests is inscribed, " The book of S. Columbanus of Bobio."[2] That he used his library with effect we learn from his biographer, who says of him " that he laid bare as with a cautery, and dissected the deceits of the Arian heresy;" and further, that he issued against them a book displaying a rich acquaintance with the controversy. To the possession of this hostile student of Arian literature we may trace this manuscript. It would be still more interesting if we could ascertain its author. Cardinal Mai, in editing these fragments, confesses that he is unable to point out the author of them; but of this much he is convinced,—the date of the MS. is to be placed at the end of the fourth century or at latest in the fifth; the author was a bishop;[3] but the style is unpretentious and provincial. The fragments are, in his opinion, the remains of three treatises,—one, " Concerning the Son of God"; a second, " Concerning the Holy Spirit"; and a third, " Concerning ecclesiastical questions."

The documents, thus published by Mai, have re-

---

[1] We may judge of the number of Arian documents which must at one time have existed from Hilary, *adv. Const.* 7: " impiissimis Arianorum blasphemiis plenae omnes ecclesiarum chartae, plenique jam libri sunt."

[2] Vit. S. Columb. ap. Surium, Nov. 20, chap. 29, cit. Revillout.

[3] Mai: " episcopum fuisse valde arbitror." " Stilus utriusque operis perinde humilis ac subrusticus."

cently been examined by Krafft, who came to conclusions more decided about the authorship.[1]   The
MS. belongs clearly to the fourth or beginning of the
fifth century.   The doctrine expounded therein coincides with none of the well known forms of Arianism;
it approaches most nearly to the scheme set forth by
Eunomius before the Emperor Theodosius, but there are
discrepancies even when compared with his creed.   In a
word, the only teaching with which they entirely agree
is that of Ulfilas, as set forth by Auxentius.   With
this, the correspondence is very remarkable, even in
details.   The phrase " secundum divinarum scribturarum
traditionem " is a favourite with Auxentius, and the
writer of the treatises alike.   On the subordination of
the persons of the Godhead, obedience of the Son to the
Father, and the Spirit to the Son, as well as in many
expressions used to define the Divine nature, they agree.
The anonymous writer repudiates the title of Arians
imposed upon his party, and in the exposition of his
faith justifies the disclaimer.   For he, as Auxentius
does, exalts the Son as God and Lord, while, on the
other hand, he maintains doctrines foreign to pure
Arianism, namely, that the Son did not make progress
in the character of his divinity, but was at once made
perfect;[2] and again, that though not eternal " a priori "
he was eternal " in posterum."[3]   The verbal coincidences

---

[1] Krafft, *de fontibus Ulfilae Arianismi.*

[2] " Hunc non proficientem in posterum, sed statim perfectum,"
fol. 209.

[3] " Sempiternum autem sic dicimus filium quia cum initium
habeat finem tamen non habiturum sed mansurum in aeternum,"
fol. 149; cf. Comm. on Luke i. 33.

with Auxentius are very striking, especially when we take into consideration the brevity of the exposition the latter has given. In both, we find not only the orthodox ("those who so call themselves"), but also the Homoiusians and the Macedonians condemned. And in the anonymous treatise the last receive especial attention, their distinction from the orthodox being pointed out as well as their distinction from the writer. In style also there is a remarkable correspondence; that which Cardinal Mai notes in both documents as an unpretentious and rather rustic style, to which, indeed, the anonymous writer makes an apologetic allusion at the beginning of his treatise, is characteristic of Auxentius also.[1] On the combined evidence of corresponding style, identical phrases, arguments, and quotations from Scripture, taken in connexion with the undoubted date of the MS., Krafft ascribes these fragments to the same pen as that which wrote the exposition of Ulfilas' teaching, that is, to Auxentius. The date of the composition may be ascertained approximately from a consideration of one sentence, where the writer declares his chief object of attack to be "those who call themselves orthodox, who have forced their way into our churches, and do now hold them in tyrannical fashion declaring that the Son is in all things equal to God the Father." This can only refer to a time succeeding, and probably immediately succeeding, the legal suppression of Arianism in Constantinople by Theodosius and the occupation of all the churches of the sect by their triumphant rivals.

---

[1] "Non sublimitate sermonis vel compositae orationis verbo confidentes, quorum omnino studium non habuimus."

There is not so much evidence to be found for the
other suggestion advanced by Krafft,[1] that the commentary on St. Luke is actually the work of Ulfilas.   The
style and doctrine, so far as opportunity is afforded by
the passages commented on for bringing forward pecu-
liarities of doctrine, correspond with the style and doctrine of the treatises.   Certain words differing from
the correct Latin spelling shew traces of Gothic influence,[2] and some of the characteristic teaching of the
treatise is reproduced very exactly.   Moreover, there is
one passage in the commentary which is undoubtedly
more appropriate to the circumstances of Ulfilas and
his flock than to any other church extant about the
period at which the MS. must be dated.   On Luke
v. 11, which is thus paraphrased—"And they drew
their ships to land, and left all, and followed the
Saviour and His saving words," the comment is as
follows: "I believe they were saying, 'the earth shall
receive our boats as a mother her offspring; let us
leave parents and all things, that we may find a better
parent and all things made ready; let us learn with our
ships to leave behind our bodies, and imitating the
master to consecrate our victorious spirits to a martyr's
death, that seeking sky instead of earth, instead of this
world, paradise, we may win a kingdom; and let us with
Paul boast triumphantly, I follow after, etc.'"   Though
it may be hard to say where the transition takes place

---

[1] Krafft is surely mistaken when he says "idem codex in quo
hic commentarius invenitur, alterum ut supradictum est commen-
tarium continet lingua, qua Ulfila usus est, conscriptum."   At any
rate, Mai's introduction does not bear this out.

[2] e.g. *aecclesiam* for *ecclesiam*; cf. *aikklésjo.*

here between the imagined words of the Apostles and the exhortation of the speaker to his flock, it is clear nevertheless that the flock was threatened with, perhaps in the very midst of, a persecution unto death. It may fairly be asked to what flock in Europe, except to that over which Ulfilas was bishop, could such words have been addressed during the half century within which this MS. must fall. Take further into consideration the connexion of the commentary with the treatises, and that of the treatises with the commentary on St. John in the Gothic tongue of Ulfilas, and in the absence of any evidence to the contrary, we have at least a strong presumption in favour of this theory of the authorship. But we cannot suppose that Ulfilas would compose a commentary so obviously addressed, in the first instance, to his own people in what was to most of them a foreign tongue. Rather is it probable that this is a translation from the Gothic original made either by Ulfilas himself or, as it seems more likely, by his admiring pupil Auxentius.[1]

Interesting as this investigation is, and doubly interesting though the discovery would be if it could be proved that we have here a genuine work of Ulfilas, yet the direct addition to our knowledge would be small. The very exactness of the correspondence between the treatises and the exposition of Auxentius, while it is the most striking evidence for identity of origin, at the same time subtracts from their value as sources of additional information; and the commentary

[1] That Ulfilas did write such works, and could have written one in Latin, we know from Auxentius: "qui et ipsis tribus linguis plures tractatus, et multas interpretationes . . . post se dereliquid.

yields even less to supplement the information from
Auxentius. In fact, his invaluable exposition of the
faith of his master supplies all we know, but that is all
we need to know of the position of Ulfilas in the Church
of his time, and of the faith which he handed down to
his followers.[1]

The work of Ulfilas for his people was not con-
fined to the preaching of the Gospel, the organisation of
the Church, and the civilising influence of his great
personality. Enduring as were the results of these
labours, and widely as his influence was spread thereby,
he achieved in his translation of the Bible into Gothic
a work whose issues were wider and more enduring
still. He was not only the Moses but the Luther also
of his flock; had not only led them forth out of the
land of their oppressors, but had also given them the
Bible in their mother-tongue. To believe the chroniclers,
he was their Cadmus too, and had devised the alphabet
in which their speech first became a written language.

The fact that Ulfilas had translated the Scriptures
into Gothic was vouched for by the early authorities.
Philostorgius, in the passage frequently referred to,
relates of Ulfilas, that " besides all the other ways in
which he ministered to his people, he also invented for
them letters of their own, and translated into their own
tongue the whole of the Scriptures, except indeed the
books of Kings,"[2] which he omitted because of their
stirring narratives of war, with which his people were

---

[1] Bessell, *Göttingen Gel. Anz.* 1861, p. 211, will have none
of Krafft's conjectures.

[2] Philostorgius, *Hist. Eccl.* ii. 3.

already too familiar. The other authority is that represented by a group of writers,[1] of whom we may take Socrates as representative. He says that "at that time, Ulfilas, bishop of the Goths, invented Gothic letters, and having translated the Holy Scriptures into the Gothic tongue, prepared the way for the barbarians to learn the divine teaching." The only important addition to the statement of Socrates is that the translation was made "out of the Greek."[2]

Excluding those statements of intermediate historians, which are clearly based on one or other of these authorities, there are only two traces of a version of the Bible in Gothic to be found between these early authorities and the sixteenth century. One is in a note which appears at the end of the Codex Brixianus, warning the reader not to suppose that one thing is written in the Greek and another in the Latin, or in the "so-called Gothic."[3] This indicates that a Gothic version was in existence, and held in the same estimation with the Latin, and evidently belongs to a time when, on the one hand, Greek was but little understood, while Latin and Gothic, on the other hand, had about equal acceptance, a relation between the three tongues only to be found in the era of the kingdoms of Theodoric and of Toulouse. The second allusion to a Gothic version is found in a writer of the ninth

---

[1] Socrates iv. 33; Sozomenus vi. 37; Acta Nicetae.

[2] Acta Nicetae.

[3] "Ne legenti videatur aliud in graeca lingua aliud in latina vel gotica designata esse conscripta," quoted in Gabelentz, *Prolegomena*, p. 12, with reference to Semler, *Versuch einer Erläuterung einer alten Spur einer Gothischen Uebersetzung.*

century. Walafrid Strabo, abbot of the Monastery of Reichenau in 842, referring to the Goths, says that "learned men of that nation have translated the sacred books into their own tongue," and adds that their work was then extant.[1]

After these two notices, six centuries intervene before we hear again of a Gothic Bible. Then, in the fifteenth or beginning of the sixteenth century, a manuscript is discovered in the Monastery of Werden, near Cologne, from which one visitor after another copies short extracts, which are published, and rouse the curiosity of the learned world. The Lord's Prayer was copied by Antonio Morilloni, and given by him to Becanus, who printed it in his *Origines Antverpiane* in 1569. Then the language of the new MS. was declared to be Gothic, and it was at once concluded that this was a copy of the translation of Ulfilas. At the end of the century the MS. was transferred either by purchase or by robbery to Prague, whence it was carried off after the siege in 1648, and presented by the victorious Königsmark to Queen Cristina of Sweden. From Stockholm it passed in a mysterious manner into the hands of Isaac Vossius, in whose possession it was when the first complete transcript was made and published by Franciscus Junius in 1655. It was then discovered that the manuscript had originally contained the four

---

[1] The whole passage is of interest: "Gothi, qui et Getae, eo tempore quo ad fidem Christi licet non recto itinere perducti sunt, in Graecorum provinciis commorantes, nostrum, i.e. theotiscum sermonem habuerunt, et ut historiae testantur, post modum studiosi illius gentis divinos libros in suae locutionis proprietatem transtulerunt, quorum adhuc monumenta apud nonnullos exstant."

Gospels in Gothic, arranged in the following order: Matthew, John, Luke, and Mark. But, as of the original number of 318 sheets only 118 could then be found, large portions of each Gospel were missing. Junius printed such portions as were still preserved in parallel columns with an Anglo-Saxon version, while copious notes, as well as a glossary, were added at the end. We learn from an introductory tetrastich[1] that the MS. was already known as the Codex Argenteus, a name which it has borne ever since. Its uncial letters are formed in silver upon a surface of purple vellum, and, before the silver was blackened with age and the purple faded, the MS. must have been a most brilliant one.[2] A poem, dedicatory, consisting of some three hundred lines in elegiac metre, gives a history of the Goths founded on Jordanis and the Church historians, and offers the work to the patronage of the Count de la Gardie, who had bought the MS. from Vossius and restored it to Sweden. After having it bound in a heavy silver case, he presented it to the University of Upsala, where it now lies, one of the greatest literary treasures of the north.

For many years the Codex Argenteus remained the only discovered monument of Gothic literature; and of

---

[1] Composed by "Thomas Mareschallus, Anglus," who edited the Anglo-Saxon MS., and wrote some of the notes. It runs thus:

> "Quae dudum e tenebris sacra duxit pagina Gothos
> Nunc tandem e tenebris ducitur ipsa suis.
> Aurea sic gaza ex Argenti codice cusa est
> Chalcographi, quamvis ferrea secla, typis."

[2] A similar MS. was found in Calabria, 1879,—a Greek liturgy written in silver uncials upon a purple ground; described and edited by Harnack and Gebhardt in 1880.

the translation of the whole Bible made by Ulfilas no trace had yet appeared beyond these portions of the Gospels. But in 1736 a MS. was brought to light at Wolfenbüttel, which proved to contain large portions of the Epistle to the Romans in Gothic. The letters of this, the so-called Codex Carolinus, closely resemble those of the Codex Argenteus,[1] though they appear to have been more hastily formed. Still more valuable, inasmuch as they contain passages from the Old Testament also, are the MSS. discovered in 1817 by Cardinal Mai. They had formed part of the library of Bobio, and belong apparently to the sixth century. Of these, the so-called Milanese codices, the first (Codex A) contains, beneath the homilies of Gregory Nazianzen, large portions of each of the Epistles of Paul. Codex B contains smaller portions of several epistles and the whole of 2 Corinthians. The third, which is specially known as the Ambrosian, yields portions of the Gospel of St. Matthew, some of which were lacking in the Codex Argenteus; and a fourth MS. of three sheets contains also, beneath a later writing, some verses from Nehemiah and Esdras. The fifth MS. contains the fragments of a Gothic commentary on St. John, now published and known as the Skeireins. The MSS. thus enumerated, and the portions of Scripture they contain, represent all that has yet been discovered of a Bible in the Gothic tongue. Of the New Testament there are yet lacking the Acts of the Apostles, the Catholic Epistles, and the Apocalypse. Of the Old Testament very little has been found; but indications which appear

---

[1] See the table of facsimiles in Gabelentz and Loebe.

in the Skeireins, *e.g.* a quotation from the Psalms and allusions to passages in the Books of Genesis and Numbers, leave no doubt that there was a complete version in existence in the sixth century.

' Have we then before us in these MSS. portions of the great work of Ulfilas? Few have denied this, but all must admit that it is but an assumption. "It is, in fact, difficult either to assert or to deny that the fragments which have been preserved to our time belong to that version which was completed by Ulfilas."[1] But the probability remains exceedingly strong that, in the Codex Argenteus and the Milanese MSS., we have a version of the New Testament at least, which is in the main the work of Ulfilas. That Ulfilas made such a translation, and that his translation was held in the highest authority among his own people and their descendants, makes it very improbable that any of his successors would attempt either to add or to substitute a new version. But with respect to the fragments of the Old Testament the presumption is in the other direction; for, short as they are, it can be shewn that they are translated from Italian MSS. of the Septuagint,[2] which formed the basis of the Complutensian edition.

Now, taking the material collected in these manuscripts, and assuming that in the version of the New Testament we have in the main a portion of the work of Ulfilas, we can learn much concerning his translation, its basis, its method, and its probable history. That the translation of Ulfilas was founded on Greek authorities is both directly asserted in the Acta Nicetae, and con-

---

[1] Gabelentz, *Prolegg.* xv.   [2] Ibid, xxiii.

firmed by a close examination of the Gothic text. He has even been accused of a too slavish adherence to the text of the Greek original; but the censure is easily removed on consideration, both of the only purpose that could have sustained him in such a work (namely, to make the Scriptures intelligible to his whole people), and also of several passages and phrases which deviate from a literal translation with the obvious intention of securing that that they should be understood by the unlearned folk. Nevertheless, in adhering to the order of words in the Greek, even against the rhythm of his own language, where the meaning or force could thereby be better brought out, in the frequent use of the dual number, and various other delicate characteristics, he has left good evidence to shew what was the language out of which he translated.[1]

It is true, however, that a connexion can be even more distinctly traced between these Gothic MSS. and the early Italian version. Added words and phrases, which are rejected by the Greek codices but acknowledged by the Latin, appear in the Gothic version. In many passages the readings are those characteristic of the Latin and variant from the Greek authorities. Hence the influence of Latin authority on the Gothic MSS. must be admitted. It has been explained in various ways. The opinion that Ulfilas translated from Latin sources only has scarcely been seriously held, and is refuted by the exposition of the fundamental connexion with Greek authorities. Another explanation offered has been that Ulfilas used both Greek and Latin manuscripts. .

---

[1] The doxology at the close of the Lord's Prayer is present in the Gothic, but universally absent from the Latin versions.

But apart from the improbability either that he would be at the unnecessary pains to collate authorities when all that was wanted was a simple translation of the Scripture, or that the Latin versions would be held of any authority in the east in the end of the fourth century, it can hardly be explained why, if Ulfilas had the Latin authority before him, he used it so seldom; or why he passed it over in so many places where its assistance would have helped him to avoid mistakes and mis-apprehensions. The only tenable explanation is that the work of Ulfilas, passing out of Moesia with the Goths into Italy, was there compared by later Gothic theologians with the Latin versions which they found there; that they added glosses and corrections, which afterwards became incorporated in the text, and gave it a distinctly Latin character. Thus, to take some of the more obvious additions, it must have been after comparison with the Latin version (for the corresponding words are found in none of the Greek MSS.) that the words were introduced which mark the beginning and the close of certain books.[1] The Euthalian sub-scriptions to the Epistles, some of which appear in Codex B, must have been added some time after 458, when they were first drawn up, and the immediate source of these also was probably one of the Latin versions.[2] Which of these versions it was which formed

---

[1] *Prolegg.* xxiii. Mark, " anastodeith " = *incipit*; so Luke, and with a similar word 2 Cor. and Ephesians. Romans, *ad finem* " ustauh " = *explicit*; cf. also Epistles to Galatians and Ephesians.

[2] For readings differing from the Greek MSS. and corresponding with Latin, cf. Luke i. 3: "jah ahmin veihamma"=*et Spiritu sancto*. Luke ix. 43: " Kvath paitrus, Frauja du hve veis ni mahtedum," etc.

the basis of the revision cannot be ascertained. The changes introduced in the Gothic correspond exactly with the text of no one of the known Latin versions; but the Itala and the Brixian Codex seem to have been the source of many of the new readings. With the Vulgate the Gothic corresponds more rarely than with any other of the Latin versions.[1]

The first evidence of a subsequent revision is afforded by a comparison of the MSS. where certain passages have been preserved in duplicate, which plainly indicates the existence of two recensions; and on the margin of the Gospel of St. Luke in the Codex Argenteus the various readings and glosses which appear there shew how a second recension might very easily be formed. The relations between the different MSS. and the original work of Ulfilas on the one hand, and the Greek and Latin MSS. on the other, belong to textual criticism, and require to be thoroughly sifted before it is possible to make use of the Gothic version for the textual criticism of the New Testament. It is sufficient for the present sketch to ascertain the probable origin and history of the translation, and to indicate the problems to which it gives rise.

ʻThat Ulfilas, far from slavishly adhering to his original and reproducing a Greek book clad in Gothic words, allowed himself some freedom in adapting his translation to the needs of an uninformed people, is clear from many passages and phrases. Thus, to take one example, he transposed the method of reckoning

---

[1] *Prolegg.* xix., note 54, referring, I take it, to 1 Tim. iii. 16 (not iii. 6); but, in spite of the note, the editors read "Saei" and not "Guth," which points to ὁ or ὅς, not to Θεός.

by years and new moons, which he found common in the Gospels, into the method with which his people were more familiar, and counted by "winters" and "full-moons."[1] On the other hand, many variations from the original are to be explained as due to mis-readings and false renderings, or to ignorance of the customs of the Jews. Of each of these classes of mistakes many examples have been collected by Gabelentz.

Does this translation by the great Arian bishop contain no traces of his distinctive doctrines? This is naturally a question of great interest, and the absence of all such traces from the MSS. known to him led one critic to doubt whether Ulfilas were actually the author of the translation which they contained.[2] But it must be remembered that in accordance with the exposition of Ulfilas' doctrinal position given in the last chapter, the uncompromising doctrines of the extreme Arians were absent from his creed, and there are few passages in the New Testament where he would have any opportunity or temptation to colour his translation according to his views. We have seen that he main-tained, however illogical the position may seem to us, that the Son was God and would be God to all eternity, but *in secundo gradu;* hence, there was nothing in his creed to make him shrink from applying to the Son any or all of the titles he found applied to Him in the New Testament; and it is in vain that we look for traces of his Arianism even in such passages as might

---

[1] cf. the use of "galga" for "cross" even metaphorically.

[2] See *Prolegg.* xxv.

be crucial for an extreme Arian. Unfortunately, the opening of the Gospel of St. John, which would have been particularly interesting in this connexion, is still wanting in our MSS.; but in Rom. ix. 5, the important passage is rendered without deviation from the original, —"Saei ist ufar allaim guth thiuthiths in aivam."

Nevertheless, there can be distinctly traced, in one passage at least, the effect on the translation of the translator's views. The difficult verse, Philipp. ii. 6, ὃς ἐν μορφῇ Θεοῦ ὑπάρχων οὐχ ἁρπαγμὸν ἡγήσατο τὸ εἶναι ἴσα Θεῷ, is rendered "Saei in guthaskaunein visands ni vulva rahnida visan sik *galeiko* gutha," where *galeiko*[1] represents a distinct deviation from the Greek text; for the adjective "galeiks" in all other passages corresponds to ὅμοιος, and here alone answers to a Greek ἴσος. Comparing Auxentius—"he maintained that the Son is like unto his Father according to Holy Scripture and tradition,"—we cannot avoid the conclusion that here the translation bears witness to the translator's doctrinal opinions. The substitution of likeness for equality in the description of the relation between the Father and the Son is the point most characteristic of the party to which Ulfilas belonged.

It would be another interesting enquiry how far the translation is coloured by Teutonic modes of thought, and what traces can be found in its language of their distinctive conception of the future life, of sin and of

---

[1] "Galeiks," (cf. Germ. *gleich*, Eng. *like*) = ὅμοιος; Mark xii. 31: "jah anthara galeika thizai." Luke vii. 31: "Hve nu galeiko thans mans this kunjis jah hve sijaina galeikai." On the other hand, ἴσος is rendered by "ibns," e.g. Luke xx. 36, ἰσάγγελος; and once by "samaleiks."

redemption. The apprehension of "law" in the Gothic mind, if we may judge from the word they used to express it,[1] was not that of a command issued (as "*gebot*,") or of a line of action laid down and confirmed by a superior authority (cf. *lex, law, gesetz*), but it was rather viewed subjectively and as contained in that which is known to a man, so that these Gentiles were, in a strangely exact sense, "a law unto themselves." Sin and the sinful state of man were looked at from two points of view. In the first of these, sin[2] was the transgression of the law, and exposed the transgressor to the payment of a penalty. This notion of penalty incurred by crime or sin, and the necessity of its discharge, was one of the deepest convictions of the Teutonic consciousness;[3] the notion of guilt and the notion of debt coincided, one word served for both. So also the word by which Ulfilas represented κατακρίνειν, *condemnation* either for this world or for the next, was coloured by the local circumstances and position of his people. In the age and among the tribes, where every stranger was a foe, the simplest and the worst punishment an injured community could inflict was to drive the offender from their midst. He became a wanderer on the face of the earth, or in Teutonic phrase a "vearges"

---

[1] "Vitoth," cf. "vitan" = εἰδέναι, συνιέναι; cf. "vitubni" = γνῶσις.

[2] ἁμαρτία is always rendered by "fra-waurhts" = "ver-wirkung," cf. *fro-ward*.

[3] cf. Tacitus, *Germania*, c. 12. "Distinctio poenarum ex delicto . . . . . equorum pecorumque numero mulctantur. Pars mulctae regi vel civitati, pars ipsi qui vindicatur vel propinquis ejus exsolvitur." cf. also c. 21.

or *wolf;* and Ulfilas, making use of " ga-varjan " and its derivatives, pictured the sinner after judgment as the outcast and the wanderer. To render ᾅδης he used the word " halja," *the hollow place,* knitting up the new scheme of Christianity with a fragment of the old Teutonic mythology, in which Hel was already known as the goddess of the place of darkness and the newly departed. The word γέεννα, wherever it occurred, he wisely did not attempt to translate, but transliterated it into "gaiainna." Parallel with the notion of sin as a crime, and redemption as the payment of the penalty it had entailed, was the conviction, deep rooted in Teutonic thought and language, that sin was a disease, and the Redeemer a healer. This also might be abundantly illustrated from the Gothic version. The Greek σώζειν with all its forms and derivatives, is represented by the Gothic (" nisan ") " nasjan " and its derivatives. " Salvation" was regarded as "healing"; above all the "Saviour" was the " Nasjands," " Heiland," the Healer.

Such was the gift that Ulfilas gave to his people, and to all the folk who used the same tongue; not a bald and characterless reproduction of the words of his original, but a vivid and vigorous presentation of its spirit; not careless of its true meaning, but clothing it in the idioms, even allowing it to be coloured by the earlier ideas of his people, doing everything that the book might come to them in no strange garb, but might become readily familiar and be truly a national possession. That they regarded it as such for many generations after his death we know. Goths and Vandals alike carried it with them on their " wanderings" through Europe. Whether in simple piety or in the superstitious hope of reading the future on the chance-appointed page, it was consulted on the battle-fields of Gaul before the fight began. In Italy it was diligently compared with the Latin authorities, and notes were made of the discrepancies. To Spain the Vandals carried it before the Goths, and in their hands it crossed to Africa and even came round again to Rome when Geiseric tried to win where Hannibal had failed.

In a wider sense but not less truly, Ulfilas made a great gift to the world. Though it has lain buried for so many centuries, it is none the less the foundation-stone of all Teutonic literature. Whether he invented an alphabet for the language, adapting to its needs signs taken from neighbouring alphabets, or whether he found a written language but no literature, are questions for the philologist. In either case he was the first to raise a barbarian tongue to the dignity of a literary language, and made for himself and his Goths a monument even more lasting than their deeds.

That Ulfilas was not content with having given his people a version of the Bible in their own tongue we learn from Auxentius. In the three languages, which he could wield, he composed "treatises, and made many translations for use and edifying"; and, as we have seen, certain fragments of a commentary in Latin and of doctrinal treatises which have come down to us, have been ascribed to his pen or to his dictation. Another of the Milanese MSS. contains a fragment of an exposition or a commentary on the Gospel of St. John, which is written in the same language as the version of the Bible (Moeso-Gothic), and with characters similar to those of the Codex Argenteus, while in its contents it agrees with the Latin MSS. in the form of Arianism which it upholds and displays. Hence it has been conjectured that this fragment, the so-called Skeireins, is part of one of the works of Ulfilas; but, though any evidence to the contrary is lacking, the conjecture remains one of which there is small hope of proving the truth.

If by such works as these, by the labours of his pupils and disciples, and above all by the leavening power of the Scriptures now opened to their understanding, Ulfilas carried on indirectly the work of conversion among his heathen countrymen who remained on the other side of the Danube, among his own people he moved in person, preaching and teaching the word of God, "giving thanks to God the Father through Christ with gladness." So he fulfilled the years of his bishopric. His pupil delights to compare him to David, who for thirty years was "king and prophet to rule and teach the people of God and the children of Israel"; or to Moses, by whose hand God had brought his people out of the land of bondage and caused them to pass through the Red Sea, and brought them into a land of promise; or even with the ministry of "our Lord and God Jesus Christ," inasmuch as like his Master, Ulfilas at the age of thirty began "to preach the Gospel and to feed the souls of men."

But his work was done; hardships as well as years must have combined to make him an old man, when in 381 he was sent for to Constantinople. The emperor required his presence. The reason can only be con-

jectured.[1] A split had taken place among the Arians
in Constantinople. Party riots were too common there,
and a fierce dispute over a theological dogma however
abstruse, placed the peace of the city, if not the security
of the palace, in jeopardy. Ulfilas was summoned to
meet the innovators, and either by argument or by
influence to induce them to surrender the opinion that
caused the dispute. " In the name of God," he set out
upon his way, hoping to prevent the teaching of these
new heretics from reaching " the churches of Christ, by
Christ committed to his care." No sooner had he
reached Constantinople than he fell sick, " having
pondered much about the council," and before he had
put his hand to the task which had brought him, " he
was taken up after the manner of Elias the prophet."
" Only observe the high desert of the man who by the
hand of God was brought to die at Constantinople, call
it rather Christianople, where the holy and spotless
priest of Christ might receive such strange and brilliant
honours at the hands of so great a multitude of
Christians."

The figure of Ulfilas may have seemed vaster when
less was known of him. A knowledge of his great influence with his people led historians to introduce that
figure at critical points of his nation's history, to summon
that influence to their aid to explain the problem of
the Gothic creed. But as the figure has become less
mysterious, and his influence on outward events less
universal and imposing, the man has come nearer
to us. We see him not negotiating in courts and

[1] I follow Bessell's restoration of the text of Auxentius. See
Bessell, *Ulfilas*, p. 37.

camps, but preaching the word of life with unwearied patience to his flock; not moving as an energetic missionary from the Save to the Dneister, but extending a silent influence over the whole Gothic-speaking race through his translation of the Scripture; not entering into the arena of a fierce controversy, where the champions of the different parties did open battle, or descending to the conduct of policy and intrigue which more surely secured success, but training up round him a church that cherished his name, and a band of disciples who carried forth his doctrines and fostered them among all the branches of his own nation for many generations after his death. Auxentius has described his life in outline, and lets us see the affection of the pupil as well as the admiration of a fellow-worker. But Auxentius only confirms what the master's work already proclaims. By birth thought worthy to be a hostage for his nation, by education fitted to take an enviable position among the officials of the palace or the foreign leaders of the army, at a time when the Goths were ever becoming more valuable to the throne, —Ulfilas must have thrown away ambition when he became first a humble lector and then a bishop, a missionary bishop among the Danubian tribes. To all the other qualities that make up a leader of men he added the head that planned and the patient heart that carried out the hitherto unheard-of task of clothing the story of Israel and the message of the Gospel in a barbarian tongue. He must have loved his people and he must have loved his Master. " Quem condigne laudare non sufficio, et penitus tacere non audeo."

CHAPTER VI.

THE DECLINE OF THE GOTHIC CHURCHES IN THE EAST.

AUTHORITIES FOR CHAPTER VI.

The Sources are fewer, but the accounts more detailed :

Socrates, Sozomen, and Theodoret (as before).
Chrysostom, esp. his letter to Olympias.
The letters of Nilus.
The letter of Jerome to Sunnia and Fretela.

In the latter part of the chapter the references to mediæval travellers are taken from Massmann, *Ulfilas*, etc. Krafft pays special attention to the missionary activity of Chrysostom, and to the letter of Jerome. Pallmann, p. 187, discusses the relation of parties at the court of Theodosius.

THE defeat of Valens at Adrianople was the most paralysing shock which the Roman world had received since the fatal day of Cannae. The army was utterly cut to pieces, the emperor slain, and the whole of south-eastern Europe lay open to the victors, who might turn their steps whither they pleased. The policy of the previous years, wherein the emperor had relied ever more exclusively on barbarian auxiliaries to fight the battles of the empire, now reaped a bitter fruit. The townspeople, the farmers, and the peasants of the provinces had not only been discouraged from joining the legions, but had been restrained from equipping or training themselves, had even been forbidden to leave their homesteads. And now the empire, in its hour of need, had no reserve on which to fall back, no source from which to draw new defenders. Stunned by the news of the disaster, the Western Emperor Gratian, who had been advancing to the assistance of Valens, fell back

upon Sirmium, and took the wisest and most prudent
step in summoning the young Spanish general Theodosius to take over the throne of the East, with all
its attendant perplexities and dangers.   Guided by his
military skill and political shrewdness, the Eastern
empire passed through the terrible crisis.   Fortunately
the fenced cities that defied their attack, and the booty
that destroyed their discipline and cohesion, had already
done much to diminish the once overwhelming danger
of the Gothic mastery.   The hope of conquest which
had for a moment gleamed before the Goths was
quenched when they were repulsed by a handful of
Saracens from the walls of Constantinople.   They fell
back on their original demands,—the fulfilment of the
treaty they had made with Valens, and the right to
settle in the Balkan peninsula.   Theodosius knew his
own strength too well to push the enemy to extremity.
The empire must have peace to restore its losses, and
the army time to recover from the demoralisation of
Adrianople; so both parties found relief in coming to
terms.   Perhaps a third of the fighting strength of the
nation passed over into Roman service; the remainder
settled down in the plains of Thrace and Moesia.

On the other hand, the battle of Adrianople dealt a
blow to Arianism which was nothing less than fatal.
The Homoean party, which for twenty years had been
supreme, and had all but crushed the rival sections of
the Arian body, was itself supported almost wholly on
the influence of the court.   Valens, who had been
both open in his adhesion, and zealous in lending his
support, to Arianism in its struggle with the Nicene
party, had favoured the Homoean form to the ex-

clusion of all others. At his death Homoeanism, and Arianism with it, crumbled away. Gratian, in the interval of sole government between the death of Valens and the appointment of Theodosius, issued an edict of toleration which removed from the Nicenes, at least, the pressure of the legislation of Valens. This was the first step towards their final victory. The long and dangerous illness of Theodosius was an accident which issued greatly in their favour. While he lay at Thessalonica he was converted by Ascholius, the bishop of that city, and professed the Nicene faith. He went further, and, perhaps in the expectation of death, he accepted the rite of baptism, to which even Constantine had submitted only during the illness which proved his last. Pledged then by his formal admission to the Church, and impelled perhaps by grateful zeal on his recovery, Theodosius became no inactive ally of the Nicene party. Already, in February, 380, a decree issued from Thessalonica, ordering all men to hold the Nicene faith "as committed by the Apostle Peter to the Romans, and now professed by Damasus of Rome and Peter of Alexandria." But during the illness of the emperor the new policy did not take effect. It was not till he arrived in Constantinople[1] in the end of the same year that the Arians fully experienced the change in their position involved in the change of emperors. Then the alternative was offered to the Arian bishop Demophilus,[2] either to deny his faith and accept the

[1] For a picturesque account of the position of the Nicene Church in Constantinople at this time, v. Stanley, *Christian Institutions*, p. 295.

[2] See Socrates v. 7; Gibbon, c. 27; Greg. Naziauz. *contra Arianos et de seipso.*

Nicene creed, or to surrender the cathedral and the churches of Constantinople to the opposite party. He chose the latter; and, having summoned his people to meet him in the great church, announced to them that from thenceforth they would worship outside the walls. What a reversal of position this involved for the Nicene party who entered upon the churches thus vacated may be gathered from the fact that Gregory, the Nicene bishop, at that time " was holding his meetings in a little house of prayer,"[1] which was, in fact, a dwelling-house that had been " altered into the fashion of a church by certain of his flock." But, beyond replacing the Arians by the Nicenes in the churches of Constantinople, Theodosius did not at once take measures to suppress the heretics. Not till three or four years had passed did he issue and enforce edicts of persecution. We may suppose, with some degree of confidence, that his hand was held in some measure by the consideration of his new subjects, in whom a comprehensive and determined attack on the form of faith which they professed would be certain to raise distrust and indignation that might even endanger the newly established relation. New blood had been infused into the dying party of Arianism by the arrival of the Gothic nation, and their settlements in Moesia provided at once a ready asylum for those who fled from Constantinople, and a rallying point for members of any discontented faction; while in Constantinople an ever-increasing resident body of Goths, attracted to the service of the court and of the army, would be a formidable obstacle to any high-handed measures in favour of the Nicene party.

[1] Sozomenus vii. 5.

The vacillating policy of the emperor in the years 380—387 becomes clear when we perceive the presence of a body of Arians with an ill-defined power of disturbing the peace of the empire, which might at one time seem threatening enough to induce the emperor to employ mediation rather than persecution, and at another would appear so problematical that he might boldly risk their anger. His first step, after establishing the Nicene party in the churches of the capital, was to call a general council, at which the semi-Arians were strongly represented. An attempt to reconcile them with the dominant party having failed, they had to submit to lose their churches. The triumph of the Nicene party was complete. On the other hand,[1] two years had scarcely passed before the emperor made a new and more determined attempt to secure unity in the Church, not by crushing out the heretics, but by bringing about a general reconciliation. The deprived Arians were proving troublesome in many quarters of the empire. Theodosius summoned once more the heads of the most influential sects to give and receive an account of the points on which they differed. He had his dream, like Constantine, of a strong unbroken Church, the best ally of the State; and he, too, thought that a frank discussion of the points at issue was all that was required to make all parties see their errors and accept a common basis of doctrine. His failure was even more complete. The discussion never took place. The heads of the different parties—Homoiusians, Arians, Eunomians, etc.—presented the creeds

---

[1] Sozomenus vii. 12; Socrates v. 10.

of their particular sects. But upon their followers clamouring .that these creeds did not fairly represent their faith, the emperor threw up the attempt, and the only result of the Synod of 383 was a severe decree forbidding all heretics to hold meetings, to give instructions concerning the faith, or to ordain either bishops or inferior clergy.

Evidence both of the continued numerical importance of the Arian party in Constantinople, even after their political influence had disappeared, and of the important position which the Goths held, is afforded by a controversy which broke out among them in the early years of Theodosius' reign, and the attention which is given to it by the Church historians. Though, according to its chronological position in the narrative of Socrates, the Psathyrian schism appears to take place after the Italian expedition of Theodosius—that is to say, after 387—yet it had probably broken out some years earlier. The point at issue illustrates very well the nature of many of the controversies of this whole period. It was, whether the Father was to be regarded as already Father before the Son was called into existence. A certain Marinus, who "had been summoned from Thrace" to be a bishop or leader of the Arian party (after the death of Demophilus), had for some reason or other to give way to a rival Dorotheus, who had been brought from Antioch to take his place. Dorotheus denied the eternal Fatherhood of God; Marinus, either of conviction or out of contentiousness, asserted it. The former party remained in possession of their churches; the latter, who insisted on withdrawing, had to build new ones. They were popularly

known as Psathyriani,[1] as the historians explain, because a certain Syrian cakeseller or confectioner (ψαθυροπώλης) was an energetic supporter of the party. But
they· were also known as the party "of the Goths,"
whose bishop, Selenas, held with Marinus. Here we
may see a possible explanation of the circumstances.
Marinus, "called out of Thrace," may have been the
candidate for the Arian bishopric whom the Goths
supported. His teaching of the eternal Fatherhood
would be entirely in sympathy with the doctrine of
Ulfilas, though, so far as we know, Ulfilas did not enter
upon the question. On the other hand, Dorotheus,
brought up from Antioch and denying the eternal
Fatherhood, was probably the candidate of the non-
Gothic section of the Arian Church at Constantinople;
and either through the superior number of his supporters, or through some intrigue, he was preferred to
his rival or exalted in his place.

Almost all the barbarians (*i.e.* Goths), as we learn,
followed Marinus and worshipped with his party.
Ulfilas had found a successor who bore the mantle, and
with it some of the influence of his master, in one
Selenas. He had been the amanuensis of the great
bishop, and the people accepted him and "followed him
most gladly." Hence his attachment to the cause of
Marinus ensured the adhesion of the greater number of
the Gothic Christians. This party itself shortly be-

---

[1] For the Psathyrian schism, see Socrates v. 23; Sozom. vii. 17.
The statement that the schism was healed thirty-five years after its
outbreak by Plinthas in his consulship (419) seems to refer the
dispute to 384, a date which is more probable than 387 from the
known relations between the Arians and the government.

came a prey to schism. The cause of the dispute is obscure; a certain Agapius, whom Marinus had raised to the bishopric of Ephesus, claimed the "primacy." The contention that ensued was so bitter that, we are told, many of the clergy withdrew altogether, and joined themselves to the Catholic Church. The Goths took the side of Agapius in this controversy, abandoning their allegiance to Marinus, a proceeding which, in the absence of any further information, seems quite inexplicable. The schism lasted for many years; until, for the Arians of Constantinople at least, it was healed through the mediation of Plinthas, an ex-consul, in the year 419.

The legislation of Theodosius against the Arians affected the Gothic Church in Thrace only indirectly. As "foederati," the settlers were allowed to follow their own choice in matters of religion. Nevertheless, the issue of some fifteen persecuting edicts in as many years cannot fail to have roused the sympathetic indignation of the Goths. That disturbances and remonstrance did not follow is due to the fact that these decrees were very imperfectly executed. Almost any one of the number, if rigidly carried out, would have sufficed to eradicate Arianism or, at any rate, to force its adherents to seek safety in obscurity; but they probably represent less a decided purpose of suppressing heresy than repeated concessions to the demands of the chiefs of the Nicene party. Theodosius was encouraged to disregard the feelings of his subject-allies by the opposition between two sections of the nation. There was all along a party among the Goths who adhered to the old paganism. They were especially strong in the

capital, where they furnished many valuable and
trusted officers to the court and to the army. The
Arianism of the main body estranged them from the
emperor, whereas the heathen Goths found more ready
access to his favour. Thus, over against the national
party, there appeared a court party, which latter took
rise, perhaps, with the invitation and reception of Athanaric, whose followers, heathens doubtless, remained in
the emperor's service after the death of their chief.
Theodosius could regard this antagonism with com-
placency, and even when it led to high words at his
own table between the pagan Fravitta and the Christian
Eriulf, he bore the insult with indifference. The separation of interest between Constantinople and Thrace,
which was the result of this policy, produced serious
effects after the emperor's death.

For fifteen years the Goths in Thracia lived a
settled life, learning the arts of peace, occupied with
pasturage and tillage. Here the various tribes were
gradually welded together. The sense of religious
separation fostered the growth of national consciousness. The followers and pupils of Ulfilas carried on his
work; the seeds of his teaching took root, and bore
fruit in a national character to which later historians
were to bear warm testimony.

Auxentius at Dorostorus (Silistria) and Palladius at
Ratiara (near Widdin), were working either in the midst
of or close beside the young nation. But their allegiance
was given to Selenas, who was called the successor
of Ulfilas, who, like his master, was " well-fitted to
instruct the people in the church," having command
of the Greek as well as of his mother-tongue. The

position of the clergy, and their identification with the life of the nation, is shewn by their frequent appearance as envoys and negotiators. From the time of the battle of Adrianople down to the battles on the plains of Gaul the Arian presbyters appear frequently as the representatives of their nation.

The death of Theodosius revealed the effects of the fifteen years of tranquil development. The Goths were no longer to plunder, but to conquer; to play a part on the stage of Europe no longer as a collection of tribes loosely held together by common hope of spoil or by common danger, but as a nation with a purpose. That the religious isolation into which they were thrown by the policy of Theodosius, and their resentment at the encouragement which the defection of the heathen party received from him, did much to mould their development can hardly be doubted. The Arianism of the Goths was full of consequence for the empire.

With the general break up of the nation in 395 the Gothic Church in Thracia disappears. The greater part of the nation took part in the out-wandering. Those who remained behind have left no trace. Many, no doubt, were drawn by the persuasive efforts of Chrysostom's missionaries to join the Catholic Church. In one spot alone, within the Balkan peninsula, the Gothic name and Church was recognised in the ninth century, though we cannot tell whether the little Gothic remnant, who preserved their mother speech at Tomi in the ninth century, preserved also the memory and the teaching of their great first bishop.

For half a century all parties in the Church had

been alike in the absence from their ranks of men of
commanding genius and influence, who might compare
with the heroes of the first half of the century. The
leaderships had descended from Athanasius, Arius, and
Eusebius to court intriguers and factious strivers for
political ends. No party had clean hands; all had at
one time or other been soiled by intrigue, surrender of
friends, or cowardly abnegation of teaching and principles. But at the end of the century the man at last
appeared, and appeared on the side for which victory
had already declared. Theodosius, dying in 395, was
succeeded in the east by his weakling son Arcadius.
In the early years of his reign John, called Chrysostom,
was brought a presbyter from Antioch, and made
Bishop of Constantinople. We have not to trace the
history of the succeeding years, or describe his influence
in any direction save one. He sealed the victory of the
Catholic party. He achieved what all the edicts of
Theodosius failed to do; detached the populace of Constantinople from their persistent and often tumultuous
support of Arianism, and, before the end of his brief
opportunity, made them devoted adherents of himself,
and through himself, of the Catholic Church. He extended the sphere of his diocesan work till it included
all Thracia.[1] Here he was in contact with the remnants
of the Church of Ulfilas, and no doubt added many of
the Thracian Goths to the Catholic faith. In Constantinople he laboured with especial care and devotion for
the same people.[2] A church was set apart for their
worship, and a staff of presbyters, deacons, and readers

---

[1] Theodoret, *Hist. Eccl.* v. 28.   [2] Ibid, v. 30.

of the Scriptures appointed to minister to them in their own tongue; and he himself frequently taught them from the same pulpit, using an interpreter to transmit, as well as possible, his wonderful eloquence. It is no strange thing that such efforts and such devotion met with success; for "many of them which had been deceived he recalled, shewing to them the truth of the preaching of the Apostles."

In the midst of these aggressive measures against Gothic Arianism Chrysostom was called upon to defend the Church against an attempted inroad from the same quarter. Gainas, by birth a Goth, through his good service and determination raised to be Master of the troops, made to his imperial master a request, which was equivalent to a demand, that one of the churches in the city should be transferred to the Arians, his fellow-believers. The emperor was prepared to yield, but the proposal met with most determined opposition from Chrysostom. Whether the demand was a sincere one or an insolent pretext for a quarrel,[1] the result was one of the most serious tumults that ever raged in Constantinople. During the absence of Gainas from the city the gates were shut, the populace rose and put to death seven thousand barbarians, whom they found within. The church which Chrysostom had set apart for the Goths offered them an asylum in vain. Religious hatred, added to a political distrust, had infuriated the

---

[1] That Gainas was sincere in desiring a place of worship for his followers appears most probable from the lengthy correspondence that passed between him and Nilus, the disciple of Chrysostom. See the letters of the latter, *Epp.* bk. i. 70, 79, 114, 116, 205, 206, 286, ed. Migne.

mob to such a pitch that they fired the building, and all the refugees perished in the flames.[1]

It was not long in the power of Chrysostom to labour to repair this disaster; the synod of the Oak, confirmed by the cabal under Theophilus of Alexandria, pronounced his deposition and authorised his banishment. But even from the distant wilds of Asia he continued to exercise his influence, and his interest in the Goths remained undiminished. Already, before his banishment,[2] he had received and acceded to a request from the "king of Gothia," that he would send a bishop to the Church of his country. There can be no doubt that by this "king of Gothia" we must understand the ruler of a tribe which dwelt on the north shore of the Euxine,[3] probably round the Cimmerian Bosphorus, in the modern Crimea. Here a remnant of the subjects of Hermanaric had established themselves after escaping from the Huns, or shewing such resistance as might secure them till the storm had passed. To this people Chrysostom had sent one Unila (or Wunnila) to oversee their Church. But three years later, word came to him in his banishment that Unila was dead, and a Gothic mission was once more in Constantinople to obtain a bishop for their Church. The anxiety of Chrysostom was raised lest his rival Arsacius should introduce heresy and schism into the Gothic Church by appointing an Arian to be bishop. Accordingly, he took steps to

---

[1] Socrates vi. 6; Sozomenus viii. 4; Theodoret v. 33. The accounts vary, especially in the order of events; I have not thought it necessary to attempt to reconcile them.

[2] Chrysostom, *Ep. ad Olympiadem*, xiv. 1.

[3] Procopius, *B. G.* iv. 2.

have the envoys detained by friends of his own in Constantinople, cherishing the hope that before long he himself would be recalled, and might nominate a successor to Unila. His letters to the wealthy widow Olympias, whose house in Constantinople was thrown open to bishops, monks, and churchmen, together with his letter to the deacon Theodulus,[1] shew his great affection for the Gothic Church of the Crimea, and express his gratitude to the monks who remained faithful to him, though they found him banished from Constantinople, and had to meet the persecution of Arsacius for their persistent adherence to his rival.

We have already seen reason to believe that these Goths received the seeds of Christianity from the Cappadocian captives mentioned by Philostorgius, and never deviated from the Nicene faith of their first teachers; and also that the Bishop of Gothia, who signed the Nicene creed, was the representative of the Church in the Crimea. Communications passed between this church and another father of the Church besides Chrysostom. Among the letters of Jerome is preserved a reply which he sent to two of the Gothic clergy named Sunnia and Fretela. Unfortunately, the letter which drew forth this reply has not been preserved. But it is clear that the tenor of it was to enquire concerning several passages in the Psalms where the Greek text of the Septuagint was at variance with the Latin text.[2] To Jerome they appealed to learn the

---

[1] Ibid, *Ep.* 206.

[2] Hieronym. *Opera*, ed. Erasmus, **Paris**, 1534, iii. p. 28. " Quaeritis a me rem magnae operis et majoris invidiae in qua scribentis non ingenium sed eruditio comprobetur: ut in opere Psalterii

true significance of the Hebrew original. He opens his reply with an expression of his astonishment and thankfulness that the barbarian Gothic tongue should be seeking to know the truth of the Hebrew; and that, while the Greeks are slumbering or disputing, Germania herself is searching the Scriptures. Thereafter he explains the relation between the κοινή and his own Hexapla version, where he had carefully rendered the better text into Latin. The body of the letter is taken up with a categorical reply to their several questions, in the course of which the warning is frequently repeated to "avoid foolish and superfluous discussions where there is no actual difference of meaning involved"; and while he carefully answers the most minute questions, he interjects general comments on the true method of translation.

The nation of Goths, from whom the letter to Jerome had proceeded, was known to the Greeks as the τετραξῖται. They maintained considerable intercourse with Constantinople, and were in alliance or subject-alliance with the Emperor Justinian,[1] to whom they made application that he should send them a bishop. This he did, and from that time forward the Church of the Crimea was connected with the Byzantine Church. The seat of the bishopric was at Kapha, and the name of the bishop appears as ὁ Γοτθίας in the acts of the Byzantine Synod down to the eighteenth century.[2]

juxta distinctionem schedulae vestrae, ubicunque inter Latinos Graecosque contentio est, quid magis Hebreis conveniat, significem."

[1] Procopius, *B. G.* iv. 4, 5.

[2] Massmann, Introduction, xxvii., cites *Notitia graecorum episc. Leonis*, and *Oriens Christiana, Le Quien*, i. 1240.

One of their bishops, Johannes of Parthenope, was present at the Church Council at Nicaea, and keenly opposed the Iconoclasts.

Traces of the people, if not of the churches, are found at intervals throughout the middle ages. The Minorite Ruysbroeck of Flanders, on the journey which he undertook for Louis IX. in 1253, found, "between Chersun and Soldaja," forty villages, among whose inhabitants he says there were many Goths, whose language was "deutsch." Later still Josafa Barbaro,[1] sent by the republic of Venice to the Black Sea in 1436, mentions Goths who spoke "deutsch" as dwelling in "Gothia," with whom his German servant could converse freely. In the next century they attracted the attention of three travellers,[2] the last of whom, Busbek, though he did not visit their country, met two of their envoys in Constantinople, and obtained information from them concerning the manners and customs of their countrymen. He collected from them a number of words and phrases, which prove to be not only distinctly Teutonic, but in some cases indisputably Gothic in form and root. Joseph Scaliger states, moreover, that the remnant of the Goths, who dwelt among the Pericopean Tartars, possessed the Scriptures of both the Old and the New Testament in the same lan-

---

[1] Josafa Barbaro, *Travels to Tana and Persia*, by J. B. and Ambrogio Contarini, published by Hakluyt Society, 1873.

[2] Matthias von Miechow, Monk of Cracow; *Tractatus de duabus Sarmatiis.* Conrad Gesner, Mithridates, 1555. Busbequius Augerius, *The Four Epistles of A. B. concerning his Embassy into Turkey* (London, 1694). New translation by Forster and Daniell, 1881, vol. i. p. 355.

guage and the same characters as those of Ulfilas' translation.[1]

Lastly, in 1750, a Jesuit monk of Vienna,[2] named Mondorf, conversed with a galley slave whom he bought from the Turks, and learnt that among his countrymen in the Crimea, where a language related to the German was still spoken, the Christian faith had become extinct, and the worship of the people was paid to a log of wood. The small Christian community in the Crimea lost its connexion with the Christian world when the Eastern empire fell; and the intrusion between it and the West of the Tartar and Ottoman tribes produced an isolation which indefinitely weakened the resisting power of the faith. The tide of heathenism, in which all the countries round the Black Sea were engulfed, overflowed also the little Church which had received first, and possessed longest, the simple faith of the Gospel.

Note on Bessell's Emendation "Psathyropolistae."—
The document of Auxentius contained in the Parisian marginal MS., which was edited by Waitz, is unfortunately most seriously defaced at the account of the last journey of Ulfilas to Constantinople. As recovered by Waitz, the passage appears thus: "qu . c . . precepto imperiali completis quadraginta annis ad Constantinoplitanam urbem ad disputationem . . . . . . contra p . . . ie . . . . . t . stas perrexit," etc. Waitz suggests "qui cum" or "itaque cum" for the first words, but leaves the rest without comment, merely remarking that the second letter before the "t . stas" looks like a "p." Bessell, who attacks the whole passage and restores it with great ingenuity, proposes for the part quoted above, "qui cum precepto

---

[1] Joseph Scaliger, *Isagog.* iii. 347.

[2] Büsching, *Geographie Universelle* (Strasburg, 1785; London, 1762).

imperali, etc., ad disputationem . . . . . . contra psathyropolistas per-rexit." "Psathyropolistas" he defends as a legitimate form of Psathyriani, comparing the double use of "Apollinariani" and "Apollinaristae"; also the fact that in Socrates the god-father of the sect is actually described as ψαθυροπώλης. Ulfilas, he con-cludes, was summoned by the emperor to meet these disturbers of ecclesiastical peace and reconcile them with their brethren.

The brilliancy of the restoration is obvious; the letters corres-pond in number with what would be required to fill the space shewn in Waitz's reproduction: from Waitz's " p," two places before the "t" to the end of the word the only change required for the reading, " polistas " is the obvious one of "t" to "l"; the rest of the word is more entirely conjectural.

Yet there are some serious objections in the way of the accept-ance of the restoration. It will be noticed that Bessell has left blank the space before "contra," which might represent a word which would alter the effect of the sentence. But the reasons for withholding assent are as follows:

1. Accepting, as we have done, the date fixed by Bessell for the death of Ulfilas, namely 381, and very early in that year, this reading pushes back the controversy too far; for it must already have reached serious dimensions before the emperor took steps to allay it. But, according to its position in the narratives of Sozomen and Socrates, we might put the breaking out of the controversy in 387, since it appears after the narrative of Theodosius' Italian expedition; and though there are good reasons for disregarding this consideration (firstly, because Plinthas in 419 healed the breach thirty-five years after it arose; secondly, because in 387 the relations of the Arian party to the empire would scarcely admit of the public disruption of the kind), yet the supposition that it is misplaced by seven years is hardly to be justified.

2. Since the strife must have broken out some time before Ulfilas was summoned, and therefore at least before Demophilus surrendered the churches in Constantinople, how comes it that two new men appear as heads of the opposite party, one of whom had been brought from Antioch to be (in the *room of the other*) chief of the Arian party in Constantinople, for "Dorotheus quidem qui Antiochia accitus in locum Marini Arianis praesidebat"? (Sozome-nus vii. 17.)

3. The effect of the proposed reading is to bring Ulfilas to oppose the Psathyropolistae; but this is hardly credible, not only because their doctrine that the name Father was to be ascribed to God the Father from eternity is altogether consonant with what we know otherwise of Ulfilas' views, but also because we are actually told that this Psathyrian party was the one to which both the Goths, as a body, and their bishop, Selenas, attached himself. Can it be supposed that the Goths and their bishop became the notorious supporters of a cause which their great leader, a few years before, had gone up to Constantinople to attack?

It appears, therefore, that Bessell's theory of the date of Ulfilas' death and his proposed reading of Psathyropolistae in the text of Auxentius are not compatible.

CHAPTER VII.

THE GOTHIC CHURCHES IN ITALY AND GAUL, AND THEIR DECLINE.

AUTHORITIES FOR CHAPTER VII.

SOURCES:

Salvianus Massiliensis, *de Gubernatione Dei.*
Cassiodorus, *Historia tripartita* (ed. Migne).
Sidonius Apollinaris.

LITERATURE:

Dahn, *Könige III., Verfassung des Ostgoth. Reichs in Italien.*
   ,,   ,,   *V. and VI., Äussere Gesch. und Verfassung der Westgothen.*
Hodgkin, *Italy and her Invaders,* vols. i. and ii.
Kohl, *Zehn Jahre Ostgothischen Geschichte,* 526—536.
Kaufmann, *Ueber das Foederatverhältniss des tolosanischen Reichs zu Rom.*
   Deutsch Forsch. VI.
Fauriel, *Histoire de la Gaule Méridionale sous la domination des Conquérants*
   Germains.
Zschimmer, *Salvianus der Presbyter von Massilia und Seine Schriften.*
Baret, *Oeuvres de Sidoine Apollinaire.*
Loening, *Geschichte des Kirchenrechts in Gallien.*
Revillout, *de l'Arianisme des peuples Germaniques qui ont envahi l'empire*
   Romain.

THE death of Theodosius in the year 395 marks the close of an epoch in the world's history. The powerful hand was then removed which for one moment had placed arrest on the decline of the empire. Called first to govern in the East, he had displayed foresight, tact, and determination in the rescue of the State from the perils of the Gothic invasion. Thence his influence had been extended beyond the Eastern empire, and he was the last to hold in one grasp the undivided empire from the Bosphorus to the pillars of Hercules. His policy was approved by success in his lifetime, and might have prospered still had his successors possessed a little of his genius or a spark of his determination.

But under the nominal government of Arcadius and
Honorius the empire rushed impetuously to its fall.

Within the year of the death of Theodosius the
Gothic nation was in arms against the empire. Arcadius had withdrawn or reduced the subsidy which
Theodosius had prudently paid to his subject-allies.
The young nation, who knew their strength and saw
their opportunity, caught the pretext, and threw off the
irksome allegiance which bound them to the empire.
The next five years saw all South-eastern Europe laid
waste by the host of Alaric. From the walls of Constantinople to the plains of Argos, from Athens to
Sirmium, they carried war and desolation. Then came
the decision, on whose issue two emperors might well be
trembling. The fate of the East and of the West was
in the balance, one against the other. Constantinople
escaped. The word was given to march on Italy, and
in 401 the storm broke on the devoted land.

Alaric himself was no stranger to its northern
frontier, and the Goths had played a part already in the
political and ecclesiastical history of North Italy. Part
of the auxiliaries, who took service with Theodosius at
the peace of 380, had been sent to garrison Milan, and
had appeared in the background of the struggle between Justina and Ambrose. The Western Church
found her Chrysostom a few years earlier than the
Eastern, in Ambrose. There is a strange correspondence
between the history of Milan in 385 and of Constantinople in 400. Events and figures are alike in both.
The central figure is the bishop who resists the empress,
refuses a demand to permit one of the churches to be
set apart for Arian believers, and triumphs over the

court through the affection and enthusiasm of the populace. And in both dramas the Arian Goths form the background; they are the pretext, real or ostensible, of the demand, and on them the fury of the populace is poured out.

The Arians had held Milan for at least twenty years in the person of their bishop, Auxentius, when he died in 374. In his successor, Ambrose, they found an opponent no less able than determined, and to Justina, the widow of the former emperor and mother of the young Emperor Valentinian, they had to look for credit and support in their falling state.[1]

The activity of the Arian party in Milan, however, which specially marks the years 385 and 386 corresponds with the presence of Gothic auxiliaries, whose Arianism would at once attach them to the cause of the empress. An Arian,[2] named Mercurinus, was appointed bishop of the party in Milan, and took the name of his predecessor, Auxentius. The reproach addressed to him by Ambrose that he was only bishop in the estimation of a handful of foreigners points to the Goths at the court of Justina, who probably represented the extent of his diocese. The empress then moved the emperor to demand of Ambrose the use of the Basilica " in Porta Romana," which was outside the walls of the city; but the bishop stoutly refused. A second demand for possession of a new church within the walls met with the same repulse.[3] By order of Justina the new church was surrounded by soldiers, probably Goths, who were

[1] cf. esp. J. H. Newman, *Historical Sketches*, ii. 339 seqq.
[2] Tillemont x. pp. 165, 746; Ambr. *Ep.* 13, p. 201.
[3] Sozomenus vii. 13.

interested in this attempt to assert the rights of their
faith, and preparations were made within the building
that on the succeeding Sunday, which was Easter Day,
Auxentius might celebrate the offices of the day. But
the opposition of the populace became so threatening
that the emperor had to withdraw the troops, and
abandon the attempt to force the consent of Ambrose.
Justina, persisting in her support of the Arians, induced
Valentinian to issue an edict granting free right of
assembly to all who accepted the creed of Arianism,[1]
which had been confirmed at Constantinople, and
menacing with death all those who put obstacles in
their way. The Catholics resented this edict, which
placed the heretics on the same footing with themselves, and denounced it as an edict of persecution.
The attempt, which was renewed under cover of this
law, to obtain the church of Porta Romana for the
Arians, and the persistent opposition of Ambrose, issued
in the plot to seize the bishop and the famous siege,[2]
which he and his devoted people sustained in the
cathedral and episcopal palace. It may be left undecided whether it was the discovery of famous relics
within the beleaguered Church and the redoubled enthusiasm of the people, or the news of the death of
Gratian, and the political troubles which followed, that
compelled the empress-mother and her son to yield.
The victory of Ambrose was complete; but it was not
till two years later, when the death of Justina had

---

[1] Sozomenus vii. 13; Cod. Theod. xvi. 4, 1. The edict was
issued January 21st, 386, having been dictated by Auxentius. See
Tillem. x. 177.

[2] See Gibbon, c. 27.

removed the principal obstacle, that Theodosius "set in order the ecclesiastical affairs in Italy."[1] Perhaps he withdrew the obnoxious Gothic garrison.

If the Wisigoths who overran Italy under Alaric left no political monument of their presence after their withdrawal under Athaulf in 412, it can hardly be expected that there are many traces of that Arian Church of which they were in some sense the representatives. They suffered doubly at the hands of the historians,— as barbarians and as heretics. While nothing too scornful could be said of them as barbarians, nothing was too harsh to say of the heretics. What might have been to their credit as Christians is ascribed to their childishness and inexperience as barbarians; what stains their name with violence and bloodshed as barbarians is attributed to their wickedness and perversity as heretics. We are asked to believe that many acts of clemency, many withdrawals from a doomed city, were due to the effect on the barbarian mind of the gorgeous pomp and solemnity of a religious procession. But the Wisigoths were not children, wild and untutored savages fresh from the forests of central Europe. For thirty years and more they had been dwelling within the empire, living a settled and peaceful life. Some had tilled the plains of Thrace, and had held frequent communications with Constantinople; while others had visited the chief cities of the empire as garrison troops, had fought under Theodosius as legionaries, and with him had conquered Maximus. These were not the people to be

---

[1] Sozomenus vii. 14. After the death of Maximus, καὶ τὰ περὶ τῆς ἐν Ἰταλίᾳ ἐκκλησίας εὖ διέθηκε· συνέβη γὰρ καὶ Ἰουστίναν ἀποθανεῖν.

overawed by a procession, however imposing. It is fair
to suppose that with them self-control meant something
more than childish awe, and clemency was not due alone
to superstition, however skilfully played upon.

Of the heretic Gothic Church itself only one trace
has come down to us. The upstart Attalus,[1] whom it
suited Alaric's purpose for a moment to use as a
puppet-emperor, though still at heart a heathen, found
it to his interest to seek baptism and admission to
a Christian Church. The Church, of course, was the
Arian-Gothic, and there was found with the Gothic
host a bishop, Sigesarius, who administered the rite
" to the great gratification of the Goths, and of Alaric
himself."

We may argue, from this case and from the general
practice of the Vandals,[2] that the Gothic army, as well
as the people who followed, was accompanied even to
the field of battle by their bishops. The external form
and rites of the Church were necessarily adapted to the
circumstances of the people. We have already observed
the use of a tent-church among the Goths, when, during
the persecution of Athanaric, an erection of this kind
was destroyed by fire, together with all those who had
sought asylum within. To a portable building of a
similar kind Ambrose, no doubt, alluded in the sarcastic
remark that "those had formerly used wagons for
dwellings, now used a wagon for a church."[3]

If the traces of the Gothic Church at this time are

---

[1] Sozomenus ix. 9.

[2] Hieronym. *Ep. ad Heliodorum.*

[3] Ambr. *Ep.* xx. 12: "Quibus ut olim plaustra sedes essent
ita nunc plaustrum ecclesia."

very few, we may yet observe the working of the Christianity which it fostered. The siege and "sack" of Rome, either as a whole or in detail, may be taken as testimony to a spirit and a character which were strangely modified from the early savagery of the barbarians.[1] It were a shallow criticism that should object at the outset that war, conquest, and plunder should altogether have been shunned by a Christian people. It would be difficult in modern, as it would be impossible in ancient history, to point out a siege and sack, of which such episodes are recorded as distinguished the capture of Rome by Alaric. Augustine himself points out that Rome did not suffer so severely in the days that followed the capture by Alaric as under the avenging return of Marius or Sulla.[2] Far from emulating the cruelties of the latter, the Goths "spared so many senators that it was rather a matter of observation that they slew some."

Though it was not in Alaric's power to deny the spoil of the great city to his long restrained troops, he gave orders that fire was not to be applied to any of the buildings, and proclaimed that he and his people would respect the right of asylum, especially in the churches of SS. Peter and Paul.[3] It is true that the first of

---

[1] For capture of Rome, see Gibbon, c. 31; Pallmann i. 310; Hodgkin i. c. 8; Sozomenus ix. 10; Hieronym. *ad Principiam*; Orosius vii. 39; Procop. bk. v. i. 9.

[2] Aug. *de civitat. Dei*, iii. 20: "Gothi vero tam multis senatoribus pepercerunt ut magis mirum sit quod aliquos peremerunt." Ibid: "Syllana porro tabula plures jugulavit senatores, quam Gothi vel spoliare potuerunt."

[3] Orosius vii. 39; cf. Augustine, *de civit. Dei*, v. 29, 23.

these orders failed to secure its object; much damage was caused by fires, which were raised either by accident or by design. But the second general order which, as Augustine remarks, was "contrary to all custom of war in previous wars," was honourably observed. If we may judge from a somewhat obscure sentence in Augustine,[1] the Goths shewed much more hostility to the heathens, and wreaked their fury on the many remains of heathen worship and edifices. Even the heathen inhabitants of the city, who had been most clamorous against the Christians during the siege, were not slow to take advantage of the asylum which was secured in their churches. In all the scene of terror and confusion, in all the opportunity for cruelty and rapine, lives were spared, women's honour was respected, nuns were conducted by Gothic soldiers to a place of safety.[2] One episode which is related at length by Orosius is very remarkable. A soldier had burst into a house and found there an aged nun in charge of the great sacred vessels of the Church of SS. Peter and Paul. Amazed at the value of his discovery, but warned by their guardian that he would lay hands on them at his peril, he sent word to Alaric. The Gothic chief despatched at once an escort of soldiers by whom the vessels were protected as they were transferred across the city to the place of asylum, the Church to which

---

[1] Augustine, *de civitat. Dei*, v. 23: "ipsisque daemonibus atque impiorum sacrificiorum ritibus, de quibus ille praesumserat, sic adversarentur pro numine christiano ut longe atrocius bellum cum eis quam cum hominibus gerere viderentur."

[2] Sozomenus ix. 10. He carefully points out the Arianism of the Goths, and the Catholicism of the nuns.

they belonged, followed by a great crowd of Christians and pagans who were drawn by the strangeness of the spectacle. The gold and silver vessels were borne along on the shoulders of men; the Gothic escort closed in on either side and behind; and the city rang with the shouts and chants of those who followed in the procession.[1]

I have referred to these events of the capture of Rome by Alaric, because in the paucity of direct reference to the Gothic Church at the time, it has been a satisfaction to find the Goths purged from the charge of uncontrolled licence, and displaying a continence and a moderation not commonly ascribed to barbarians, which may not unreasonably be referred to the influence of Christian teaching.

Eighty years after his faithful followers had diverted the little stream beside Cosenza to bury Alaric in its bed, and then turned their backs upon Italy which he had conquered, to seek a home in Gaul, another section of the Gothic race became masters of Italy. The Ostrogoths had been swept along with the wave of Huns in their westward course, had faced their Wisigothic kinsmen on the field of Châlons, and out of the wreck of the Hunnish confederacy which was dissipated at the death of Attila, they had risen an independent and powerful people. Under their noble prince Theodoric they overthrew the semblance of a government which existed in Italy, and established the kingdom of the Ostrogoths. Then began that most interesting experiment, the

[1] Orosius vii. 39, describes the procession with much detail.

attempt of Theodoric to combine two races in one kingdom, and by blending Gothic vigour and bravery with Roman traditions and cultivation, to restore the famous empire to some of its old prestige.[1] It was a great scheme and it was pursued with a persistency and a patience which surely deserved success, and renders almost pathetic the failure that was the all but inevitable issue. There were many obstacles to such a scheme, and it may be that the methods of Theodoric were not most wisely chosen for its execution, but the rock on which it split was the difference of faith. The Ostrogoths, like their brethren the Wisigoths before them, were Arians. Once more an Arian-Gothic Church stood up against the Catholic-Latin Church, and once more the latter was victorious. The Latin Church was the greatest and the most consolidated power which faced Theodoric in Italy, and in its unrelenting opposition to the Arian king lay the secret of his failure.

Theodoric was the first genuine apostle of toleration; he was willing even to suffer for the principle. Firm in maintaining his own faith, he was no less determined in protecting the liberty of others. He defended the Jews from the malice and persecution of the Italians, enforcing a general levy to compensate their losses in a riot. Towards the Catholics he shewed the greatest consideration, accepted the post of arbitrator between rival candidates for the Papacy, and decided with most careful judgment; paid honour to their saintly men, and sent contributions to their famous shrines. Had he been a pagan he would have been extolled. He might

---

[1] Gibbon, c. 39; Dahn, *Könige* ii. 123; Hodgkin, *Italy* ii.

have been led through a form of conversion, celebrated as
defender of the faith, and ultimately canonized.   Being
a heretic, his best efforts were accepted with sullen
distrust; he earned nothing but misapprehension and
dislike.   His watchword was enough to condemn him,[1]
—" We cannot impose a religion by command because
no one can be compelled to believe against his will."
The elevation of Justinian to the throne of the East,
an orthodox emperor pledged to root out heresy, brought
about a *rapprochement* between the Church of Italy
with the shadowy senate at Rome and the Byzantine
court, and this was an alliance fatal to the projects of
Theodoric.[2]   This silent opposition, impervious to all his
advances and threatening the future of his throne and
house, embittered the last years of the great king.   The
extravagant honours paid by the Byzantine Court to
Pope John on his mission to Constantinople, conveyed,
as no doubt they were intended to convey, to Theodoric
the sense of his own isolation and of the hopelessness of
his task.   He became suspicious of all his envoys, even
of his true friends Symmachus and Boethius; and their
imprisonment and death at the close of his reign have
stained a noble record for ever.

The purpose of this fatal embassy concerns our
subject.   The orthodox emperors, Justin and Justinian,
had given proof of their attachment to the true Church
by a determined attempt to suppress heresy.   An

---

[1] Var. ii. 27: "religionem non imperare possumus, quia nemo
cogitur ut credat invitus."   cit. Dahn.

[2] On the relation between the Church and the Roman senate at
this period, see Usener, *der Römische senat und die Kirche in
der Ost-gothenzeit.*

earlier decree, directed against the survivors of the
Arian party, had made an express exception in favour
of the Goths, but the new alliance between the Eastern
court and the Latin Church encouraged a bolder policy ;
and the subsequent decree which issued in 523 or 524, exposed to persecution the Arians throughout the empire
without any exception. This was a direct blow at Theodoric, who had hitherto observed some semblance of
political dependence on the Eastern emperor. The
isolation of the Goths as heretics was proclaimed and
emphasised, and his own policy of toleration rendered
hopeless, if not ridiculous. Moreover, while for his
own subjects there was no danger of persecution, there
remained within the jurisdiction of Justinian many
Goths whom he was bound, if possible, to protect.[1]
Hence the necessity of sending the embassy, for which
he selected men of the highest rank and influence. The
Bishop of Rome was sent, perhaps because he could
best represent the danger of retaliation upon the
Catholics in Italy.[2] Three senators and a patrician were
his colleagues. Whether the bishop sincerely urged the
request of Theodoric for the removal of the obnoxious
decree, and the toleration of his fellow-countrymen and
believers, or only arranged with the emperor a common
plan of operations against the heretic king, their mission
failed of its object. The envoys returned with empty
hands, and the king, in anger or suspicion, threw the
pope into that prison whence he was released only by

---

[1] The Moeso-Goths who had retained their settlements together
with Ostrogoths and other Wisigoths, who had not joined the
general out-wandering.

[2] So Dahn.

death. The obsequious senate tried, and condemned unheard, their own member Boethius, whose sentence, at first mitigated by the clemency, was afterwards enforced by the frenzied suspicion of Theodoric. The king's own death following shortly afterwards was hailed as the judgment of God, and good Catholics believed with satisfaction that their heretic benefactor was consigned at once to the volcano furnace of Lipari.

After the death of their great king the Ostrogoths struggled against their fate for nearly thirty years. But, at last worn out by victories and defeats alike, they yielded finally to Narses, and the last remnant of them entered the Byzantine service.

Of the Church among the Ostrogoths in the period of their rule in Italy almost no record is preserved. It is mentioned by Cassiodorus that Theodahat shewed great liberality towards his own Church,[1] and enriched it with lavish gifts; and some records have been discovered which 'refer to clergy, churches, and churchlands.[2] The first of these is found at Naples, and belongs to the reign of Totila, about the year 550. The Gothic Church of S. Anastasia had received an advance of 120 "skillings" from a certain Petrus Defensor, in security for which they pledged a piece of marsh land to the value of 180 "skillings." On receiving the balance of 60 "skillings" they surrendered possession of the land by the document which has been preserved. In the

---

[1] Cassiod. XII. *Ep.* ii. "Veniamus ad illam privatae Ecclesiae largissimam frugalitatem quae tantam procurabat donis abundantiam."

[2] Bernhardt, *Gotische Bibel*, etc. (Halle, 1884), p. 216; *Gotische Urkunden.*

list of signatures, which are partly in Latin and partly
in Gothic, there occur the names of a presbyter (who,
through weak eyesight, was unable to sign with his own
hands), a "papa," a deacon, a sub-deacon, and certain
other clergy. We have here the record of a Gothic Church
with a large staff of clergy, and lay officers (*ustiarii*)
holding land as a corporation, and conducting their
affairs through a notary, all which points to a long
established Church, which was itself, no doubt, one of
many such. A very similar record of a similar trans-
action was found at Arezzo, but has since been lost;
our imperfect facsimile shews that a certain deacon sold
to another deacon some part of the farm of Caballaria.

But the presence and power of the Gothic Church is
manifested apart from any other records by the influence
it exerted on the policy and life of Theodoric, and
on the whole history of the Ostrogothic kingdom. It
cannot be supposed that the Church, for whose faith
Theodoric sacrificed a sound basis for his kingdom, and
the success of his whole policy, existed only in the past.
Nor did his successors flinch from the position he had
taken up; and these records are only a material proof
of the existence of the Church which must have nourished
the Arian faith, to which they adhered till the end.

The great king of the Ostrogoths was not the first
who had cherished the noble idea of resuscitating a
Roman empire, in which Roman forms and traditions
should provide a framework for the vigour of his own
young race, and barbarian license and impetuosity be
restrained and moulded by having incorporated with it

the heritage of the past. Athaulf, who led the Wisi-goths from the grave of Alaric to find in Gaul a home which they had sought in vain elsewhere, began his reign with "an ardent desire to blot out the Roman name and make all Roman soil an empire of the Goths,"[1] in which himself should play the rôle of Augustus. But having learnt by long experience that his people would not be bound by the laws of a state, "without which a state is no state," he determined " to seek glory for himself by restoring to its former glory the Roman name" by infusing the hardihood of his own race into the decrepit members of the decaying empire. The scene of this experiment was in the south of Gaul, whither the Wisigoths withdrew two years after the death of Alaric. Honorius must have seen with relief the departure of his dangerous guests, and it is quite possible, though it can hardly be proved, that they were encouraged to turn their steps in that direction by a treaty with the emperor and a concession of land for settlement. Such a concession could be of but slight actual value, implying little more than leave to hold what land they could conquer for themselves; but it was characteristic of the Goths that they desired

---

[1] Orosius vii. 43. "Se in primis ardenter inhiasse ut obliterato romano nomine romanum omne solum Gothorum imperium et faceret et vocaret, esset que, ut vulgariter loquar, Gothia quod Romana fuisset fieretque nunc Ataulphus quod quondam Caesar Augustus; atque ubi multa experientia probavisset neque Gothos ullo modo parere legibus posse propter effrenatam barbariem, neque reipublicae interdici leges oportere, sine quibus respublica non est respublica, elegisse se saltem ut gloriam sibi restituendo in integrum augendoque romano nomine Gothorum viribus quaereret," etc. See Dahn, *Könige*, v. 64, on the passage.

nothing so much as settlement under the shadow of the empire. The old name of Rome had not lost its glamour, and very striking is the eager willingness of the barbarians to accept all the responsibilities of self-defence and nominal dependence for the shadowy privilege of the imperial alliance. It was this strange sentiment alone, whether we call it awe, reverence, or affection, that secured the barbarians to Rome as childlike dependents rather than as ungovernable destroyers. Unmanageable, of course, they were, and the empire could make no pretence to chastise them, but the fiction of the " foedus " was always maintained. Quickly disregarded by the stronger party whenever it saw its advantage, it was as readily revived after each escapade. We do not require to follow the windings of policy and intrigue on either side, during which the circle of Roman influence steadily contracted at the same time as its power within that circle as steadily diminished. The Goths, on the other hand, under a succession of able and warlike rulers,[1] gradually extended their boundaries at the expense of the Roman province, and differentiated their power from that of the empire till their king became no more, even ostensibly, the channel of delegated authority, but, in name as well as in fact, an independent sovereign.

Under Athaulf and Wallia, the kings first and third in succession to Alaric, the Pyrenees were passed by the whole nation, and it seemed for a moment as if Spain was the destined seat of the next Gothic kingdom. But the Wisigothic kingdom in Spain was not to rise for a century yet, and after overrunning the greater part of

[1] See Table of Wisigothic kings.

the peninsula as far as Cadiz, and making an unsuccessful attempt to carry out Alaric's cherished idea of seeking a home in Africa, the Goths turned back and retraced their steps to the eastern side of the Pyrenees. Here, in the Roman province of *Aquitanica fecunda,* they settled. It suited Roman policy at the time to attach the barbarians as dependent allies within the reach of nominal control rather than to leave them free to carve out a kingdom for themselves in distant Spain. To the Goths,[1] on their part, no doubt the fertile plains of Aquitaine were more attractive than the less luxuriant fields of Spain. By the treaty concluded between Wallia and Honorius, the whole basin of the Garonne was open to the Goths for settlement. With this territory there came into their hands the towns of Bordeaux, Angoulême, Poictiers, and others; and the famous city of Toulouse, in which Wallia established his capital, afterwards gave its name to the kingdom.

The kingdom of Toulouse lasted for close on a hundred years. Under four kings in succession the alternations of peace and war with the empire issued alike to the advantage of the Goths. On the field of Châlons, Wisigoths fighting with and for the Romans, met Ostrogoths marshalled under the banner of Attila. The second Theodoric proclaimed and supported Avitus as Roman emperor in succession to Maximus. Now with, and now without, the pretext of Roman authority, the Goths made expeditions to Spain, and gradually established there a claim to supremacy in the peninsula.

---

[1] Salvian, *de Gub.* vii. 2. "Nemini dubium est Aquitanos ac Novempopulos medullam fere omnium Gallianum et uber totius fecunditatis habuisse." cf. also c. 5.

But the kingdom reached its widest limits, and the Goths their most brilliant position, under the successor of Theodoric, his brother Euric. The changes in the Western empire which had afforded transient opportunities to his predecessor, were now so frequent as to give this vigorous prince almost continuous occasion to profit by the distraction and vacillation of the nominal sovereigns of Gaul.[1] In fact, the real obstacle to the complete conquest of Southern Gaul by the Goths was found not in the desire or determination of the emperors to maintain their hold over their fertile province, but in the stubborn resistance offered to the barbarians by the provincial nobility, and to the heretics by the Catholic clergy. The flood of barbarian conquest had swept over the plains of Narbonne and Lower Auvergne long before it reached Upper Auvergne, where Ecdicius, representing the Roman laity, and Sidonius Apollinaris, the bishop of Clermont, held the high table-land for Roman civilisation and Catholic unity.[2] But when Julius Nepos, last but one on the roll of Western emperors, formally withdrew the claim of Rome to the territory which his predecessors had for so long neglected to defend, Ecdicius and Sidonius abandoned their untenable post, and the Gothic kingdom was now only bounded by the Loire, the Rhone, and the two seas.

It was at this time that the kingdom of Toulouse reached its climax. Four years before the death of Euric another race had hailed as chief a young prince, before whom the Gothic power in Gaul should crumble to dust. Before Euric had been dead a year, the Franks,

---

[1] Jordanis, c. 45.
[2] Situation well sketched by Baret, *Sidoine Apoll.* p. 42.

under Chlodwig, had crushed in the thin bulwark of Roman rule that lay across the centre of France, and there stood face to face the two peoples, to one of whom the dominion of the West must fall. It is not too much to say that the issue of this momentous contest was never in doubt, that it was decided in advance by one fact,—the Arianism of the Gothic Church.

The Gothic kings of Toulouse and their people had remained faithful to the teaching of Ulfilas, and the Arianising form of doctrine which had been transmitted to them by their fathers. But the difficulty of presenting an adequate picture of the Gothic Church in Gaul is not less than in the case of the Church in Italy, and arises from the same causes.[1] The disappearance of the nation, the extinction of the Church, the malignity of their opponents, have ensured the destruction of all the records and monuments on the side of the heretics; while lack of sympathy, or of any interest deeper than the polemical, debarred the victorious party from leaving any adequate or trustworthy account of the Church of their rivals. Nevertheless, we may perceive from a number of slight indications that the Gothic Church in Gaul had a well-developed organisation, providing for its adherents throughout the kingdom the offices and ministers of a regularly established Christian Church. In the works of Gregory of Tours there is mention of controversies, both public and private, between bishops and presbyters of the two parties, and these so frequent

---

[1] Revillout, p. 96. "Il est donc bien difficile d'établir avec de pareils secours la comparaison des deux Eglises, et l'historien se trouve le plus souvent réduit en l'absence de faits concluants, à hasarder des inductions et des conjectures."

as to pre-suppose the existence of two bodies of clergy similar in numbers, organisation, and distribution.[1] Few of the Arian clergy appear by name in the records of their opponents. Yet we know that Sigesarius, the bishop who baptized Attalus at Rome, accompanied Athaulf to Gaul and Spain, and had charge of his children at the time of their father's death. That the Arian Church distributed its clergy over the country, and placed them side by side with, or sometimes in place of, the Catholic clergy, may be seen from one or two indications given by Gregory. Thus, in the diocese of Arisitum, the fifteen parishes of which it was composed had all been held by Gothic presbyters.[2] Near the town of Reuntium (Rions) the Goths had possessed themselves of a Catholic church, and "transferred it to the foul service of their sect."[3] Here, on the eve of Easter, they proceeded to baptize the children of the village, in the hope that as the Catholic priest was denied the opportunity of baptizing, "the people might be more easily entangled with their sect." The Catholic party, not to be foiled, held their baptismal service in a large house adjoining, and their triumph was complete when all the children who had been baptized by the heretics died within the octave of Easter. Whereupon the Arians restored the church to the Catholic party.

[1] e.g. Greg. Tur. *Mirac.* i. 80, where presbyters of the rival parties met at supper. Ibid. 81: "Arianorum presbyter cum diacono nostrae religionis altercationem habebat," etc.

[2] Greg. Tur. *Hist. Franc.* v. 5.

[3] Greg. Tur. *de gloria confess.* c. 48, "villa est in qua cum esset ecclesia Catholica, advenientibus Gothis, ad suam sectae immunditiam transtulerunt."

The Arian worship and ritual seems not to have differed very much from that of the Catholic Church; scarcely more, perhaps, than various uses within the Church differed from one another. Some of the variations which can be traced owed their presence to the Eastern connexions of the Gothic Church. Certain offices which took place with the Catholics during the morning were celebrated by the Arians at daybreak (*antelucani*). It was this office which, as Sidonius[1] tells us, Theodoric, the successor of Wallia, attended daily. The connexion of this early service with Arian use is curiously illustrated by the accusation of Arian practices which was laid against a certain Pamphilus;[2] the complaint against him was that he devoted himself to holy offices from midnight onwards, but ceased at daybreak. It was also a custom peculiar to the Arian Gothic Church that a special cup was provided for the royal family at the communion.[3]

While the Arian Church thus strove to present itself as highly organised and as efficient for ministering to its adherents as its rivals, it did not neglect opportunities for propagating its tenets among the neighbouring peoples. Sidonius[4] reports having seen one Modaharius, "brandishing darts of heresy," working as a missionary of the Arians among the Burgundians. Thus, wherever

---

[1] Sid. Apoll. *Ep.* i. 2, "antelucanos sacerdotum suorum coetus minimo comitatu expetit."

[2] Bolländ, *Vit. S. Pamphili,* April 28: "quapropter plerique civium rem inique aestimantes illum Ariani ritus apud pontificem criminantur."

[3] Greg. Tur. *Hist. Franc.* iii. 31.

[4] Sid. Apoll. *Ep.* vii. 6.

we catch a glimpse of it, the Gothic Church is seen to be acting out in its methods and organisation the theory of its existence as stated by Salvian[1]—"so firmly do they consider themselves to be Catholics that they insultingly distinguish us by the title of heretic."

The controversies, of which many are recorded, are unfortunately recorded only by pronounced partisans. They all result in the same way. The heretic is silenced. Similarly the tests and ordeals which are proposed declare invariably and unmistakably for the Catholic side, while the efforts of the heretics to produce miracles or undergo ordeals are futile, or worse than futile. Gregory accuses the Goths, moreover, of cowardice and timidity, which are characteristics scarcely to be looked for in a people with such a history.

Another contemporary writer, on the other hand, has drawn a picture of Gothic character, and described a state of public and private morals, which bears testimony to the efficacy of their belief, if not to the theological accuracy of their creed. Salvian, the presbyter of Marseilles, in his book on *The Government of God*, when he is upbraiding the feebleness, and lashing the vices, of the Roman and Catholic Christians, again and again places before them, as examples of Christian life and practice,[2] the "ill-instructed" barbarians who sojourned in the land. Their life was better than

---

[1] Salvian, *de Gub.* v. 2: "Nam in tantum se Catholicos esse judicant, ut nos ipsos titulo haereticae appellationis infament."

[2] Salvian, *de Gub.* v. 3: "ut quandoque haereticos patientia Dei faciat plenam fidei noscere veritatem, maxime cum sciat eos forsitan Catholica non indignos fide quos videat Catholicis vitae comparatione praestare."

their creed; how much worse was that of his own flock. "As concerns the 'conversation' of the Goths and Vandals," he says, "wherein could we either prefer or compare ourselves? To speak first of love and charity, —all barbarians, one may say, who are of one race and under one king, love one another; all Romans mostly persecute one another. The poor are pillaged, the widows mourn, the orphans are trampled under foot, so much so that many of them flee to the enemy,—seeking, I suppose, Roman humanity among the barbarians when they could no longer bear barbarous inhumanity among the Romans. So, in spite of differences of worship and habits, they pass over to the Goths." "Treacherous, but chaste," is the label which Salvian attaches to the Goths in his list of races;[1] and elsewhere he enlarges on the fact that they scorned the licentiousness and debauchery that was undermining Roman vigour, and was such a foul blot even upon the Church itself.

The attitude of this Arian people and government towards the Catholic inhabitants of their country was, on the whole, one of great tolerance. Princes[2] and people[3] alike treated the Catholic clergy with honour and reverence. Portrayed as their conduct is, by those who were alien by race and by creed, and likely to

---

[1] *de Gub.* vii. 15: "Gothorum gens perfida sed pudica est. Ibid. vii. 6: "Impudicitiam nos deligimus, Gothi exsecrantur. Esse inter Gothos non licet scortatorem Gothum; soli inter eos permittuntur impuri Romani." See this fully worked out in Isaac Taylor, *Ancient Christianity*, ii. 64, seqq.

[2] *e.g.* Greg. Tur. *Hist. Franc.* ix. 24. (Fronimius episcopus) a Leuvane magnifice est receptus.

[3] Salvian, *de Gub.* vii. 9, "cum illi (Gothi) etiam in alienis sacerdotibus Deum honorarent, nos etiam in nostris contemneremus."

resent and recal the smallest tyranny or attempt at
compulsion, there is nevertheless no trace in the records
of the earlier kings of any measure of repression or open
hostility.   Nor was this for lack of provocation.   There
must have been a deliberate purpose in the policy of the
kings of Toulouse,—patiently to live down the opposition of the Catholic clergy, or to bring about the
supremacy of the Arian Church by careful fostering and
gradual spread of its doctrines.   It cannot be that king
after king who reigned at Toulouse was blind to the
fact that the greatest hindrance to union and tranquillity within his kingdom, and to extension beyond
it, lay in the resistance, passive or active, of the Catholic
clergy.   The semi-feudal constitution of the nation
placed over against the king a body of nobles, from
amongst whom he himself frequently had been raised
to the throne, and whose jealousy and insubordination
were rendered formidable by their independent following
of vassals.   In the Catholic clergy, who had learnt
independence and to know their own power under the lax
government of the declining empire, the Gothic kings
found a new and unexpected factor with which they had
to reckon.   Always in opposition so long as the kings
remained heretics, pitilessly immoveable by any concessions short of complete submission, this third party
checked the king at every step.   They provided a
rallying-point for Roman laity and disaffected Goths
within the kingdom, and a fulcrum for any crafty foe
without.   We shall not be surprised, therefore, to find
that the king who had the greatest ambition, shewed
the highest state-craft, and enjoyed the most favourable
opportunities, found himself compelled to abandon as

untenable the position of toleration taken up by his predecessors, and adopt a policy of repression against the Catholics. This repression, which might conceivably be justified as politically necessary, has been magnified and distorted in the hands of the annalists till it appears as a ruthless and unjustifiable persecution. Euric is branded with the name of persecutor, and his reign supplies dates for many martyrdoms; yet it is more than doubtful whether he can fairly be regarded as a persecutor or his victims as martyrs.

To Sidonius Apollinaris we owe a graphic account of this persecution of the Catholics by Euric.[1] In a letter addressed to Basil, the bishop of a neighbouring diocese, he describes the condition of the Church under Euric. After a complimentary preface, he opens his subject by saying: "I do not do wrong in bewailing to you the way in which that wolf, who fattens on the sins of perishing souls, is gnawing at the entrances of the Church biting in secret with a tooth as yet un-noticed." He accuses himself, with other shepherds, of having given the enemy an advantage by slumbering at his post; in spite of the pain it gives him he will set forth the whole truth. Euric (Evarix) is not to be judged by himself or his correspondent for defending or extending his frontiers; but it is a case of Dives and Lazarus, of Pharaoh marching with his diadem, and the Israelite with his basket; of Assur thundering in royal insolence, and Jeremiah with his people bewailing the spiritual Jerusalem. He comforts himself with the

---

[1] Euric had built a church at Briuda (Brivas) in honour of St. Julian. Dahn, *Könige*, v. 101, note ref. to Sid. Apoll. *Ep.* ii. 1; but I have not been able to find the reference.

reflection that this is not what he deserves, and that
affliction purifies the soul. He must, however, confess
that he is in dread that Euric is likely to undermine
not so much Roman bulwarks as Christian institutions.[1]
"The mention of the name of Catholic acts like vinegar,
they say, on his face as on his heart, so that you cannot
tell whether he is more truly chief of his nation or of his
sect." Then after characterising Euric as distinguished
as a warrior, as a statesman, and as a man of affairs,
he gives a list of nine dioceses whose bishops or arch-
bishops have been "cut off by death";[2] and as no other
bishops have afterwards been appointed in their place
(by whom, of course, the lower orders of clergy are appointed), wide-spread spiritual ruin has been the result.
"This ruin would move even an arch-heretic, spreading
as it does, while the fathers are dying, day by day.
The parishes are without priests. The churches are
falling into decay; alas, even round the altar-stones the
cattle may be found cropping the grass. Look more
deeply into the injury inflicted on the spiritual members,—it is clear that the more bishops are removed,[3] the
more of your people will find their faith endangered.
I forbear to mention your own colleagues, Crocus and
Simplicius, who have been removed from the chairs
that were entrusted to them."[4] He concludes with an

---

[1] "Sed, quod fatendum est, praefatum regem non tam Romanis
moenibus quam Christianis legibus insidiaturum pavesco."

[2] "Summis sacerdotibus ipsorum morte truncatio nec ullis
deinceps episcopis in defunctorum officia suffectis (per quos utique
minorum ordinum ministeria subrogabantur) latum spiritualis
ruinae limitem traxit."

[3] "Quanti subripiuntur episcopi tantorum fidem periclitaturam."

[4] "Cathedris sibi traditis eliminatos."

appeal to Basil to devise with his colleagues some remedy for the unhappy state of matters in the vacant dioceses.[1]

This famous account of the "persecution" of Euric has been reproduced at some length, in order that its tone may be apprehended as well as the facts which it contains; for in the tone we fail to find the earnestness of those who have "resisted unto blood" for conscience' sake, and are led to doubt whether, on calm examination, even the facts related justify a charge of persecution against the king. For what is described here except a political struggle between the Gothic government and the third party in the state, who were using their position as spiritual princes for political ends? We have here, in fact, the prototype of the *kulturkampf* of the nineteenth century. The method adopted by the State in its contest with the Church is identically the same. The episcopal sees as they fall vacant are not allowed to be filled up; the ordinations of the lower clergy cannot take place; and the consequence of a few years of bloodless conflict is that many country parishes are found without spiritual officers, the services of the Church are suspended, and the churches fall into disrepair.[2] But a policy like this is not to be placed in the same category with the attempts of Decius

---

[1] Sid. Apoll. *Ep.* vii. 6.

[2] It is interesting to observe the use that can be made of these authorities: *e.g.* Maimbourg, *History of Arianism* (Eng. trans. 1729), ii. 179. "Evarix (misprinted, Odoacer) turned his arms against the true religion, expelled the bishops and pastors from their churches, some he put to death, caused most of the churches both in town and country to be destroyed, etc." cf. *Revillout*, p. 138, seqq.

or Diocletian to suppress Christianity, or of the Stuarts
to enforce prelacy upon the Scottish Covenanters.   If
"persecution" means the tyrannical and cruel application
of temporal power to control or crush liberty of opinion
and spiritual independence, the word cannot also be used
without qualification to describe the action of the State
in an imperative attempt to grapple with high treason
in the Church.   That was the justification of the
policy of Euric, and the issue of the struggle in the
reign of his successor only confirmed it.[1]

Nor do the details of the persecution, which may
be gleaned from the pages of Gregory, invalidate this
conclusion.   The passage in Gregory,[2] which is chiefly
relied on, is obviously a digest of the letter of Sidonius,
to which, indeed, express reference is made at the end
of the chapter; and a careful examination and comparison would shew that even if its authenticity be
admitted, it is of no value as an independent authority.
Passing from this, the individual cases of the persecution which are alleged all resolve themselves into
measures of precaution against ecclesiastics who were
suspected, and, as the event proved, only too justly
suspected, of holding treasonable intercourse with the
Franks.   In the records of the bishops of his own diocese of
Tours, Gregory mentions two who were banished from

---

[1] Those who maintain the cruelty of the " persecution," and
that it was an attempt " faire prévaloir partout l'arianisme " (Revillout), infer from the expression of Sidonius, " truncatis morte," that
the bishops suffered a violent death; but this certainly requires
proof, which is not forthcoming, especially when compared with
other expressions in the same letter, passim,—e.g. " per singulos
dies morientum patrum," " excessu pontificum," etc.

[2] Greg. Tur. *Hist. Franc.* ii. 25, cit. Revillout.

their see by the Goths.[1] In each case the reason was the same; they were "suspected of desiring to submit themselves to the rule of the Franks." But the interval of eleven years, during which the second ruled unmolested, does not at least betoken any undue impatience or nervousness on the part of the Gothic king.

The conversion of Chlodwig was the decisive event for the history of Gaul. Henceforward the whole weight of Catholic influence was given to the Franks. The struggle between a heathen nation with a heathen chief and the united forces of Gothic and Roman Christianity might have been a doubtful one; but the submission of the Frank to the Catholic Church secured him the friendship of a party within the camp of the Goths, whose influence, thanks to their organisation and tenacity of purpose, was out of all proportion to their numbers. "Thy faith is our victory," said the Catholic to the new convert; and a very few years proved the truth of the prophecy.

Euric had been succeeded by a son who had neither the ability nor the tenacity of his father (A.D. 485). When Alaric weakly surrendered Syagrius to Chlodwig, he made a fatal confession of weakness,[2] by which the Frank was not slow to profit. The interview with the chief of the Franks, sought and obtained by Alaric, produced only a very transient security. The Catholic Church in the south was waiting eagerly for their champion to

[1] Greg. Tur. *Hist. Franc.* x. 7, 8. Volusianus and Verus; both appear to have died natural deaths.

[2] Greg. Tur. *Hist. Franc.* ii. 27, "at ille metuens, ne propter eum iram Francorum incurreret, ut Gothorum pavere mos est, vinctum legatis tradidit."

take the first step towards their freedom; "all men were desiring with anxious longing that they should reign."[1]   Nor did Chlodwig hesitate to take up the rôle thus assigned to him.   "It likes me not at all that these Arians should hold any part of Gaul.   Let us march by the help of God, overthrow them, and subject the country to our own rule."[2]   With this address to his men Chlodwig opened the campaign.   No opportunity was overlooked of keeping up the religious character of the struggle.   Parties sent to neighbouring shrines along the route brought back the encouraging responses of the Church; and Catholic clergy with the army marched to meet their brethren, who were oppressed by the hand of the heretics.[3]

The conduct of Alaric at this crisis might be ascribed either to the exasperation of conscious weakness or to cool calculation and discrimination.   What might be branded as feeble inconsistency in the one view might equally be regarded as determined and far-sighted policy in the other.   On the one hand he suppressed with promptitude more than one revolt which the impatience of some of the bishops brought prematurely to a head.[4]   Other outbreaks were nipped in the bud by the removal from their sees of other bishops,— Caesarius from Arles, Quintian from Ruthena, and Verus from Tours.   The appointment some years later

---

[1] Greg. Tur. *Hist. Franc.* ii. 23, "omnes eos amore desiderabili cuperent regnare." Ibid. 36, "Multi jam hinc ex Galliis habere Francos dominos summo desiderio capiebant."

[2] Greg. Tur. *Hist. Franc.* ii. 37.

[3] Detailed with naive admiration by Maimbourg, bk. x.

[4] e.g. Galactorius of Bearn, and in Tortosa. See Dahn v. 104.

of Quintian to the bishopric of Clermont by the Franks is a measure of the justness of the king's suspicions. On the other hand, he formally abandoned the attempt of his father to force them to compliance with his rule by systematic repression. He permitted vacant bishoprics to be filled up at Bearn, Bigorre, and many other places, and sanctioned the assembling of a council at Agde. This combination of firm and judicious policy failed to avert the doom of the Gothic kingdom of Toulouse. Chlodwig, always rapid in his operations, was determined to anticipate the arrival of the Ostrogothic reinforcements, for which Alaric had appealed to Theodoric. Alaric's captains resented his cautious policy of withdrawal towards the coming succour. The Catholics of Clermont, the town which had been the last to submit to the Goths, fought bravely and obstinately for their conquerors.[1] But the forces of Alaric were no match for the Franks and their allies, the Burgundians. At the battle of Vouglé the king himself fell fighting, and was spared the pain of seeing his country overrun by the enemy and the destruction of his kingdom.[2] "By the help of God," as the Catholic historian puts it, the orthodox barbarian had won the victory and secured Gaul for the Franks.

[1] Description of the battle in Greg. Tur. *Hist. Franc.* ii. 37, "rex Chlodvechus deo adjuvante victoriam obtinuit."

[2] A. D. 507.

CHAPTER VIII.

THE GOTHIC CHURCH IN SPAIN, AND ITS DECLINE.

AUTHORITIES FOR CHAPTER VIII.

SOURCES :
  Isidorus Hispalensis.
  Joannis Biclarensis.
  Paullus Emeritensis.
  Gregorius Turonensis.
  Canons of the Council of Toledo III.

LITERATURE :
  Dictionary of Christian Biography, Articles " Euric," " Leovigild."
  Pius Gams, *Kirchengeschichte von Spanien.*
  Helfferich, *Entstehung und Geschichte des Westgothenrechts.*
      „   *Der Westgothische Arianismus, und die Spanische Ketzergeschichte.*
  Lembke, *Geschichte Spaniens.*
  Menandez y Pelayo, *Historia de los Heterodoxos Españoles.*
  Görres, *Die Anfänge des König's Leovigilds* in *Deutsche Forsch. XII. and XIII.*
      „   *Kritische Untersuchungen über den Aufstand und das Martyrium des*
            Hermenegild in *Zeitsch. für Hist. Theol.* 1873.
      „   *Leovigild's Stellung zum Katholicismus und zur Arianischen Staats-*
            kirche, ibid.

THE disastrous day of Vouglé put an end to the Gothic kingdom of Toulouse. The death of the king on the field of battle, the youth and immaturity of his legitimate heir, and the disputed succession which followed, exposed the country to the ravages of Frankish armies, unchecked by any opposition from a regular government. The issue of many complications was that, after long delay, Theodoric, the Ostrogoth, interfered to protect his kindred, gradually cleared Southern Gaul of the Frankish troops, and established a boundary between Goths and Franks which roughly corresponded with the course of the Garonne. He saw, moreover, that it concerned the safety of his own kingdom that there should be a strong and stable government in

Southern Gaul to hold these new foes in check; and accordingly, under pretext of guardianship of Amalaric, son of the late king Alaric, and his own grandson, Theodoric took into his own hands the Wisigothic government. But the home of the Wisigothic folk was no longer chiefly in Gaul, but in Spain. Large numbers of them had been forced across the Pyrenees by the southward pressure of the Franks, and by their occupation of Gallia Gothica; and these being added to the numerous bands of earlier conquerors and settlers, it came about that the bulk of the Wisigothic stock was planted in Spain, and Gallia Gothica became a dependency of a new Spanish-Gothic kingdom. This, however, was not fully established till the death of Theodoric, when his daughter and his grandson, Amalasuntha and Athalaric, recognised, not unwillingly, Amalaric's ability to govern his own kingdom, and the Ostrogothic control ceased. Only that part of the old kingdom of Toulouse which was east of the Rhone remained in the hands of the Ostrogoths; and the province of Narbonne or Septimania, west of the Rhone and south of the Garonne, became an adjunct to the new Gothic kingdom in Spain.

Here, in Spain, was played the last act of this long drama in ecclesiastical history. This was the third of the Gothic kingdoms of the West. One of these had already crumbled to ruin, sapped by religious strife and disaffection. A second laboriously-erected kingdom, that of Theodoric, in spite of the military success and skill of its founder, after thirty years of his fostering care was at this very moment beginning to totter, and about to shew, by one more instance, the hopelessness of the attempt to build a throne above the quicksand of ecclesiastical schism. Now the same problem was once again presented under new circumstances. It was solved in a new way. The Spanish monarchy, after a long struggle to maintain the ancient faith, saved itself by submission to the Catholic Church. In the kingdom of Toulouse the Goths had tried first by toleration to conciliate, then by repression to disarm, the enemies who hated them even worse as heretics than they despised them as barbarians. In Italy the attempt to find a *modus vivendi* was yet more patiently and perseveringly pursued, the Gothic government giving to the Catholic Church all the pledges of impartiality and all tokens of respect. In Spain the Wisigoths at last confessed themselves beaten; overcome by the subtle unrelenting pressure of organised, though often passive, resistance. There are but three forms which the relations between two such parties can take. Two of these had been tried in turn by the temporal power of the Goths; toleration had been rejected, repression had failed, there remained only submission.

But even after Vouglé it took eighty years of contest and disaffection to bring this fact home to the nation. They were years of confusion and insecurity. Of the earlier kings belonging to this portion of Wisigothic history little or nothing has come down to us, "except their names and the manner of their violent deaths."[1] Not one of the first six who occupied the throne established his house even for two generations. Hardly do they seem to have contemplated it. The indifference to the future, which this fact implies,

[1] Dahn.

explains much of the history, and especially how so
many princes cherished their old creed, without dis-
covering it to be a hopeless obstacle to their policy.
They had no policy. The first who had a policy, and
aspired to found a dynasty, came at once into sharp
collision with the Catholics, towered by the force of
genius and determination, and fell. His son succeeded
him, it is true, but only to surrender to the Catholic
party, and conform with all his people to the Catholic
faith.

Little is recorded of the kings who reigned before
Leovigild, but there remains enough to shew that they
adhered obstinately to the creed of their fathers. Amalaric, no doubt, followed a prudent policy when he allied ·
himself with the Frankish court by marrying Chroti-
child, a daughter of the Merowings. But the refusal of
his bride to conform to her husband's creed caused the
king to break out in such a persecution of herself and
her fellow-Catholics that, instead of an alliance, he
brought down upon himself the vengeance of her brother
Childibert. Of another of these kings, Athanagild, it was
said that he was secretly a Catholic before he died; but
the authority is insignificant.[1] He it was, however,
who, while yet a pretender to the crown, took the fatal
step of summoning the Byzantines to his aid. Justinian
was only too ready to accept the opportunity thus
offered of planting his foot within the breach of another
Gothic kingdom. Athanagild gained his purpose, but
sixty years afterwards his successors were still struggling
to dislodge the Byzantines, and loosen their grasp upon

---

[1] See Aschbach, 196; Lembke i. 65; Dahn v. 126. The only
authority is Lucas of Tuy.

the land.[1] Two daughters of Athanagild and his wife, Gosvintha, were sought in marriage by two of the Merowing princes; each of these, on her arrival at her bridegroom's home, was induced to abandon the Arian creed and accept the Catholic faith of her husband.[2] In the same reign the collective Arianism of the Germanic races suffered a serious loss, and the pressure on the remaining adherents of the creed in Spain was much increased by the conversion of the king of the Suevi and the whole body of his subjects to the Catholic faith. The isolation of the Wisigoths was now complete. On every frontier they were hemmed in by nations whose racial antipathy was embittered by dogmatic separation. To the north-east lay the Franks, ever pressing southward and westward. On the north the Suevi were on the alert to turn the internal dissensions of the kingdom to their own advantage and aggrandisement. And the cities of the south, and along the coast, contained many nests of Byzantines and Byzantine sympathisers, who kept open the communications between the disaffected in the Gothic kingdom and the ever-watchful Eastern emperor.

To rule this kingdom, watched by so many jealous eyes without, and racked by such distractions within, Leovigild was called first as coadjutor, and afterwards as successor, to his brother Liuva. His reign "marks the last attempt to firmly establish the Gothic dominion according to its inherited character, by the most strenuous application of all available remedies against its similarly

---

[1] Isid. *de reb. Goth.* p. 124; "quos postea submovere a finibus regni molitus non potuit, adversus quos huc usque confligitur."

[2] Greg. Tur. *Hist. Franc.* iv. 27, 28.

inherited perils."[1] Five months of interregnum had only increased the difficulties of his task. Yet he attacked them with equal boldness and sagacity. Foreign foes and domestic rebels alike felt the effects of his vigorous policy, and acknowledged a worthy successor of Theodoric and Euric. He was the first Gothic king of whom it could truly be said that he was master of the Iberian peninsula.

Towards the Catholic Church the attitude of this Arian prince was, throughout the first ten years of his reign (569—580), one of consistent toleration.[2] This absence of a persecuting spirit in Leovigild is needed to give colour to the story, which was current in later times, that he married for his first wife an undoubted Catholic,[3] Theodosia, a sister of the famous bishops, Leander and Isidore. Apart from the unimportant testimony of Lucas of Tuy, there is no reason to suppose that the king's first wife was anything but an Arian like himself. They had two sons, Hermenegild and Reccared, but their mother died before Leovigild came to the throne.[4] In a second marriage he took to wife Gosvintha, the widow of his pre-

[1] Dahn.

[2] Persecution of the Catholics by Leovigild is asserted to have taken place *before* the revolt of Hermenegild by Külb, " Johannes von Biclaro" in *Ersch und Gruber*, and by Helfferich, *Westgothenr.* p. 11; discredited by Dahn v. 136, and Görres, *Leovigild's Stellung*, p. 518.

[3] The statement appears first in Lucas of Tuy; it is accepted by Aschbach, 203, Dahn v. 135, vi. 366, and Helfferich; contested by Görres, *Anfänge Leovigilds*, p. 593. Helfferich supposes that, under the guidance of Leander, Theodosia brought up her two sons as Catholics.

[4] Joann. Bicl. *Ann. vii. Justini*, "duos filios suos ex amissa conjuge."

decessor Athanagild, a woman notoriously and fanatically
Arian.[1] To the fanatical influence of this woman some
have ascribed the blame for most of the evils which followed. But it is unnecessary to see in Gosvintha the sole
cause of events, for which many other agencies were pre-
paring the way. In the heart of the king himself the
promptings of his wife against the Catholics would only
sound familiarly as the echoes of his own experience.
His task of government was infinitely complicated by the
double antipathy of race and of creed between the two
sections of the people whom he ruled. His policy
during the earlier part of his reign, when he was mainly
occupied in reducing to obedience ambitious and tur-
bulent vassal-nobles, had naturally produced great
discontent, and raised against him a number of re-
bellious-minded chiefs, whose power for mischief was
not destroyed, though he had forced them to a show of
submission. With these, as well as with all other
enemies of his throne, he found the Catholics ever
ready to make common cause. A network of intrigue
was spread over his whole kingdom, the ends of which
communicated with his enemies beyond its borders, with
the Suevi within the peninsula, with the Franks in Gaul,
with the Byzantines in the coast-cities, and, through
them, with the court of the Eastern empire. It would,
therefore be no matter for surprise if there grew up in
the mind of Leovigild a sense of the impossibility that
his own government could co-exist with so formidable and
hostile a power as that wielded by the Catholic Church.

But it was neither this growing conviction of the king

---

[1] Joann. Biel. *Ann. viii. Mauricii*, "Goisvintha Catholicis semper
infesta"; Greg. Tur. v. 39, "caput hujus sceleris Goisvintha fuit."

nor the persuasions of Gosvintha that led to the actual
crisis. Nevertheless this arose within the family of the
king.[1] Leovigild, like some of his predecessors, had sought
to strengthen his house by an alliance with the Franks,
and had obtained, as a wife for his elder son Hermenegild, Ingundis, daughter of Sigebert and Brunichild, that
Brunichild, who, being a Wisigothic princess, had become
a Catholic on her marriage. According to that precedent,
and according, no doubt, to the expectation of her
husband's nation, Ingundis should have taken his faith
when she came to be his wife. But she had been brought
up by her mother as a strict Catholic; and, moreover, on
her journey to Spain, passing through the diocese of Agde,
she had been specially warned by Fronimius, the bishop,
to shun the Arian heresy as poison. She accordingly
refused to change her creed. A sharp quarrel ensued
between Ingundis and her grandmother, Gosvintha (who
had now become her stepmother-in-law). The princess
was little more than a child, but she remained obstinately true to her creed. A story of barbarous cruelty,
inflicted on her by Gosvintha, is told by Gregory of
Tours. It finds no place, however, in the chronicles of
our most sober and trustworthy authority for this period,
John of Valclara, who was also a contemporary witness;
and the truth of the story has latterly been called
in question.[2] Nevertheless, this refusal of Ingundis

---

[1] For a detailed account, with analysis of the authorities, see
Görres, *Kritische Untersuchungen über den Aufstand und das
Martyrium Hermenegilds*, in the *Zeitschrift für hist. Theol.*
1873.

[2] Görres, *Untersuchungen*, p. 7. Gregory's own authority is
vague, "ut asserunt multi": so Wachter, "Ingundis" in *Ersch
und Gruber*. Dahn v. 137, and Helfferich p. 11, (undecided).

to conform to the religion of her adopted country was a severe blow to the policy of Leovigild. His long struggle with his nobles and his neighbours was at last concluded.[1] He had brought peace to his people, and looked forward now to years of tranquillity and the peaceful succession of his son. But a yet greater blow fell on him. In the same year that his son was married, Leovigild appointed him viceroy or governor of part of his kingdom, probably the province of Baetica, where he resided in Seville, the capital.[2] Here he came under the combined influence of his wife and of Leander, afterwards bishop of Seville, a most able and persuasive champion of the Catholic faith. The announcement of his conversion to the orthodox Church followed in the same year.[3]

The significance of this step was greater than belongs, at first sight, to the simple change of creed. In the political situation of the kingdom the transfer of the allegiance of the heir apparent from the Arian to the Catholic confession both involved and proclaimed a withdrawal of his allegiance to the king. This ecclesiastical defection was necessarily accompanied by a political rebellion. All the elements of opposition in the country

---

[1] Joann. Biel. *Ann. ii. Tiberii*, "extinctis undique tyrannis, et pervasoribus Hispaniae superatis sortitus requiem propria cum pace resedit."

[2] Joann. Biel. *Ann. iii. Tib.*, "provinciae partem ad regnandam tribuit"; Greg. Tur. v. 39, "dedit eis unam de civitatibus, in qua residentes regnarent."

[3] Greg. Magn. *Dial.* iii. 31: "Sicut multorum, qui ab Hispaniarum partibus veniunt, relatione cognovimus, nuper Hermenegildus rex ab Ariana haeresi ad fidem Catholicam Leandro praedicante conversus est." So Greg. Tur. *Hist. Franc.* v. 39.

would rejoice at the new prospects opened up by the conversion of Hermenegild; orthodox neighbouring princes, Roman provincials mindful of their conquered state, Catholic clergy determined with iron will to use every means to root out the detested heresy, Gothic nobles smarting under the bonds and strokes of discipline, one and all regarded the new convert as the hope and mainstay of their cause.

To Leovigild himself there was but one course open at this time. His former policy of toleration was no longer tenable; and between the two extremes of intolerant Arianism and intolerant Catholicism, he had no longer any choice. Even if he had ever been inclined to consider the advisability of submitting to the Catholic party, the action of his son had made such a step henceforward impossible. If the success and comparative ease with which his second son and successor carried out that course might lead us to think that Leovigild would have been wiser had he recognised the fatal hopelessness of prolonging the struggle, we have only to remind ourselves how the national pride of the king, and the injured pride of the father, would certainly outweigh counsels which could only appeal to a far-sighted politician in his coolest mood. From this time forward his policy in Church matters was one consistent attempt to exalt Arianism to be the sole creed of the country to the destruction of the Catholic Church, which, either by force or by persuasion, should be gradually absorbed in the State-Church.

Into the details of the political strife which followed the conversion of Hermenegild we do not require to enter. The son became a rebel by the very force of circumstances. After a prolonged struggle the father prevailed, Hermenegild surrendered, and was exiled to Valentia. A year later (585) he was imprisoned at Tarragona, and there put to death.[1] Whether his father was directly responsible for his death cannot be ascertained. The principal chronicler is unaccountably silent on this point; but public opinion a few years later was obviously against Leovigild.[2] The Catholic Church acknowledged Hermenegild as one of her martyrs when he was canonised by a decree of Pope Sixtus VI.

Leovigild had succeeded in crushing the rebellion headed by his son, but his attempt to undermine the Catholicism, from whose support the rebellion had derived its strength, met with very partial and transient success. Keeping firmly in view this one end, the absorption, voluntary or compulsory, of the Catholic in the Arian Church of his kingdom, he used all the means that offered to that end. He pursued alternately, or it might be simultaneously, a policy of coercion and of conciliation. He has been branded as a cruel persecutor; and were we called upon to accept in all its details the picture drawn by Gregory of Tours,[3] the justice of the charge could hardly be denied. But in the vagueness of this writer's authority, in the obvious connexion of the passage with the account of Gosvintha, which is drawn up with

---

[1] Joann. Biel. *Ann. iii. Maur.*, "in urbe Tarraconensi a Sisberto interficitur."

[2] Fully discussed in Görres, *Untersuchungen*, p. 59.

[3] *Hist. Franc.* v. 39: "Magna eo anno in Hispaniis Christianis persecutio fuit, multique exsiliis dati, facultatibus privati, fame decocti, carcere mancipati, verberibus affecti, ac diversis suppliciis trucidati sunt."

unsparing, perhaps unscrupulous, hostility, and in the absence of corroboration for the details, we may find good grounds to suppose that the picture is over-drawn.[1] There is no evidence whatever of a general persecution of the Catholics.

The king's coercive measures affected mainly, if not exclusively, the higher clergy; and for checking the activity of these he could plead such justification in their political conduct as might well acquit him of the charge of religious persecution. Leander, whom he sent into exile, had been the instrument of the conversion of Hermenegild, and indirectly the cause of the civil war that inevitably followed. During that war he had even journeyed to Constantinople[2] to invoke, on behalf of the rebels, the help of the Byzantine emperor. Froninius,[3] bishop of Agde, escaped out of the dominions of Leovigild, either at the instance of an accusing conscience, or because he heard that Leovigild had sent out assassins to slay him. Against two other prominent men, whom the king banished from their respective cities, there is no suspicion of complicity in the rebellion or of political disaffection. But Mausona of Merida and Joannes, afterwards of Valclara, were both Goths by birth, and nothing was likely to embitter the king more than to find his policy checked by the apostacy, as it seemed to him, of his own subjects.

---

[1] Dahn v. 141: "Die von Leovigild in dieser Zeit nothwendig verhängte Verfolgung der Kirche hat man sehr übertrieben;" vi. 366, "theils Nothwehr, theils Ausübung des Strafrechts."

[2] Greg. Magn. *lib. mor. in lib. Job. praefatio.* See esp. Görres, *Untersuchungen*, p. 103.

[3] Greg. Tur. *Hist. Franc.* ix. 24.

Leovigild had made great efforts[1] to bring over Mausona
to the Arian side ; and when they failed, he sent one
Sunna, a violent upholder of Arianism, to be bishop in
the same see. Fierce disputes naturally followed, and
on the representation or misrepresentation of Sunna,
Mausona was banished to Complutum. One other case
of persecution was charged against Leovigild. A cleric,[2]
whose name is not known, is said to have been first
tempted with bribes, and then, as he would not submit,
put to the torture by Leovigild, and actually beaten to
death in his presence. This is a good example of the
evidence on which exaggerated reports[3] of the cruelties
of the persecution are based. The story as it stands,
even in Gregory, is that the man rejected the king's offer
saying, " I abhor thy gifts as filth "; whereupon
Leovigild ordered him to be scourged ; but so far was
he from being killed (and this is the only instance that
can be alleged as evidence of bloody persecution)—" he
departed rejoicing, and returned to Gaul."

Leovigild is further charged with appropriating to
the public treasury Church revenues, and annulling the
immunities of the clergy.[4] And this is confirmed by the
statement made by two authorities, that Reccared his

---

[1] The story is told with much fanatical exaggeration by Paüll.
Emerit. 12, 14, 17. See Görres in *Zeitsch. für wissentsch. Theologie*, 1885.

[2] Greg. Tur. *de Glor. Mart.*, i. 82.

[3] *e.g.* Maimbourg, ii. 215 ; Revillout, p. 237 : " Il fit assassiner
les plus redoubtables [des évêques] et se débarassa de presque tous
les autres par l' exil ; il détruisit les priviléges des églises et s'empara
de leurs revenus, les laissant ainsi sans chefs et sans pouvoir."

[4] Isid. *Hist. Goth.* aera 606, "ecclesiarum reditus et privilegia
abstulit."

son, restored to the Church the estates which his father
had impounded.   But the persecution of Leovigild
resolves itself into the banishment from their sees of
certain violent and intriguing Catholics, and the con-
fiscation for public use of certain Church property.

On the other hand, Leovigild never ceased to shew
to the shrines and offices of the Catholic Church the
respect which was due from all Christians.   Those who
accused him of being a barbarous persecutor, taunted
him also with hypocrisy because he offered prayers at
the shrines of the martyrs, and in the Catholic churches.[2]
Nor did he hesitate to make known his own faith in a
form which shewed the distinction between the Catholic
and the so-called Arian faith narrowed to a single point.
A Frankish ambassador to the court of Leovigild informed
Gregory of Tours that the king proclaimed his faith in
Christ, the Son of God, as "equal with the Father; but
the Holy Spirit I do not believe to be God; because he
is not said in any of the Holy Scriptures to be God."
This admission of the equality of the Son may have
been a momentary concession of the king, and is not to
be taken as defining the position of the Gothic Church
in Spain.   For it is at variance with another passage in
Gregory, where one of the acts of persecution is represented as beginning with an entreaty of the king to a
Catholic that he would confess both the Son and the
Spirit to be inferior to the Father.   It is also a departure
from the creed of Ulfilas, hitherto so unflinchingly
maintained by the Goths; and if such a concession had

[1] Greg. Tur. *Hist. Franc.* vi. 18.   "Sed rex novo nunc ingenio
eam [catholicam fidem] nititur exturbare, dum dolose et ad sepulcra
martyrum et in ecclesiis religionis nostrae orare confingit."

been permanent or general it would certainly have been formulated at the Council of Toledo, where so great a stride towards unity could not have been overlooked.[1]

For apart from a personal attitude, thus ostentatiously friendly to the well-disposed Catholics, the king took public measures also to bring about an absorption of the Catholics in the Arian Church. One of the obstacles which hindered the admission to the Arian Church of Catholics, otherwise disposed to conform, was the requisition that the new converts should submit to re-baptism. This had always been a serious check on the growth of the Arian Church, and Leovigild resolved that it should be removed. Accordingly he summoned a council of Arian bishops and clergy[2] with some or all of the Gothic notables to meet at Toledo, and from them he procured a decree that, "Converts from the Roman faith to our Catholic faith need not be baptized; but require only to be purified by the laying on of hands and partaking of communion, and to give glory to the Father *through* the Son *in* the Holy Ghost." In this way was the obnoxious formality dispensed with, and the transfer of allegiance from the one confession to the other made to look as insignificant and to be as

[1] See Görres, *Leovigild's Stellung*, p 560. Maimbourg, *Hist. of Arianism* (transl.) ii. p. 287, asserts that this was actually proclaimed by Leovigild's Council; but he quotes no authority, nor can I find such.

[2] Joann. Biel. *Ann. iv. Tib.*: "Synodum episcoporum sectae Arianae congregat, et antiquam haeresim novello errore emendat dicens de Romana religione venientes ad nostram Catholicam non debere baptizari." See Helfferich, *Westg.*, 5; Dahn v. 142. The horror against the practice of re-baptism—"abominatio gehennae"—can hardly have been universal; *e.g.* the chronicle of Fredegar describes Reccared as admitted to the Catholic Church by baptism.

perfunctory as possible. Great pressure was now brought
to bear on the Catholics to induce them to make use of
the new opportunity of making submission to the wish
of the king. No doubt bribes and cajoleries were freely
employed, and a certain specious and temporary success
was obtained. Large numbers of Catholics, both clergy
and laity, passed over to the Arian side,[1] and one of the
bishops, Vincent of Saragossa, was found among the
converts.

It is clear that this council at Toledo was the master
stroke of Leovigild's ecclesiastical policy. It caused
disunion and uncertainty in the Catholic camp, and
probably lightened effectively the task of suppressing
the rebellion. But although large numbers of individual
Catholics may have been gained to the Arian Church,
Leovigild was as far as ever from achieving his main
object. This policy, at once the boldest and the most
cunning which a Gothic king had yet devised to meet
his inherited difficulty, produced but little result in the
direction of union of the discordant elements, or con-
solidation of the kingdom. The attempt to arrive at a
fair idea of the relations between the two parties,
Catholics and Arians, to recover traces of their respective standards—intellectual, moral, and doctrinal—
is checked in this province of Gothic history, as in
others, by the entire absence of material for estimating
one party from their own works, and the consequent

---

[1] Joann. Bicl. l.c.: "per hanc ergo seductionem plurimi
nostrorum cupiditate potius impulsi in Arianum dogma declinat."
Isid. *Hist. Goth.* aera 124: "plerosque sine persecutione illectos auro
rebusque decepit . . . . . et non solum ex plebe, sed etiam ex
sacerdotalis ordinis dignitate, sicut Vincentium Caesaraugustanum,"
&c. See Görres *Leovigild's Stellung*, p. 568.

impossibility of viewing the relation from more than one side. With the single exception of the record of the Council of Toledo just referred to, the Gothic Arianism of Spain has not left any literary monument of its existence. Yet it is impossible to believe that a century and a half of Gothic occupation had passed without producing some literary fruit, or that the controversy which raged through all these years left no monument in the shape of polemical pamphlets and tractates. What became of the liturgies, the copies of the version of Ulfilas, the commentaries, of which we had a specimen in the Skeireins, the apologies and expositions of the Arian creed, and the Church records? The entire disappearance of all these records of the existence of an Arian Church could only be ascribed to an organised and successful attempt to destroy every trace of the heresy. So we are not surprised to find it recorded that the next king, in the fresh ardour of his conversion to Catholicism, ordered all the Arian books to be gathered and handed over to him.[1] They were then piled together, set fire to, and consumed to ashes.

The Gothic Church in Spain, like its sister-churches elsewhere, has thus to be judged entirely on the evidence of its opponents, and scrupulous fairness to an adversary was not a common characteristic in churchmen of the sixth century. Nevertheless, we may get a glimpse of the character of the Arianism upheld by the

---

[1] Fredegar, *Chronicon.* c. viii.: "Omnes libros Arianos [Richaridus] praecepit ut sibi praesententur: quos in una domo collocatos incendio concremare jussit." See Görres, *Leovigild's Stellung*, p. 555; Dahn iv. 367; aliter Aschbach, p. 221.

Spanish Church, and of the arguments by which they defended it, from two interesting passages from Gregory of Tours.[1] He describes, at some length, the discussions which he held with two several ambassadors of Leovigild to Chilperic, who had halted at Tours on their journey. The bishop-naturally gives greater prominence to his own share in the conversations, and perhaps states his own case with more force than that of his collocutors, while he is not superior to the temptation to depreciate both their natural ability and their accomplishments;[2] nevertheless, some valuable light is thrown by these narratives on the Arianism of the time. Both discussions are concerned with the old question of the equality of the first and second Hypostases of the Trinity. On the first occasion, Agila, the Arian envoy, bases his position on the text "My Father is greater than I";[3] on the sorrow of Jesus at the approach of death, and on His commending His spirit to the Father, "as though possessed of no power in Himself"; and he concludes that "the Son is always inferior to the Father." To this the bishop replies both with text and with argument; whereupon the Arian turns the discussion to the question of the equality of the Holy Spirit in the Godhead. "The Holy Spirit, whom ye put forward as equal to the Father and the Son, is regarded (by us) as inferior. For no one promiseth except that which is subjected to his control; and no one sendeth except one inferior to himself,—as He Himself saith in the Gospel, 'If I

[1] Greg. Tur. *Hist. Franc.* v. 44; vi. 40.
[2] "Virum nullius ingenii aut dispositionis ratione peritum."
[3] John xiv. 28.

go not away, the Comforter will not come unto you ; but
if I go, I will send him unto you.' " To this, again, the
bishop makes his reply, and the discussion is conducted
with calmness until the Catholic stirs the indignation of
the heretic by citing the death of Arius as a proof of
God's displeasure at his doctrine. " Blaspheme not the
law which thou dost not observe," he breaks in ; " We,
who believe not what you believe, nevertheless blaspheme
not ; for with us it is not accounted an offence to worship
this and that. For we say in our common speech, ' It is
no harm if a man, passing between heathen altars and
a church of God, make his reverence in both directions.' "
A conception of religion so broad as this passed the
apprehension of a bishop of the sixth century, who
began to adjure the heretic by the law and the prophets
to abandon so dangerous a creed, by professing his faith
in the Trinity, and receiving the benediction from his
own hands. Agila, however, angrily declared that he
would rather die than receive the benediction from
" any priest of your creed." So the conversation broke
up, the bishop referring with great distinctness to the
saying about the pearls and the swine.

Oppila, the Arian champion in the second case,
began by announcing that he believed " what the
Catholics believe," by going to the Catholic church on
Easter Day, and attending the celebration of the mass.
But he refused to give the kiss of peace, or to partake
of the elements, and the bishop found that he had
uncloaked an Arian. At supper Gregory asked him
once more to state his belief, and why he did not com-
municate. He replied that it was because of the form
in which the Catholics repeated the Gloria, and pro-

14

ceeded to maintain that the Arian form, "Glory to the Father *through* the Son," was more scriptural. Where-upon Gregory, at some length, justifies the practice of the Church in giving "Glory *to* the Son."

We observe in both these narratives, and especially in the former, what has claimed our attention already,—the strongly practical way in which the Arian theology appealed to the Gothic religious sense. The simple texts, in which emphasis is laid on the human nature and humiliation of Christ, were proof sufficient for them of a scheme of subordination, which was recommended already by its consonance with the principles of Teutonic mythology. There is no trace here, or anywhere else in the history of Gothic Arianism, of the speculations based on the absolute Being, and Simplicity, of an unbe-gotten God, or of other philosophical refinements into which Arians, like Aetius and Eunomius, proceeded. Both these narratives present to us a Church tenacious, after two centuries of opposition and failure, of the creed left to them by Ulfilas, yet willing to manifest, by fellowship and common worship, how much they held in common with their opponents. Theirs was a more stunted creed, but they had worked out a larger tolerance. It does seem a strange freak of language, or perhaps a monument to the misrepresentations of their adversaries and historians, that this nation should lend its name (Wisigoth) to the modern tongues of Europe as a synonym for religious *intolerance*—'bigot.'[1]

Leovigild survived his elder son but one year, during which he met with some success in an attempt

---

[1] Dahn : "pas sans probabilité" (Littré); so "cagot " = "canis Gothicus " (Littré, Dahn).

to recall his new subjects, the Suevi, to their former
Arian faith.[1] The Catholic writers have a story about
a deathbed repentance for the murder of his son, and
submission to the Catholic Church with which he had
struggled so long.[2] But the report, which, when it first
appears, is admittedly based on rumour only,[3] finds no
countenance in the best contemporary annalists, and
bears on the face of it the stamp of improbability. The
source of the story may readily be found in the desire
of the new king, his successor, and his councillors, to
throw down something to bridge the chasm over which
they were about to step and lead the Gothic people.
A well-circulated report of Leovigild's repentance and
conversion would do much to soften the severity of the
change, when his creed and his policy came to be
condemned and abandoned, and would weaken the will
of the Arians to resist this new departure. In fact, this
application of the story peeps out from Gregory's report,
in which the repentant king adjures his hearers " that
no one may be found adhering to that heresy." But
the report of such a conversion is implicitly condemned
by one of the contemporary records, wherein Paul of
Merida, after describing the death of the king, contem-
plates with amiable satisfaction the doom of his soul

---

[1] Evidence and examination in Görres, *Leovigild's Stellung*,
p. 584.

[2] Greg. Mag. *Dial.* iii. 31, and Greg. Tur. *Hist. Franc.* viii. 26.
Accepted by Maimbourg ii. 286, with reserve by Revillout, 248;
rejected by Aschbach, 216; Dahn v. 156; Görres, *Leovigild's
Stellung*, 590.

[3] Greg. Tur. l.c.: " ut quidam asserunt, poenitentiam pro errore
heretico agens, et obtestans ne huic haeresi quisquam reperiretur
consentaneus."

"to suffer the everlasting tortures of Erebus," and to "boil in waves of bubbling pitch."[1]

Leovigild was succeeded by Reccared, the younger brother of the murdered Hermenegild. This prince, who had more of the character of a diplomatist than that of a warrior, cut the knot which his predecessors had struggled so long to undo, by abandoning the Arianism which had so long entangled their steps, and making full submission to the Catholic Church. That he was already secretly a Catholic before the death of his father is, in the light of his relation to his brother, very improbable.[2] But the experience of a few months of government, added to the knowledge of affairs which he had gained during his father's life-time, convinced him that any attempt to follow up the lines of his father's policy would end in failure. In the tenth month of his reign Reccared professed himself a Catholic, and was admitted to the Church by the rite of Confirmation.[3]

---

[1] Paull. Emerit. xvi. This writer's rancour against Leovigild and the Arians is almost incredible. Two examples out of many: c. xi.—"Crudelissimus tyrannus, vas irae fomesque vitiorum, ac frutex damnationis." c. xvi.—"Igitur cum non praesset sed obesset, magis perderet quam regeret, Leovigildus Hispaniam." For a just and appreciative estimate of the king's career, see Revillout, p. 218. In ecclesiastical matters: "Il ne su jamais comprendre l'esprit religieux de son temps, et provoqua un pouvoir auquel appartenait l'avenir."

[2] Aliter Aschbach, p. 222, with those who hold the king's mother to have been a Catholic, Theodosia.

[3] Joann. Biel. *Ann. v. Maur.*: "primo regni sui anno mense X. Catholicus Deo juvante efficitur." Greg. Tur. ix. 15: "se Catholicae legi subdidit, et accepto signaculo beatae crucis cum chrismaretur unctione, credidit Dominum Jesum Christum aequalem Patri."

While making all due allowance for the reality and influence of his personal conversion, it is fair to observe what considerations of policy would combine with growing conviction to urge upon him this step. The church-policy of Leovigild had met with that comparative success which is little better than absolute failure. The Arian Church was still far from outnumbering its rival in adherents, and markedly inferior to it in the culture of its clergy and in intensity of purpose. The best reply to the charge of barbarous persecution against the late king was the present state of affairs. If he had really executed so many bishops and banished all the rest, how came it that the sees were full at his death? It was, no doubt, a great grievance that, in many dioceses, he set up Arian bishops alongside of the Catholic ones; but it would be strange to insist upon this charge if he had already slain or banished all the latter. Leovigild's enticing methods had more effect, and withdrew not a few Catholics from the Church; but these were her weakest members, and, as a power in the State, Leovigild left the Catholic Church nearly as he found it, but with all the added prestige of persecution. Moreover, the creed which they cherished exposed the Goths to an isolation from help and sympathy, which, as they settled down into a civilised state, must have been very irritating to an ambitious king.

But nothing was so effective to open the eyes of a ruler to the disadvantage of adhesion to the heretic creed as the ambition to found a dynasty; nothing, on the other hand, so calculated to display the advantages of alliance with the Catholic Church. In the absence of any acknowledged hereditary claim to the throne the ruler in the Gothic State for the time being was at best "primus inter pares." The nobles who had chosen him, or suffered him to usurp the crown, held a position that bordered dangerously near on independence. Leovigild had spent the first ten years of his reign in a continuous struggle to establish his royal authority over these vassals in name, but rivals in effect. It was a mark of his success that his son succeeded unchallenged to the throne. But the new king, knowing with whom he had to deal, and shrewdly casting about for an alliance to strengthen the power of the crown, would naturally set his eye on the Catholic Church. He would observe how strong it was in that highly developed organisation which has always proved so elastic, yet so unbreakable, a framework. He would perceive, too, that in the growing influence of the papacy, the centralisation of Christianity at Rome, and the continuity and coherence which followed for the Church at large, there was promise of ever-increasing power for the Catholic Church in Spain. Compared with this widely ramified and highly organised system, the Arian Church had nothing to offer by way of support to the throne. The position of entire dependence on the king which German tradition imposed upon it, checked all independent growth. It could offer no profitable alliance to the king, who was already its head. Some influence, too, must be allowed to the character and cultivation of the Catholic clergy compared with their rivals. However good Christians the Gothic clergy might be, yet, as men of the world, they were no match for highly-trained cosmopolitans, of whom Leander is a type; and in being reconciled to the Church, Reccared would not only secure the alliance and support of the only organised power which could balance the influence of the nobles, but he would also obtain for himself and his house the counsel and support of the most polished intellects and most highly-trained statesmen of his kingdom.

The public announcement of the conversion of the king was variously received by different sections of the nation. The most thoughtful and observant must have been ripe for the change; the careless would follow indifferently where the king was pleased to lead. Hence we are told that, when Reccared summoned the Arian clergy to meet him, and "in a wise address" expounded his new views, he readily overcame their scruples, and induced a large number of them to follow the example which he had set.[1] Many of the nobility also followed in the steps of the king and the clergy, and more tardily, but not less surely, the common folk were gathered in. The Catholic Church wisely refrained from requiring re-baptism, and converts were admitted by the laying-on of hands. Confirmation of the rumoured repentance and conversion of Leovigild would be given by the execution at this time of Sisbert,[2] who had been instrumental in the death of Hermenegild. Whether Leovigild were really guilty of the death of his son, or had it unjustly imputed to him, the execution of this official, who was said to have acted

---

[1] Joann. Biel. *Ann. v. Maur.*: "Sacerdotes sectae Arianae ratione potius quam imperio converti ad Catholicam fidem facit." "Secuti dominum nostrum ad dei ecclesiam transivimus," say the Gothic bishops at the Council of Toledo.

[2] Joann. Biel. l.c.: "Sisbertus interfector Hermenigildi morte turpissima perimitur."

on authority, was an indication of Reccared's having utterly broken with his father's policy, and a shock to the Arian party.

On the other hand, opposition to the new departure, and that of a strenuous kind, was not wanting. Many of the bishops and clergy were not prepared so hastily to give up their cherished creed. Many of the nobles viewed this momentous step of Reccared, not unnaturally, as a breaking with the national tradition as well as with the national creed, and a betrayal of the national consciousness to the ambition of the royal house. No less than three distinct risings took place in different parts of the country; each of these was headed by a bishop of the Arian Church. The most serious was one that broke out in Narbonne, where Athalocus and two of the nobles threw off their allegiance, and, with support from the Burgundian Franks, made war on the Catholics of the province. At the opposite end of the kingdom Sunna, Leovigild's bishop of Merida, with Segga and Witteric, headed a conspiracy of determined Arians, whose object was to dethrone Reccared and replace him by Segga. Still a third rising occurred in the same year. The king's step-mother, Gosvintha, after momentarily conforming with the faith of her son, joined an Arian bishop, Uldila, in alliance with the Franks, to attempt to dethrone Reccared and restore Arianism. But the prompt measures taken by the king were sufficient to repress these risings, one by one, before they became really formidable. Athalocus died, it was said, of a broken heart; Gosvintha died, either by her own hand or by the sword of the executioner; Sunna, made prisoner, and offered pardon and replacement in a bishopric, if he would repent and renounce his Arian error, indignantly refused, saying: "Repentance I know not, and a Catholic I will never be; but in the form in which I have lived I will live, or for the religion in which I have remained from my earliest years I will most gladly die."[1] He withdrew into exile in Africa, and with his departure the Arian-Gothic Church ceased to exist.

There remained only to write its epitaph, and to ratify the conversion of its members. This was done in 589, when Reccared summoned a general council of the Catholic Church in his dominions to meet at Toledo.[2] At the first sitting of the council the king addressed the members, recalling the long period during which Spain had "struggled with the errors" of heresy, and the change which had been beneficially effected since his accession, and recommending them to take measures for the restoration of discipline, which had suffered from long disuse. On another day the king again appeared, and delivered, to be read to the council, a written document in the form of a speech from the throne.[3] In this he set forth, at great length, a statement of his own faith, and concluded by reciting the creeds of Nicaea and "Constantinople," and the Formula of Chalcedon. To these both Reccared and his wife, Baddo, testified their assent by affixing their signatures.

Then followed a public recantation of their errors by

[1] Paull. Emerit. c. xviii.

[2] Mansi ix. 977; Dahn vi. 425.

[3] This "tomus" was ordered to be prefixed to the Acta of the Council.

the Gothic clergy and the noble laics, who had been present at Leovigild's council in 580, and had subscribed to the "detestabilis libellus," then drawn up and promulgated "for the perversion of Romans to the Arian heresy."[1]   This recantation and profession of the orthodox faith is signed by eight formerly Arian bishops, and was subscribed also by "the rest of the presbyters and deacons who were converted from the Arian heresy,"[2] and by several of the nobles.   In the two and twenty anathemas which they were called on to pronounce, they condemned, besides Arius and all his adherents with their works, the "detestabilis libellus" of Leovigild and the "sacrilegious practice of re-baptism."   The canons of the council, which then proceeded with its work, deal chiefly with discipline.   In connexion with the repentant Arians, it was ordained that their clergy should put away the wives, whom they had been suffered by their former discipline to take,[3] and that the Arian church-edifices should pass into the hands of the Catholic bishops, in whose dioceses they were severally situated.[4]   It would appear that those bishops and presbyters of the Arian Church who made their submission on this occasion were received into the ranks of the Catholic clergy.

The second Council of Saragossa, which met three years later, decreed that "presbyters who have been

---

[1] Conc. Tolet. III. Anath. xvi.: "Quicunque libellum detestabilem duodecimo anno Leovigildi a nobis editum, in quo continetur Romanorum ad haeresem Arianam transductio," etc.

[2] Conc. Tolet. III.; Mansi ix. p. 979.

[3] Ibid. Can. v.

[4] Ibid. Can. ix.

converted to the holy Catholic faith from the Arian heresy, if they have maintained pure faith and holy lives, are to be ordained afresh by the presbyterate, and discharge their office in purity and holiness."[1] Those who had failed to fulfil these conditions, were to be deposed from their office. The same rule was to apply to deacons also.[2] This council further decreed that "all relics of the Arian heresy," wherever they might be found, should be handed over by the clergy of the Church where they were discovered to the bishop, that they might be "tried by fire," an ordeal which we have seen reason to suppose that none of them survived.[3] The offence of concealing any such relics was punished by excommunication. Finally, all churches which had been consecrated by Arian bishops were to be consecrated anew by the Catholic. In this way the Council of Saragossa took measures not only to eradicate the Arian heresy, but also to blot out all traces of its existence,—so completing the work of the Council of Toledo.

It was surely fitting that one of the acknowledged leaders at the great Council of the Conversion should be Leander, the great bishop of Seville, who saw now the consummation of his life's work in the conversion of the Gothic conquerors of Spain, and the union of

---

[1] Conc. Caesar Aug. II. i.: "Accepto denuo benedictione presby-teratus."

[2] This admission of converted heretics to the orders of the Church was in contradiction to the decision of the Synod of Elvira (Can. li.). "Ex omni haerese fidelis si venerit, minime est ad clerum promovendus: vel si qui sunt in praeteritum ordinati sine dubio deponantur." See Dale, *Synod of Elvira*, p. 79.

[3] Conc. Caesar Aug. II. ii., "ut reliquiae de Ariana haeresi . . . . igne probentur."

"Romans" and "barbarians" under the banner of the Catholic Church.

The last of the Gothic Churches was now extinct. Its members had been absorbed within the great organisation which covered Southern Europe from Byzantium to Cadiz with a network of Christian influence. The struggle to maintain an independent existence had been a long one; but the Arians had had the losing side since the death of Valens. The causes of their failure lie on the surface of the foregoing account, but may be briefly summed up. The faultiness and inadequacy of their system of Christian doctrine was of course at the base of their defeat. To this was added—weakness of organisation compared with the complete and elaborate system of their opponents; the entire dependence of the clergy on the court, which was traditional since the time of Valens and a fundamental characteristic of Teutonic society; the stern and unyielding opposition of the Catholic Church, bearing upon Arianism both directly, and indirectly through the government, with irresistible pressure; and, finally, the lack of men of conspicuous ability and commanding influence. It is true that the proper records of the Church were lost at its downfall, and we know its leaders not at all, or only through the pages of their adversaries. Nevertheless, it is a striking and suggestive fact that, so far as we know, there appeared only once in the Gothic Church a man of grandeur, and a true leader of men. But the influence of that man for good and for evil moulded the destiny of his people for more than two hundred years.

APPENDIX

APPENDIX.

I.

AUTHORITIES CONNECTED WITH LIFE OF ULFILAS.

1. Philostorgius, *Hist. Eccl.* II. 5 :

Ulfilas brings across the Danube a great body of persecuted people—origin of their Christianity—captives from Gothic inroads—Ulfilas descended from Cappadocian captives—how he came to be bishop—he invents Gothic letters and translates the Scriptures—except the books of Kings—a favourite with the emperor—"the Moses of our age."

Ὅτι Οὐρφίλαν φησὶ κατὰ τούτους τοὺς χρόνους ἐκ τῶν πέραν Ἴστρου Σκυθῶν, οὓς οἱ μὲν πάλαι Γέτας, οἱ δὲ νῦν Γότθους καλοῦσι, πολὺν εἰς τὴν Ῥωμαίων διαβιβάσαι λαὸν, δι' εὐσέβειαν ἐκ τῶν οἰκείων ἠθῶν ἐλαθέντας· χριστιανίσαι δὲ τὸ ἔθνος τρόπῳ τοιῷδε. βασιλεύοντος Οὐαλεριανοῦ καὶ Γαλλιηνοῦ, μοῖρα Σκυθῶν βαρεῖα τῶν πέραν τοῦ Ἴστρου διέβησαν εἰς τὴν Ῥωμαίων. καὶ πολλὴν μὲν κατέδραμον τῆς Εὐρώπης· διαβάντες δὲ καὶ εἰς τὴν Ἀσίαν, τήν τε Γαλατίαν, καὶ τὴν Καππαδοκίαν ἐπῆλθον, καὶ πολλοὺς ἔλαβον αἰχμαλώτους, ἄλλους τε καὶ τῶν κατειλεγμένων τῷ κλήρῳ· καὶ μετὰ πολλῆς λείας ἀπεκομίσθησαν οἴκαδε. ὁ δὲ αἰχμάλωτος καὶ εὐσεβὴς ὅμιλος συναστραφέντες τοῖς βαρβάροις, οὐκ ὀλίγους τε αὐτῶν εἰς τὸ εὐσεβὲς μετεποίησαν, καὶ τὰ χριστιανῶν φρονεῖν ἀντὶ τῆς Ἑλληνίδος δόξης παρεσκεύασαν. ταύτης τῆς αἰχμαλωσίας γεγόνεσαν καὶ οἱ Οὐρφίλα πρόγονοι, Καππαδόκαι μὲν γένος, πόλεως δὲ πλησίον Παρνασσοῦ, ἐκ κώμης δὲ Σαδαγολθινὰ καλουμένης. ὁ τοίνυν Οὐρφίλας οὗτος καθηγήσατο τῆς ἐξόδου τῶν εὐσεβῶν, ἐπίσκοπος αὐτῶν πρῶτος καταστάς· κατέστη δὲ ὧδε. παρὰ τοῦ τὴν ἀρχὴν ἄγοντος τοῦ ἔθνους ἐπὶ τῶν Κωνσταντίνου χρόνων εἰς πρεσβείαν σὺν ἄλλοις ἀποσταλείς—καὶ γὰρ καὶ τὰ τῇδε βάρβαρα ἔθνη ὑπεκέκλιτο τῷ βασιλεῖ—ὑπὸ Εὐσεβίου

καὶ τῶν σὺν αὐτῷ ἐπισκόπων χειροτονεῖται τῶν ἐν τῇ Γετικῇ
χριστιανιζόντων. καὶ τά τε ἄλλα αὐτῶν ἐπεμελεῖτο, καὶ γραμμάτων αὐτοῖς οἰκείων εὑρετὴς καταστὰς, μετέφρασεν εἰς τὴν αὐτῶν
φωνὴν τὰς γραφὰς ἁπάσας, πλήν γε δὴ τῶν βασιλειῶν, ἅτε τῶν
μὲν πολέμων ἱστορίαν ἐχουσῶν, τοῦ δὲ ἔθνους ὄντος φιλοπολέμου,
καὶ δεομένου μᾶλλον χαλινοῦ τῆς ἐπὶ τὰς μάχας ὁρμῆς, ἀλλ᾽
οὐχὶ τοῦ πρὸς ταῦτα παροξύνοντος· ὅπερ ἰσχὺν ἔχει ταῦτα
ποιεῖν, σεβάσμιά τε μάλιστα νομιζόμενα, καὶ πρὸς τὴν τοῦ Θείου
θεραπείαν τοὺς πειθομένους καταρυθμίζοντα. ἱδρύσατο δ᾽ ὁ
βασιλεὺς τὸν αὐτόμολον τοῦτον λαὸν περὶ τὰ τῆς Μυσίας χωρία,
ὡς ἑκάστῳ φίλον ἦν. καὶ τὸν Οὐρφίλαν διὰ πλείστης ἦγε τιμῆς,
ὡς καὶ πολλάκις ὁ ἐφ᾽ ἡμῶν Μωσῆς λέγειν περὶ αὐτοῦ.

λίαν δὲ οὗτος τὸν ἄνδρα θειάζει, καὶ τῆς αἱρετικῆς αὐτοῦ δόξης
ἐραστὴν αὐτόν τε καὶ τοὺς ὑπ᾽ αὐτὸν ἀναγράφει.

2. The Last Journey of Ulfilas to Constantinople:

Vid. supra, pp. 36—44, and p. 138; Bessell, *Ulfilas*, p. 34
seq. The account of his master's last journey, given by
Auxentius, is much defaced in the MS. of Waitz. With the
lacunae filled up according to the conjectures of Bessell, it
would read thus: "Qui cum precepto imperiali, conpletis
quadraginta annis (*scil.* espiscopatus) ad Constantinopolitanam
urbem ad disputationem . . . . . contra p[sathyropoli]stas
perrexit et eundo in [dni di n nomine ne xpi eccl]esias sibi a
x[po dedi]tas docerent et contestarentur, intrabat, et ingr[es-
sus in] supradictam civitatem, recogitato ei im . . . . de statu
concilii, ne arguerentur miseris miserabiliores, proprio judicio
damnati, et perpetuo supplicio plectendi, statim coepit in-
firmari."

The concluding passage in Waitz's MS. is important.
Palladius, addressing his opponent Ambrosius, challenges him
to a meeting and a public disputation between the Arians
and the Catholics on the points at issue; he concludes thus:

"Et quamvis Auexenti ita meministi, ut non indicares, de
quo dixeris, utrum de superstite, id est Dorostorensi, an de
Mediolanensi, qui sine successore decessit, tamen scito tam

. . . . Palladium Ratiarensem, Auxentium inter ceteros con-
sortes, sancto et omni reverentia digno ac fidelissimo doctori
Demofilo ubicumque examen haberi placuerit, Deo omnipo-
tente per unigenitum suum Jhesum dominum auxilium ferente,
glorioso ac salutari certamini non defuturos.

"Unde et cum sancto Hulfila ceterisque consortibus ad
alium comitatum Constantinopolim venissent, ibique etiam et
imperatores adissent, adque eis promissum fuisset concilium,
ut sanctus Auxentius exposuit, agnita promissione, prefati
prepositi heretici omnibus viribus institerunt, ut lex daretur,
quae concilium prohiberet, sed nec privatim in domo nec in
publico vel in quolibet loco disputatio de fide haberetur, sicut
textus indicat legis." [Here follow the two decrees cited from
the Codex Theodosianus, ut supra, p. 41.]

.

II.

CONVERSION OF THE WISIGOTHS IN THE HISTORIANS.

1. Socrates, *Hist. Eccl.* iv. 33, 34:

Strife between Athanaric and Frithigern—Frithigern, with aid
of Valens, victorious—Frithigern in gratitude becomes a Christian
and an Arian—Ulfilas invents Gothic letters, translates the Scriptures, and teaches the people—persecution of Athanaric—interval of
peace—arrival of Huns—Valens permits Goths to settle in Dacia—
no mention of conditions.

Οἱ πέραν τοῦ Ἴστρου βάρβαροι οἱ καλούμενοι Γότθοι, ἐμφύ-
λιον πρὸς ἑαυτοὺς κινήσαντες πόλεμον, εἰς δύο μέρη ἐτμήθησαν
ὦν τοῦ ἑνὸς ἡγεῖτο Φριτιγέρνης, τοῦ δὲ ἑτέρου Ἀθανάριχος·
ἐπικρατεστέρου δὲ τοῦ Ἀθανάριχου φανέντος, Φριτιγέρνης προσ-
φεύγει Ῥωμαίοις, καὶ τὴν αὐτῶν κατὰ τοῦ ἀντιπάλου ἐπεκαλεῖτο
βοήθειαν. γνωρίζεται ταῦτα τῷ βασιλεῖ Οὐάλεντι καὶ κελεύει
τοὺς ἐνιδρυμένους κατὰ τὴν Θράκην στρατιώτας, βοηθεῖν τοῖς
βαρβάροις κατὰ βαρβάρων στρατεύουσι· καὶ ποιοῦνται νίκην
κατὰ Ἀθαναρίχου πέραν τοῦ Ἴστρου, τοὺς πολεμίους εἰς φυγὴν

τρέψαντες. αὕτη πρόφασις γέγονε τοῦ χριστιανοὺς γενέσθαι τῶν
βαρβάρων πολλούς· ὁ γὰρ Φριτιγέρνης χάριν ἀποειδοὺς ὧν
εὐεργετεῖτο, τὴν Θρησκείαν τοῦ βασιλέως ἠσπάζετο, καὶ τοὺς ὑφ'
ἑαυτῷ τοῦτο ποιεῖν προετρέπετο· διὸ καὶ μέχρι νῦν πλείους οἱ
Γότθοι τῆς Ἀρειανῆς Θρησκείας ὄντες τυγχάνουσι, τότε διὰ τὸν
βασιλέα ταύτῃ προσθέμενοι. τότε δὲ καὶ Οὐλφίλας ὁ τῶν Γότθων
ἐπίσκοπος γράμματα εὗρε Γοτθικά· καὶ τὰς θείας γραφὰς εἰς
τὴν Γότθων μεταβαλών, τοὺς βαρβάρους μανθάνειν τὰ θεῖα λόγια
παρεσκεύασεν. ἐπειδὴ δὲ Οὐλφίλας οὐ μόνον τοὺς ὑπὸ Φριτιγέρνην, ἀλλὰ καὶ τοὺς ὑπὸ Ἀθανάριχον ταττομένους βαρβάρους
τὸν χριστιανισμὸν ἐξεδίδασκεν, ὁ Ἀθανάριχος ὡς παραχαραττομένης τῆς πατρῴου Θρησκείας, πολλοὺς τῶν χριστιανιζόντων
τιμωρίαις ὑπέβαλλεν, ὥστε γενέσθαι μάρτυρας τηνικαῦτα βαρβάρους ἀρειανίζοντας. ἀλλὰ Ἄρειος μὲν πρὸς τὴν Σαβελλίου τοῦ
Λίβυος δόξαν ἀπαντῆσαι μὴ δυνηθεὶς τῆς ὀρθῆς ἐξέπεσε πίστεως,
πρόσφατον Θεὸν τὸν υἱὸν τοῦ Θεοῦ δογματίσας· οἱ δὲ βάρβαροι,
ἁπλότητι τὸν χριστιανισμὸν δεξάμενοι, ὑπὲρ τῆς εἰς Χριστὸν
πίστεως τῆς ἐνταῦθα ζωῆς κατεφρόνησαν· ταῦτα μὲν περὶ τῶν
χριστιανιζόντων.

Οὐκ εἰς μακρὰν δὲ οἱ βάρβαροι φιλίαν πρὸς ἀλλήλους σπεισά-
μενοι, αὖθις ὑφ' ἑτέρων βαρβάρων γειτνιαζόντων αὐτοῖς τῶν
καλουμένων Οὔννων καταπολεμηθέντες, καὶ τῆς ἰδίας ἐξελαθέντες
χώρας, εἰς τὴν Ῥωμαίων γῆν καταφεύγουσι, δουλεύειν τῷ
βασιλεῖ συντιθέμενοι, καὶ τοῦτο πράττειν, ὅπερ ἂν ὁ Ῥωμαίων
προστάξειε βασιλεύς. ταῦτα εἰς γνῶσιν ἧκε τοῦ Οὐάλεντος· καὶ
μηδὲν προϊδόμενος, κελεύει τοὺς ἱκετεύοντας οἴκτου τυχεῖν, πρὸς
ἓν τοῦτο μόνον οἰκτίρμων γενόμενος. ἀφορίζει οὖν αὐτοῖς τὰ
μέρη τῆς Θρᾴκης, εὐτυχεῖν τὰ μάλιστα ἐπὶ τούτῳ νομίσας· ἐλογί-
ζετο δὲ ὡς εἴη ἕτοιμον καὶ εὐτρεπὲς κτησάμενος κατὰ πολεμίων
στράτευμα· ἤλπιζε γὰρ βαρβάρους Ῥωμαίων φοβερωτέρους ἔσεσθαι φύλακας. καὶ διὰ τοῦτο ἠμέλει τοῦ λοιποῦ, τοὺς Ῥωμαίων
στρατιώτας αὐξῆσαι· καὶ τοὺς μὲν ἤδη πάλαι στρατευομένους, καὶ
κατὰ τοὺς πολέμους γενναίως ἀγωνισαμένους ὑπερεώρα· τὸν δὲ
συντελούμενον ἐκ τῶν ἐπαρχιῶν κατὰ κώμας στρατιώτην ἐξηργύ-
ρισεν, ὀγδοήκοντα χρυσίνους ὑπὲρ ἑκάστου στρατιώτου τοὺς
συντελεστὰς ἀπαιτεῖσθαι κελεύσας, οὐ πρότερον τὰς συντελείας
κουφίσας αὐτοῖς. τοῦτο ἀρχὴ γέγονε τοῦ δυστυχῆσαι τότε πρὸς
ὀλίγον τὴν Ῥωμαίων ἀρχήν.

2. Sozomenus, *Hist. Eccl.* vi. 37:

Goths driven in by Huns cross the Danube—legends concerning the Huns—Gothic embassy to Valens—Ulfilas at the head of it—Valens accedes to their request—no condition mentioned—strife between Athanaric and Frithigern—Frithigern, with aid from Valens, victorious—in gratitude he becomes a Christian and an Arian, and persuades his people to do the same—this not the only cause of Gothic Arianism—Ulfilas—first a Catholic—how he became an Arian—his great influence—inventor of their letters and translator of the Scriptures—the cruel persecutions by Athanaric—details.

Γότθοι γὰρ, οἳ ἐν πέραν Ἴστρου ποταμοῦ τὸ πρὶν ᾤκουν, καὶ τῶν ἄλλων βαρβάρων ἐκράτουν, ἐξελαθέντες παρὰ τῶν καλουμένων Οὔννων, εἰς τοὺς Ῥωμαίων ὅρους ἐπεραιώθησαν. τοῦτο δὲ τὸ ἔθνος, ὥς φασιν, ἄγνωστον ἦν προτοῦ Ὀραξὶ τοῖς παρὰ τὸν Ἴστρον καὶ Γότθοις αὐτοῖς· ἐλάνθανον δὲ προσοικοῦντες ἀλλήλοις, καθότι λίμνης μεγίστης ἐν μέσῳ κειμένης, ἕκαστοι τέλος ξηρᾶς ᾤοντο εἶναι τὴν καθ᾽ αὑτοὺς οἰκουμένην· μετὰ τοῦτο δὲ θάλασσαν καὶ ὕδωρ ἀπέραντον. συμβὰν δὲ βοῦν οἰστροπλῆγα διαδραμεῖν τὴν λίμνην, ἐπηκολούθησε βουκόλος· καὶ τὴν ἀντιπέραν γῆν θεασάμενος, ἤγγειλε τοῖς ὁμοφύλοις. ἄλλοι δὲ λέγουσιν, ὡς ἔλαφος διαφυγοῦσα, τισὶ τῶν Οὔννων θηρῶσιν ἐπέδειξε τήνδε τὴν ὁδὸν, ἐξ ἐπιπολῆς καλυπτομένην τοῖς ὕδασι· τοὺς δὲ τότε μὲν ὑποστρέψαι, θαυμάσαντας τὴν χώραν, ἀέρι μετριώτερον, καὶ γεωργίᾳ ἥμερον ἔχουσαν· καὶ τῷ κρατοῦντι τοῦ ἔθνους ἀγγεῖλαι ἃ ἐθεάσαντο· δι᾽ ὀλίγων δὲ τὰ πρῶτα καταστῆναι εἰς πεῖραν τοῖς Γότθοις· μετὰ δὲ ταῦτα, πανδαμεὶ ἐπιστρατεῦσαι, καὶ μάχῃ κρατῆσαι, καὶ πᾶσαν τὴν αὐτῶν γῆν κατασχεῖν· τοὺς δὲ διωκομένους, εἰς τὴν Ῥωμαίων περαιωθῆναι· καὶ τὸν ποταμὸν διαβάντας, πρέσβεις πέμψαι πρὸς βασιλέα, συμμάχους τοῦ λοιποῦ ἔσεσθαι σφᾶς ὑπισχνουμένους, καὶ ἐσομένους συγχωρεῖν αὐτοῖς ᾗ βούλοιντο κατοικεῖν· ταύτης δὲ τῆς πρεσβείας ἄρξαι Οὐλφίλαν, τὸν τοῦ ἔθνους ἐπίσκοπον· κατὰ γνώμην δὲ αὐτοῖς προχωρησάσης, ἐπιτραπῆναι ἀνὰ τὴν Θρᾴκην οἰκεῖν· οὐ πολλῷ δὲ ὕστερον πρὸς σφᾶς αὐτοὺς στασιάσαντας, διχῇ διαιρεθῆναι· ἡγεῖτο δὲ τῶν μὲν Ἀθανάριχος, τῶν δὲ Φριτιγέρνης. ἐπεὶ δὲ πρὸς ἀλλήλους ἐπολέμησαν, κακῶς πράξας ἐν τῇ μάχῃ Φριτιγέρνης, ᾐτεῖτο Ῥωμαίων βοηθεῖν αὐτῷ· τοῦ δὲ βασιλέως ἐπιτρέψαντος βοηθεῖν καὶ συμμα-

χεῖν αὐτῷ τοὺς ἐν Θράκῃ στρατιώτας, αὖθις συμβαλὼν ἐνίκησε, καὶ
τοὺς ἀμφὶ Ἀθανάριχον εἰς φυγὴν ἔτρεψεν. ὥσπερ δὲ χάριν ἀποδι-
δοὺς Οὐάλεντι, καὶ διὰ πάντων φίλος εἶναι πιστούμενος, ἐκοινώ-
νησε τῆς αὐτοῦ θρησκείας· καὶ τοὺς πειθομένους αὐτῷ βαρβάρους
ἔπειθεν ὧδε φρονεῖν. οὐ τοῦτο δὲ μόνον οἶμαι αἴτιον γέγονεν,
εἰσέτι νῦν πᾶν τὸ φῦλον προστεθῆναι τοῖς τὰ Ἀρείου δοξάζουσιν·
ἀλλὰ γὰρ καὶ Οὐλφίλας ὁ παρ' αὐτοῖς τότε ἱερωμένος, τὰ μὲν
πρῶτα οὐδὲν διεφέρετο πρὸς τὴν καθόλου ἐκκλησίαν· ἐπὶ δὲ
τῆς Κωνσταντίου βασιλείας, ἀπερισκέπτως οἶμαι μετασχὼν τοῖς
ἀμφὶ Εὐδόξιον καὶ Ἀκάκιον τῆς ἐν Κωνσταντινουπόλει συνόδου,
διέμεινε κοινωνῶν τοῖς ἱερεῦσι τῶν ἐν Νικαίᾳ συνελθόντων· ὡς
δὲ εἰς Κωνσταντινούπολιν ἀφίκετο, λέγεται διαλεχθέντων αὐτῷ
περὶ τοῦ δόγματος τῶν προεστώτων τῆς Ἀρειανῆς αἱρέσεως,
καὶ τὴν πρεσβείαν αὐτῷ συμπράξειν πρὸς βασιλέα ὑποσχο-
μένων, εἰ ὁμοίως αὐτοῖς δοξάζοι, βιασθεὶς ὑπὸ τῆς χρείας,
ἢ καὶ ἀληθῶς νομίσας ἄμεινον οὕτω περὶ Θεοῦ φρονεῖν, τοῖς
Ἀρείου κοινωνῆσαι, καὶ αὐτὸν καὶ τὸ πᾶν φῦλον ἀποτεμεῖν τῆς
καθόλου ἐκκλησίας. ὑπὸ διδασκάλῳ γὰρ αὐτῷ παιδευθέντες οἱ
Γότθοι τὰ πρὸς εὐσέβειαν, καὶ δι' αὐτοῦ μετασχόντες πολιτείας
ἡμερωτέρας, πάντα ῥᾳδίως αὐτῷ ἐπείθοντο· πεπεισμένοι μηδὲν
εἶναι φαῦλον τῶν παρ' αὐτοῦ λεγομένων ἢ πραττομένων· ἅπαντα
δὲ συντελεῖν εἰς χρήσιμον τοῖς ζηλοῦσιν. οὐ μὴν ἀλλὰ καὶ
πλείστην δέδωκε πεῖραν τῆς αὐτοῦ ἀρετῆς· μυρίους μὲν ὑπομείνας
κινδύνους ὑπὲρ τοῦ δόγματος, ὅτι τῶν εἰρημένων βαρβάρων
ἑλληνικῶς θρησκευόντων· πρῶτος δὲ γραμμάτων εὑρετὴς αὐτοῖς
ἐγένετο, καὶ εἰς τὴν οἰκείαν φωνὴν μετέφρασε τὰς ἱερὰς βίβλους·
καθότι μὲν οὖν ὡς ἐπίπαν οἱ παρὰ τὸν Ἴστρον βάρβαροι τὰ
Ἀρείου φρονοῦσι, πρόφασις ἥδε. κατ' ἐκείνου δὲ καιροῦ, πλῆθος
τῶν ὑπὸ Φριτιγέρνην διὰ Χριστὸν μαρτυροῦντες, ἀνῃρέθησαν· ὁ
γὰρ Ἀθανάριχος, καὶ τοὺς ὑπ' αὐτῷ τεταγμένους Οὐλφίλα
πείθοντος χριστιανίζειν ἀγανακτῶν, ὡς τῆς πατρῴας θρησκείας
καινοτομουμένης, πολλοὺς πολλαῖς τιμωρίαις ὑπέβαλε· καὶ τοὺς
μὲν εἰς εὐθύνας ἀγαγὼν, παρρησιασαμένους ἀνδρείως ὑπὲρ τοῦ
δόγματος· τοὺς δὲ, μηδὲ λόγου μεταδούς, ἀνεῖλε. λέγεται γὰρ
ὥς τι ξόανον ἐφ' ἁρμαμάξης ἱστὼς, οἵ γε τοῦτο ποιεῖν ὑπὸ
Ἀθαναρίχου προσετάχθησαν, καθ' ἑκάστην σκηνὴν περιάγοντες
τῶν χριστιανίζειν καταγγελλομένων, ἐκέλευον τοῦτο προσκυνεῖν
καὶ θύειν· τῶν δὲ παραιτουμένων σὺν αὐτοῖς ἀνθρώποις τὰς

σκηνὰς ἐνεπίμπρων. περιπαθέστερον δὲ τότε καὶ ἕτερον συμβῆναι
πάθος ἐπυθόμην· ἀπειρηκότες γὰρ πολλοὶ τῇ βίᾳ τῶν θύειν
ἀναγκαζόντων, ἄνδρες τε καὶ γυναῖκες, ὧν αἱ μὲν παιδάρια ἐπή-
γοντο, αἱ δὲ ἀρτίτοκα βρέφη ὑπὸ τοὺς μαζοὺς ἔτρεφον, ἐπὶ
τὴν σκηνὴν τῆς ἐνθάδε ἐκκλησίας κατέφυγον· προσαψάντων δὲ
πῦρ τῶν Ἑλληνιστῶν, ἅπαντες διεφθάρησαν. οὐκ εἰς μακρὰν δὲ
οἱ Γότθοι πρὸς ἀλλήλους ὡμονόησαν· καὶ εἰς ἀπόνοιαν ἐπαρθέν-
τες, τοὺς Θρᾷκας ἐκακούργουν, καὶ τὰς αὐτῶν πόλεις καὶ κώμας
ἐδήουν.

3. Theodoretus, *Hist. Eccl.* iv. 33:

Goths cross the Danube and make treaty with Valens—Eudoxius
offers to bring them to the Arian faith—he fails in dealing with the
chiefs—but brings over Ulfilas—partly by bribes—and persuading
him, as he afterwards persuaded his people, that the controversy
turned upon phrases.

Ἐγὼ δὲ προὖργον νομίζω, διδάξαι τοὺς ἀγνοοῦντας, ὅπως οἱ
βάρβαροι τὴν Ἀρειανικὴν εἰσεδέξαντο νόσον. ὅτε τὸν Ἴστρον διαβάντες, πρὸς τὸν Οὐάλεντα τὴν εἰρήνην ἐσπείσαντο, τηνικαῦτα
παρὼν Εὐδόξιος ὁ δυσώνυμος, ὑπέθετο τῷ βασιλεῖ πεῖσαι αὐτῷ κοινωνῆσαι τοὺς Γότθους· πάλαι γὰρ τὰς τῆς θεογνωσίας ἀκτῖνας δεξάμενοι, τοῖς ἀποστολικοῖς ἐνετρέφοντο δόγμασι· βεβαιοτέραν γὰρ,
ἔφη, τὸ κοινὸν τοῦ φρονήματος τὴν εἰρήνην ἐργάσεται. ταύτην
ἐπαινέσας τὴν γνώμην ὁ Οὐάλης, προὔτεινε τοῖς ἐκείνων ἡγεμόσι
τῶν δογμάτων τὴν συμφωνίαν, οἱ δὲ οὐκ ἀνέξεσθαι ἔλεγον τὴν
πατρῴαν καταλείψειν διδασκαλίαν. κατ' ἐκεῖνον δὲ τὸν χρόνον,
Οὐλφίλας αὐτῶν ἐπίσκοπος ἦν, ᾧ μάλα ἐπείθοντο, καὶ τοὺς
ἐκείνου λόγους ἀκινήτους ὑπελάμβανον νόμους· τοῦτον καὶ
λόγοις κατακλήσας Εὐδόξιος, καὶ χρήμασι δελεάσας, πεῖσαι
παρεσκεύασε τοὺς βαρβάρους τὴν βασιλέως κοινωνίαν ἀσπάσασ-
θαι· ἔπεισε δὲ, φήσας ἐκ φιλοτιμίας γεγενῆσθαι τὴν ἔριν, δογμάτων δὲ μηδεμίαν εἶναι διαφοράν. οὗ δὴ ἕνεκα μέχρι καὶ τήμερον
οἱ Γότθοι μείζονα μὲν τὸν Πατέρα λέγουσι τοῦ Υἱοῦ· κτίσμα δὲ
τὸν Υἱὸν εἰπεῖν οὐκ ἀνέχονται, καίτοι κοινωνοῦντες τοῖς λέγουσιν.
ἀλλ' ὅμως οὐ παντάπασι τὴν πατρῴαν διδασκαλίαν κατέλιπον· καὶ
γὰρ Οὐλφίλας Εὐδοξίῳ καὶ Οὐάλεντι κοινωνῆσαι πείθων αὐτούς,
οὐκ εἶναι δογμάτων ἔφη διαφοράν, ἀλλὰ ματαίαν ἔριν ἐργάσασθαι
τὴν διάστασιν.

4. Orosius, *Hist. adv. pag.* vii. 33 (immediately after an account of the death of Valens):

"Gothi antea per legatos supplices poposcerunt, ut illis episcopi, a quibus regulam Christianae fidei discerent, mitterentur. Valens imperator exitiabili pravitate doctores Ariani dogmatis misit. Gothi primae fidei rudimentum, quod accepere, tenuerunt. Itaque justo Dei judicio ipsi eum vivum incenderunt, qui propter eum etiam mortui vitio erroris arsuri sunt."

5. Jordanis, *de reb. Get.* c. 25:

"Vesegothae . . . . quidnam de se propter gentem Hunnorum deliberarent, ambigebant, diuque cogitantes tandem communi placito legatos ad Romaniam direxere ad Valentem imperatorem, fratrem Valentiniani senioris, ut, partem Thraciae sive Moesiae si illis traderet ad colendum, ejus legibus viverent, ejusque imperiis subderentur.

"Et, ut fides uberior illis haberetur, promittunt se, si doctores linguae suae donaverit, fieri Christianos. Quo Valens comperto mox gratulabundus annuit, quod ultro petere voluisset, susceptosque in Moesiae partibus Getas quasi murum regni sui contra ceteras gentes statuit; et quia tunc Valens imperator Arianorum perfidia saucius, nostrarum partium omnes ecclesias obturasset, suae partis fautores ad illos dirigit praedicatores, qui venientibus rudibus et ignaris illico perfidiae suae virus infundunt. Sic quoque Vesegothae a Valente imperatore Ariani potius quam Christiani effecti. De cetero tam Ostrogothis quam Gepidis, parentibus suis, pro affectionis gratia evangelizantes, hujus perfidiae culturam edocentes, omnem ubique hujus linguae nationem ad culturam hujus sectae invitavere. Ipsi quoque, ut dictum est, Danubium transmeantes, Daciam ripensem, Moesiam Thraciasque permisso principis insedere."

c. 26, *ad finem*: "Imperator . . . . crematus est: haud secus quam dei prorsus judicio, ut ab ipsis igne combureretur, quos ipse veram fidem petentes in perfidiam declinasset, et ignem caritatis ad gehennae ignem detorsisset."

6. ISIDORUS, *Chron. Goth.* era 416 :

"Et merito ut ipse (Valens) ab eis vivens temporali cremaretur incendis, qui tam pulcras animas ignibus aeternis tradiderat."

III.

TABLE OF DATES CONNECTED WITH GOTHIC HISTORY.

238	First Gothic inroad.	
251	Decius defeated by the Goths.	
270	Claudius defeats the Goths at Naissus.	.
311		Birth of Ulfilas. al. 318.
331	Gothic war of Constantine.	
337	Death of Constantine.	
341		Ulfilas ordained bishop.
348		Ulfilas and his flock migrate into Moesia.
360		Arian council at Constantinople.
364	Valens emperor.	
367	First Gothic war of Valens.	
370		Second persecution of Christians in Gothia.
376	Wisigoths under Frithigern cross the Danube.	
378	Battle of Adrianople; death of Valens.	
379—395	Theodosius emperor.	381 Death of Athanaric.
395	Revolt of the Goths under Alaric.	381 Death of Ulfilas. al. 388.
410	Capture of Rome by Alaric.	398—404 Chrysostom, archbishop of Constantinople.
412—507	Gothic kingdom of Toulouse.	
493—526	Theodoric, king in Italy.	
507	Battle of Vouglé; Alaric II. slain.	
507—711	Wisigothic kingdom in Spain.	
553	End of Ostrogothic kingdom in Italy.	586 Conversion of Reccared.

IV.

CHRONOLOGICAL TABLE OF WISIGOTHIC KINGS.[1]

Alaric I.	... ...	395—410
Athaulf	... ...	410—415
Sigrich...	... ...	415
Wallia ...	... ...	415—419
Theodoric I. ...	...	419—451 killed at Châlons.
Thorismund ...	...	451—453
Theodoric II....	...	453—466
Euric ...	... ...	466—485
Alaric II.	..: ...	485—507 killed at Vouglé.

{ Gesalic...	...	...	507—511 } 507-526, Theodoric
{ Amalaric	...	...	507—531 } the Great as regent.
Theudis	...	...	531—548
Theudigisel	...	...	548—549
Agila ...	...		549—554
Athanagild	...		554—567
{ Leova I.	...		567—572
{ Leovigild			567—586
Reccared	...		586—601

[1] See Dahn, *Könige*, v. Appendix.

INDEX

INDEX.

J. PALMER, PRINTER, JESUS LANE, CAMBRIDGE.